Agents of Revolution

John and Thomas Gilbert— Entrepreneurs

———

Peter Lead

———

Staffordshire Heritage Series
Editor J. H. Y. Briggs

Volume II

Centre for Local History
University of Keele, Staffordshire
ST5 5BG

FOR MY MOTHER
BEATRICE MARY LEAD

ISBN No. 0-9513713-1-2
ISSN No. 0950-7345
Printed by J. H. Brookes (Printers) Ltd.
141-149 Lower Bryan Street, Hanley, Stoke-on-Trent, England

CONTENTS

Publication of this volume has been made possible by the generous financial support of the following:

The Barracks Trust, Newcastle-under-Lyme
The Professor S. H. Beaver Fund, University of Keele
British Waterways Board
The Marjorie A. Cruickshank Fund, University of Keele
The Lilleshall Company
The Manchester Ship Canal Company
Newcastle-under-Lyme Borough Council

ACKNOWLEDGEMENTS

As an undergraduate student I read Hugh Malet's *The Canal Duke* (1st edition) and I was intrigued to learn that two Staffordshire entrepreneurs —John and Thomas Gilbert—had played such a key role in promoting the 'Canal Age.' So much so, that before taking a first degree I already knew what I wanted to research for a higher degree. I was fortunate enough to have the opportunity to undertake research in the History Department of the University of Keele and also to benefit from the encouragement and guidance given to me by John Briggs. After some sixteen years of research, I hope that this book will help to secure greater national recognition for these self-effacing men and their enormous contribution to our early industrial development.

During the period of my research I have received unstinting help from a great many libraries and archive collections, which I have acknowledged in the notes to the text. But I owe an especial debt to the staff at the William Salt Library and the County Record Office at Stafford, in particular Dr. Fred Stitt (the former County Archivist) and his successor Dudley Fowkes.

I would also like to record my debt to Dr. Hugh Torrens of the Geology Department, University of Keele, who not only turned up a vast collection of Gilbert references but who also never failed to respond to my many questions about eighteenth century scientific life. I would also like to record my gratitude to Dr. Hugh Malet, who fuelled my interest in the Gilbert brothers and provided the portrait of John Gilbert, which was seen for the first time in his *Bridgewater: the Canal Duke* (1977).

So many people have helped me in a host of ways with my research, but here I would particularly like to mention: Anthony M. Carr; the late Professor W. H. Chaloner; the late Herbert A. Chester; the late Norman A. Cope; Michael Corfield; the late Olive A. Dale; Godfrey Downs-Rose; David Dyble; the Editor, the *Evening Sentinel*; Arnold Gibson; Charles Hadfield; John Hancock; Dr. J. R. Hollick; Bill Jack; Alan Jeffrey; Mr. R. M. Larking; Mrs. B. M. Lead; Philip R. Leese; Mrs. Lynn Miller; Frank Mullineux; the late Dr. David E. Owen; Lindsay Porter; Dr. John Robey; Dr. Marie Rowlands; the Rev. Canon Howard Senar and Derek Wheelhouse.

Peter Lead   Stone, Staffordshire (July 1989)

5

ABBREVIATIONS

B&WP	Boulton & Watt Papers, Birmingham Reference Library.
BPDMHS	Bulletin of the Peak District Mines Historical Society.
EHR	Economic History Review.
HRL	Hanley Reference Library.
JHC	Journal of the House of Commons.
JSIAS	Journal of the Staffordshire Industrial Archaeology Society.
KEELE	University Library, University of Keele.
PRO	Public Record Office.
SHC	*Collections for a History of Staffordshire.*
SPRS	Staffordshire Parish Register Society.
SRO	Staffordshire Record Office.
T&JG	*Thomas and John Gilbert: A study in Business Enterprise and Social Mobility in Eighteenth Century England.* (M.A. Thesis, University of Keele, 1982)
TM	Trent and Mersey Canal.
TNSFC	Transactions of the North Staffs. Field Club.
WSL	William Salt Library, Stafford.

I. ORIGINS

The surname of Gilbert was not uncommon in the central and northern parts of Staffordshire during the sixteenth and seventeenth centuries. One particular concentration of people bearing this name was in the triangular tract enclosed by the villages of Alton, Ellastone and Rocester. The precise ancestry of the two eighteenth century entrepreneurs, Thomas and John Gilbert has proved difficult to establish, but without question their ancestors were well established in this area by 1600.[1] Their branch of the family was centred on the village of Ellastone, later to be immortalised in literature by George Eliot. Her father, Robert Evans spent his early life here and as Hayslope it was the scene of some of the incidents in *Adam Bede*.[2] The first reference to the Gilbert family concerns a 'Rycharde Gylbarte', who was buried at Ellastone in 1589; and this unusual spelling of the family surname is consistently followed in the Ellastone Parish Registers until the incumbent changed.[3] Another source records a George Gilbert who was an 'Alekeeper' at Rocester in 1599.[4]

This area on the edge of the Staffordshire Moorlands was a rugged one whose physical nature limited the scope of human activity. Agriculture could perhaps be best described as marginal and this point is strongly reinforced by the name of one house in the Ellastone area which was known as 'World's End'[5] Doubtless improvement of the land was undertaken, but in such a moorland area this would have been less spectacular because it was less complete. For the most part the moorland was not strictly speaking 'reclaimed' at all; for it was used more or less in its natural state for rough-grazing. Though animals grazing there would have modified the natural vegetation, they would not have transformed it. Some idea of the nature of the agricultural holdings in the area can be obtained from the details of a law suit which involved a member of the Gilbert family:—

'On the Morrow of Holy Trinity 5 James I

Between Thomas Gilbert, complainant, and Robert Meverell, armigor, and Elizabeth, his wife and Thomas Nabbes and Jane, his wife, deforciants of a messuage, a garden, an orchard, 10 acres of land, 10 acres of meadow, 10 acres of pasture, 60 acres of furze and heath, and common of pasture for all kinds of cattle in Caldon.

The deforciants remitted all rights to Thomas and his heirs, for which Thomas gave them £60.'[6]

The area of the Staffordshire Moorlands from which the Gilbert family originated. As shown on a map of 1775. *(Author's Collection)*

10

The economic exploitation of such a holding obviously laid emphasis on pastoralism, the concentration, then as now, being laid on the keeping of cattle rather than sheep. Up-and-down husbandry was probably practiced in part, some land being alternatively used for arable and pastoral purposes.[7] Clearly there was a dependence on marginal grazing in the "furze and heath" and on the common pasture at Caldon, so it is evident that in this area husbandry was practiced in a largely open-field setting.

Despite the vaguely grandiose claims made in the illuminated account of the life of Thomas Gilbert, MP, exhibited in the small chapel at Cotton;[8] the earliest known members of the Gilbert family were of a modest standing in their community. The Rychards Gylbarte (who died in 1589) may have been either a labourer or a husbandman. His son, Richard certainly belonged to the second group as he was described as a 'husbandman' in 1599 at the time of his marriage to Margarye Slacke; and in a number of subsequent entries in the Ellastone Registers up to 1610.[9] Richard was also one of the two Churchwardens at Ellastone for the year 1606-7, which says something of his standing in the community;[10] for 'All churchwardens or Questmen in every parish shall be chosen by a joint consent of the Minister and Parishioners,...but if they cannot agree...then the Minister shall choose one and the Parishioners another.[11]

The Thomas Gilbert who was involved in the litigation in 1606 may well have been Richard's brother. He would appear to be of at least yeoman status, as he was able to buy off rival claimants to a farm and 90 acres of land.

The office of Churchwarden at Ellastone was also filled by Richard's son, George (born 1601); who served in this capacity for the years 1630-31 and 1643-44.[12] Little is known of his life although he lived through the local smallpox epidemics of 1636 and 1641; and the storming of Wootton Lodge without apparently being affected by any of these events.[13] The Gilbert family do not figure in either the Order Book of the Staffordshire County Committee[14] or the list of Active Parliamentarians of 1662.[15] This is merely negative evidence, but the family's links with the Cheadle Corporation suggest that the family sympathised with the royal house of Stuart. George Gilbert lost his first wife in 1635 and within three years he had married for a second time.[16] Neither of the marriages took place at Ellastone, and this indicates that George was looking farther afield for his wives, possibly with a view to improving his position and fortunes.[17] He arranged a very good marriage for his son, Thomas; in whose marriage settlement, George is described as a 'Yeoman of Ramsor', and it was at

Ramsor that he died in 1664.[18] The family holdings around Ramsor were centred on the farmhouse at Lickshead, which continued to be held by the family into the eighteenth century. Aerial photographs of the farm show two period farmhouses and it is possible that it was the base for an extended family.

Aerial view of Lickshead Farm, c.1960.   *(The late Herbert A. Chester)*

Thomas Gilbert (1628-1694) followed in the footsteps of both his father and grandfather, serving as Churchwarden at Ellastone in 1668/69 and again in 1669/70.[19] He married very well in 1661, when he wed Elizabeth Morrice of Lockwood Hall (near Kingsley) and this may have occasioned a removal to what is now Cotton Hall.[20] The original house at Cotton appears to date back to 1630 and was probably built by the Morrice family.[21] As late as 1742, one of the main holdings at Cotton was known as 'Morrices Liveing', and this seems to strengthen the view that the Gilberts acquired their initial interest in Cotton through this marriage.[22] Thomas was definitely living at Cotton in 1687, when he was described in a marriage settlement as a 'Yeoman of Nearer Cotton';[23] and the modern Ordnance Survey map confirms that Near (or Nearer) Cotton is the name given to the area around Cotton Hall.[24] Another indication of this movement of the main family home is provided by the Ellastone Parish

12

Registers, for in the 1670s Gilbert entries became scarcer and it is clear that the family started to use the parish church at Alton.[25]

Thomas was succeeded in the estate by his son, George; who broke all family records by marrying three times.[26] One important development was occasioned by George's first marriage to Ellen Whieldon of Blackbank (Ipstones) in 1687.[27] Through this marriage the Gilberts acquired an interest in the Cloughead Colliery which they worked with the Bill family for about forty or fifty years, mainly as a source of fuel for lime burning at Caldon Low and later for the smelting mill at Alton.[28] George and his son Thomas, also witnessed an agreement between Joseph Banks and John Philips, for Philips to work the coal measures near 'Churche Gorse', Kingsley. This agreement was signed and sealed in September 1721,[29] some ten years after Thomas Gilbert had married Elizabeth Philips.[30] Such patterns of family partnership were to become common and fundamental to the development of the family's fortunes in the years to come. Another contemporary document describing the Gilbert holdings mentions a lead mine in the parish of Alton which yielded £9 per annum, but it is impossible to link George Gilbert with this enterprise.[31]

During his father's lifetime, Thomas lived 'at Farley' (possibly at Lickshead), whilst George occupied the embryonic Cotton Hall. Apart from their own lands they rented land from the Earl of Shrewsbury; but at the same time they were increasing their own holdings through enclosure. George Gilbert made at least two such enclosures at Farley and in this he was clearly following a well established pattern laid down by his ancestors.[32] The solid nature of the Ramsor holdings is indicated by the election of a Churchwarden at Ellastone in 1702/03 for 'Gilberts tenement'; and similar references are made in contemporary tithe records.[33]

George Gilbert was probably the first member of the family to be included in the ranks of what John Aikin termed the 'little country gentleman'.[34] As such he became an Alderman of Cheadle Corporation in January 1701/02; a society set up in September 1699 and open to 'honest gentlemen who were free and willing'. Thomas Pape considered that the society owed its origin to the sympathy felt by the clergy and landed gentry for the Stuarts. By 1699, when the Cheadle Corporation was founded, Parliament was considering a possible successor to William and subsequently Anne. The outcome of these deliberations was the Act of Settlement in 1701, which decided in favour of the Protestant House of Hanover. The troubled state of England following Queen Anne's death in

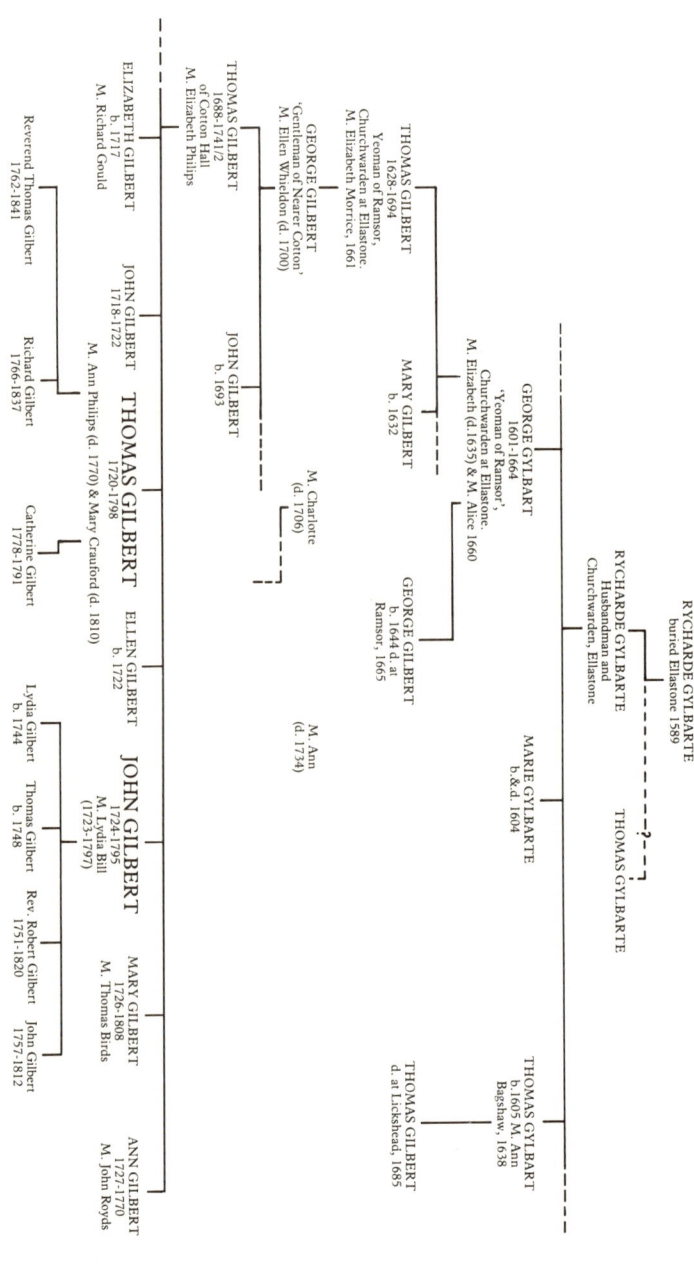

Extract from the Gilbert Family Tree

RYCHARDE GYLBARTE
buried Ellastone 1589

RYCHARDE GYLBARTE
Husbandman and
Churchwarden, Ellastone

THOMAS GYLBARTE

MARIE GYLBARTE
b. & d. 1604

THOMAS GYLBART
b. 1605 M. Ann
Bagshaw, 1638

THOMAS GILBERT
d. at Lickstead, 1665

GEORGE GYLBART
1601-1664
'Yeoman of Ramsor',
Churchwarden at Ellastone.
M. Elizabeth (d.1635) & M. Alice 1660

THOMAS GILBERT
1628-1694
Yeoman of Ramsor,
Churchwarden at Ellastone.
M. Elizabeth Morrice, 1661

GEORGE GILBERT
'Gentleman of Nearer Cotton'
M. Ellen Whieldon (d. 1700)

THOMAS GILBERT
1688-1741/2
of Cotton Hall
M. Elizabeth Philips

ELIZABETH GILBERT
b. 1717
M. Richard Gould

Reverend Thomas Gilbert
1762-1841

MARY GILBERT
b. 1632

JOHN GILBERT
b. 1693

JOHN GILBERT
1718-1722
M. Ann Philips (d. 1770)

Richard Gilbert
1766-1837

M. Charlotte
(d. 1706)

GEORGE GILBERT
b. 1644 d. at
Ramsor, 1665

M. Ann
(d. 1734)

THOMAS GILBERT
1720-1798
M. Mary Craufurd (d. 1810)

Catherine Gilbert
1778-1791

ELLEN GILBERT
b. 1722

Lydia Gilbert
b. 1744

Thomas Gilbert
b. 1748

JOHN GILBERT
1724-1795
M. Lydia Bill
(1723-1797)

Rev. Robert Gilbert
1751-1820

John Gilbert
1757-1812

MARY GILBERT
1726-1808
M. Thomas Birds

ANN GILBERT
1727-1770
M. John Royds

14

1714 is reflected at Cheadle. There was an influx into the Corporation of new gentlemen members who lived at some distance from the town, some of which were described as 'persons of loyalty and sound principles'.[35] By 1709, both George Gilbert and John Bill (son of Richard Bill, of Alton Lodge, 'Baylife' to the twelfth Earl and Duke of Shrewsbury)[36] appear to have ceased to attend the meetings of the Corporation, although this cannot be established with certainty as the attendance lists for the society are not always complete. They may well have been early subscribers to the views expressed in John Byrom's poem, which seems to sum up the viewpoint of the whole Corporation after the failure of the 1715 Jacobite rebellion:—

> 'God bless the King—I mean our faith's defender
> God bless (no harm in blessing) the Pretender
> But who pretender is, or who is King—
> God bless us all, that's quite another thing.'[37]

In 1720, John, Lord Gower was elected Mayor of Cheadle for the following year, and this could have provided an opportunity for a first contact between the Leveson-Gower family and the Gilberts.[38] However, the absence of detailed Corporation records prevent the establishment of any positive link before 1742.[39]

The Corporation at Cheadle was also a means of promoting social contact among the local gentry and business men.[40] Herbert Chester has shown how the "iron men of the Moorland Works" found time to play important roles in the Society.[41] Amongst these was John Wheeler of Stourbridge, who was initially the Foley's manager and then a partner in the Cheshire ironworks. He bought Wootton Lodge in 1700 and this purchase provided a clear statement of the degree of social and economic advancement that could be achieved through industrial activities.[42] Two members of the Foley family were also sworn as burgesses following an introduction by one of their local employees.[43] This great iron-making family provides a superb example of how progress could be made through industrial enterprise, having risen in a few generations from nail-making to enoblement by Charles II. Richard Foley, the son of a Dudley nail-maker was born in 1580 and married the daughter of William Brindley of Kinver. Brindley is credited with introducing 'the German method' of making iron in Kinver mill, the first one to be erected in England for rolling and slitting of iron. To perfect his knowledge of the slitting process, Richard Foley made two journeys into Sweden and by deception learnt the finer points of the process. On his return to England, he borrowed capital and developed a group of furnaces and forges in the Midlands. This work was carried out by his son, Thomas and his sons, Paul and Philip, so that they were able to take full advantage of the opportunities opening up in the Midland iron trade in the seventeenth ·century. By the end of the century, the family were involved in an 'industrial empire' that stretched throughout the ironworking area of the Midlands, the Forest of Dean and beyond.[44]

Cotton Hall as rebuilt by Thomas Gilbert, 1720-1798.   *(William Salt Library)*

The returns from the iron industry were considerable and provided the basis for the advancement of a number of local families:—

'In addition to the Dudleys, Levesons, Foleys, and Foulkes, the notes of Simon Degge state that the Chetwynds of Rugeley, Parkes of Willingsworth and Wednesbury, and Gorings of Bold, obtained their estates from iron works.'[45]

The Levesons were associated with ironworks on their Lilleshall and Trentham estates in the 1580s and 1590s, but they were not actively involved, preferring to lease out the ironworks to local operators.[46] But this was not the real basis of their wealth, which had been acquired in the sixteenth-century wool trade and then invested in land. They bought a great deal of monastic land, including Lilleshall and Trentham; but unlike the Chetwynds of Rugeley, they avoided further involvement in trade or industry. As a Royalist family, the Levesons suffered badly during the Civil War, but recovered sufficiently by the end of the seventeenth century to rebuild their house at Trentham. Frances Leveson married Sir Thomas Gower—and eventually in 1689, the lands of the Levesons were joined with the Yorkshire estates of the Gowers, in the hands of Sir William Leveson-Gower.[47]

The rise to affluence of such families was well known to the local gentry who were anxious to emulate their superiors. Indeed, the gentry were vital to the aristocracy who wished to develop their lands and resources, but at the same time did not wish to become too actively involved themselves. So various forms of association grew up, with the local gentry acting as agents for the aristocratic landowners, or indeed as partners in an increasingly varied number of enterprises, but mainly concerned with the extractive industries.

Copper and lead had been worked in the north-east portion of Staffordshire since at least medieval times, but serious mining only began in the early seventeenth century.[48] The Civil War interrupted operations; despite the efforts of the Staffordshire County Committee to "set on worke such myners . . . for searching and getting of leade ore within the Lordshipp of Blowre and County of Stafford being late the possessions of Wm. Marquess of New-Castle and now sequestred for the use of King and Parliament."[49] During this period the copper and brass industries were under the monopolistic control of the Company of Mines Royal, and the Company of Mineral and Battery Works, originally chartered by Elizabeth I in 1568 to encourage the home production of these metals. By the time of the Civil War and Protectorate, the Company was mainly concerned with leasing their rights to those wishing to carry on mining operations.[50] One such individual was the Third Earl of Devonshire who reopened the Ecton Mines in 1660, but was forced to close down operations due to the cheapness of imported Swedish copper.[51] A revival in the mining industry began about 1690 and it has been associated with the rescinding of the monopolistic powers under the Mines Royal Act of 1689 and 1694, which freed cooper-, lead- and tin mines. This together with the development of the reverberatory furnace for the smelting of copper using coal as fuel, and the decline of the main Swedish mine at Falun, started a major upsurge in mining activity.[52]

One such venture was launched by a partnership of five 'adventurers', including Richard Bill who leased the Ribden mines in 1692. The mineral rights belonged to the Earl of Shrewsbury who had initially tried to work the mines himself in the period after the Restoration, but the attempt proved abortive and this prompted the Earl to lease out his rights.[53] Thomas Gilbert (1688-1741/2) first became involved in mining ventures, when in January 1722/3 he took over the lease of the Calton Moor Mines from Thomas Rivett of Derby.[54] He extended his interests in 1727, when he bought out Samuel Seale's share of the Ribden lease;[55] and with his partner Anthony Hill he sublet them in the same year.[56] They again sublet their rights in 1732 to the Duke of Chandos, who was to carry on working the mines at his sole expense.[57] Meanwhile in 1730, Thomas Gilbert, in partnership with Robert Hill, obtained the lease of the Mixon Mines for twenty-one years, although nothing else is known of this venture.[58] The mines at Swinscoe were successfully leased by Thomas in 1732 from Leeke Okeover,[59] and they were sublet with the Ribden interest to the Duke of Chandos in the same year.[60] By 1737 he had acquired interests in the Thorswood mines and the Burgoyne mines at Ecton; with Robert Bill as a partner.[61] A surviving account between these two partners reveal something of the operations at the Thorswood Mines; and from this Dr. Robey has estimated that 770 tons of ore (mainly lead) were raised between 1737 and 1742, with a value of nearly £2,600.[62] At the same time expenses could be high and £169 13s 9d was expended on driving soughs at Ecton in 1739.[63] The final component in these extensive mining enterprises were the mines at Waterfall; the lease of which was negotiated by Thomas but was granted (after his death) to his eldest son, Thomas in April 1741.[64]

The rent of such mines was always a proportion of the ore and the contractors agreed to keep the mines open for a fixed period during each year. At Mixon, the partners agreed to pay 1/7th of the ore raised,[65] although another lease of 1718 specified a yearly royalty of one twelfth of the ore raised.[66] The contractors had to meet the expenses of all work and these could be of astronomical dimensions. The first stage of a sough at Ecton is said to have cost a rival group of 'adventurers' £13,000 with no return.[67] Thomas Gilbert also began the family's involvement with lead smelting mills, for in his will he left to his youngest son John:

'one 24 part of the smelting mill at Alton and of my son Thomases share of the smelting mill at Greenlow ffields.'[68] These were interests that were built up by the younger Thomas and his brother, John. The elder Thomas also worked Cloughead Colleries in partnership with Robert Bill, mainly as a source of fuel for the lime-kilns at Caldon Low, but also a small quantity for sale which realised a profit of £5 1s 6¾d in 1739.[69] At the time of the elder Thomas's death in January 1741/42, his estate was said to be

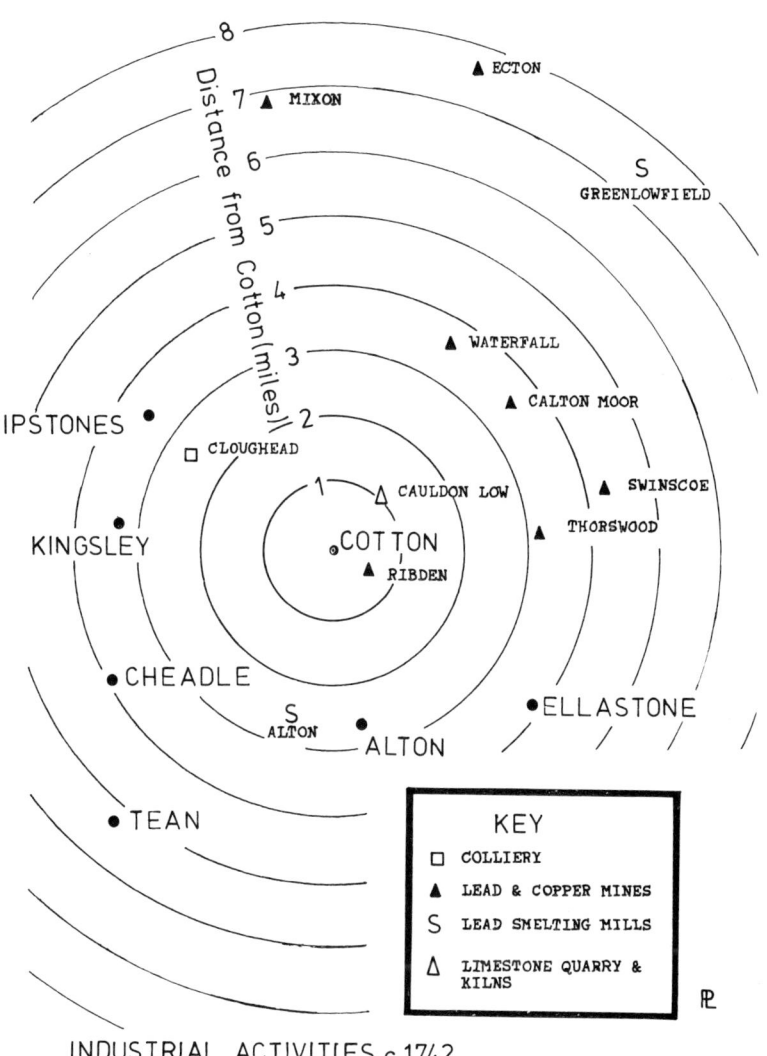

8

7 ▲ MIXON

▲ ECTON

Distance from Cotton(miles)

6

5

4

S
GREENLOWFIELD

3

▲ WATERFALL

IPSTONES •

2

▲ CALTON MOOR

□ CLOUGHEAD

1 △ CAULDON LOW

▲ SWINSCOE

KINGSLEY •

⊙COTTON
▲ RIBDEN

▲ THORSWOOD

• CHEADLE

S
ALTON

•ELLASTONE

• ALTON

• TEAN

KEY

□ COLLIERY

▲ LEAD & COPPER MINES

S LEAD SMELTING MILLS

△ LIMESTONE QUARRY &
KILNS

℞

INDUSTRIAL ACTIVITIES c.1742

worth £300 a year,[70] but his contribution to the family's ascent was not simply a financial one; for he had laid the foundations of the interests which his two sons were to develop and he also nurtured the contacts which were to be so important to his sons.

By the time of Thomas's death, the Gilberts firmly belonged to the category of smaller squires, although with an income well above that laid down by H. J. Habakkuk.[71] 'The drift of property', according to Habakkuk 'in the sixty years after 1690 was in favour of the large estate and the great lord' who expanded largely at the expense of the small squire and landed gentry. Habakkuk saw seventeenth-century legal developments relating to marriage settlements and mortgages as being the key factor in this process. In the moorland areas of North Staffordshire there is some evidence for this process, the best example being the expansion of the Earl of Shrewsbury's estates around Alton Lodge (now Alton Towers). However, families like the Bills and the Gilberts protected themselves against this trend by diversifying their interests and by careful alliances built up through marriages. In short, by employing the same tactics as those used by 'the great lord'.

The Gilberts were clearly successful in holding their estates together. Younger children were established on the estate or provided with money to establish themselves in a trade or profession. John Gilbert (1724-1795) was handsomely provided for in his father's will, for in the form of land he received:

'a certain liveing at Cotton afforesd. Called Thompson Liveing and all Morrices (but that which is my own land) and that piece of Ground which John Edge holds at ffive pounds and ffive shillings a year called Ffalknor Close and the land wch. was purchased of Barnetts at £400 now in the possession of Tunicliff and Tunicliffs wch. was purchased of Buxtons.'[72]

In addition, John received a share of his father's entrepreneurial interests, namely:

'One twenty fourth part or share of those mines at Ecton called Clayton Grove, Clay Grove, Water Work and Bowloes Grove and also one 24th part of Thorswood mines and one half of my share of the Lymekilns and one 24th part of the smelting mill at Alton and of my son Thomases share of the Smelting Mill at Greenlow ffields.'[73]

He had also been given something of even greater value, a grounding in business and an example of entrepreneurial potential. For after attending the village school at Farley, John was 'bound apprentice to Mr. Boulton'.[74] Such apprenticeships were common and took the form described by Aikin as applying to those who served apprenticeships to

Manchester Merchants. Apprentices were taken from families who could pay a modest fee, those again whom Aikin terms 'the little country gentry'. Aikin's account relates how the work could be 'laborious', but highlights the key to the merchant's prosperity:

'The improvement of their fortunes was chiefly owing to their economy in living, the expense of which was much below the interest of the capital employed.'[75] This was fundamental to entrepreneurial success and it was a lesson that John Gilbert learnt well in the years in which he was apprenticed to Matthew Boulton, Senior; father of the Matthew Boulton of Boulton and Watt fame. Matthew Boulton, Senior was a manufacturer of buckles with a workshop at the corner of Snow Hill and what is now Slaney Street, in Birmingham.[76] Doubtless part of John's apprenticeship would have been of a practical nature, but the most important element would have dealt with practical book-keeping and other aspects of daily buisness life. This was obviously a happy experience for John as in 1755 he asked Matthew Boulton to pass on his greetings to all 'My old shop mates'.[77]

The arrangement of such apprenticeships is of interest as it illustrates once again the role played by family connections. John Gilbert provides an example of such an arrangement, albeit an abortive one. In a letter to Josiah Wedgwood, written to secure an apprenticeship for a Derbyshire lad (possibly a member of the Bird family), he writes:

Worsley 9th Mrch 1769.

'Sir,

A friend of mine Desired I would recommend a near relation of his. The young man, I think is about 14 or 15 of a good family, but small fortune. I am informed he wishes a good trade.'[78]

It does not take a great deal of imagination to envisage Robert Bill, John's father's friend and partner, writing a similar letter to Matthew Boulton, around 1737. For Robert Bill was also a partner in the Cheadle Copper and Brass Company (along with his brother-in-law Robert Hurst);[79] and this company sent the greater part of its output to Birmingham and Wolverhampton. Indeed the rapid growth of the manufacture of copper and brass in England and Wales between 1690 and 1730 was closely linked with the rise of the Midland toy trades.[80]

One of Robert Bill's sons, another Robert, served a similar apprenticeship in London; and following his marriage in 1757 to Dorothy Walton,[81] he moved to the Hague in Holland where he used his wife's settlement to set himself up as a jeweller.[82] This was another practice sometimes employed by the noble families, two contemporary examples being provided by the Egerton family of Tatton Park. The second son Samuel (1711-1780) was apprenticed in 1729 to Joseph Smith, a picture-dealer based in Venice. The agreement was that Smith was to be paid £100 p.a. for the five years during which Samuel was to be under instruction and that at the end of the period, the clerk was to be taken on as partner.[83] The youngest son, Thomas Egerton was apprenticed to a Rotterdam merchant with a yearly salary of £40.[84]

Heath House (Tean), home of the Philips family.   (Mrs. M. Philips/George Short)

As Thomas Gilbert was to inherit the bulk of his father's estates and industrial interests, it seems clear that John's future either lay as a modest farmer or in some form of industrial enterprise. His father's death cut short his apprenticeship in Birmingham and determined the pattern of his future career. As his brother was still completing his legal training in London, John returned to Cotton where he ran the family estate and maintained their mining interests.[85] At the age of seventeen he began the second phase of his education, that in estate management and this early experience coupled with natural flair commended him to his future employers. Two years later, he married Lydia Bill,[86] who brought him a marriage settlement of £300. As John was not old enough to make a will, the marriage settlement made ample provision for Lydia and any children of the marriage.[87] Thomas Gilbert was forty-two years old when he married Ann Philips in 1762.[88] As Thomas's mother had also been a member of the same family, it indicates how closely alliances were forged between neighbouring families of gentry,[89] Thomas made his fiancée a present of a lottery ticket, which yielded a most unusual and fortuitous wedding present in the form of a £10,000 prize.[90] As there was a strong convention whereby a wife's portion was used to purchase land which was added to the estate settlement, it is reasonable to suppose that Thomas used the money to make purchases of land, as for example, at Goldenhill in 1760. He may also have used this windfall to finance his investments both at Lilleshall and in the Trent and Mersey Canal. If this marriage marks the success of the family's tactics in a monetary sense, then the grant of arms to Thomas Gilbert in December 1759 marked the climax of one phase of the family's social ascent.[91]

The coat of arms granted to Thomas Gilbert in 1759.   *(William Salt Library)*

II LAND STEWARDS

In medieval times, the royal household included a steward, who 'was always close to the King, an intimate.'[1] Such individuals also appeared in the establishment of the barons and the knights, where they had general oversight of their master's household and estates. As many of these estates were widely scattered and the steward was required to remain close to his master to regulate his household, it became necessary to appoint bailiffs also, who would look after component estates or farms.[2] These roles remained largely unchanged until the eighteenth century, when the increasing complexities of estate management were responsible for considerable changes in the work undertaken by such individuals. This was made necessary by the agglomeration of estates, frequently very scattered, beginning with the sale of monastic lands in the sixteenth century; and continuing with acquisitions by marriage and purchase during the following two centuries. Estate improvements of a more scientific nature meant that the people occupying these positions had to be something more than glorified husbandmen. Sometimes, a progressive landowner employed an additional functionary, in the form of a surveyor, primarily concerned with the measurement of land, but in the case of Sir Harvy Bagot (of Field, near Uttoxeter), he was involved in calculating the quantities of wood supplied to make charcoal for the local iron industry. In a list of employees, the 'Steward' appears first, followed by the 'Baylif' and the 'Surveyor'.[3]

Isolated estates were sometimes the sole concern of a bailiff as was the case with the Alton estate of the Earl of Shrewsbury. A Mr Hattfield held the position of 'baylye' there, in 1608;[4] and Richard Bill was still termed 'baylife' in 1702.[5] On many estates, Richard Bill would have been styled 'steward'; or as the eighteenth century progressed 'agent', which could be qualified by various prefixes: so chief-agent, or estate-agent, or land-agent.[6] When John Gilbert arrived at Worsley in 1759, it was to be the Duke of Bridgewater's 'steward';[7] and at that time Thomas was also described as 'steward to the duke.'[8] Meanwhile, on Earl Gower's estate at Trentham, John's brother-in-law was described as his 'agent'.[9] So it can be seen that by the eighteenth century the terms 'steward' and 'agent' had come to be virtually synonymous, local custom being the deciding factor in which one was used. The office of steward was not simply used in a rural sense, in as much as it implied someone employed to manage a country estate. Thomas Fenton was summoned to Trentham by Thomas Gilbert, in 1776, to be offered the stewardship of Earl Gower's Newcastle estate, which he readily accepted.[10] Both Fenton and his predecessor, Nathaniel Beard, had been Mayors of Newcastle, a clear indication of the relationship between the Earl's political interest in the borough and the allocation of this post which was largely urban in responsibility.[11]

Professor Mingay in his study of the eighteenth century land steward has observed that they were 'recruited from a wide field—lawyers, farmers, merchants, ironmasters, army officers, senior domestic servants—almost any persons sufficiently well known and respectable to inspire confidence as to their honesty and ability. They were essentially middle class, however, since education and some financial standing were requisites for the post.'[12] Most stewards were lawyers or farmers, the younger sons of country gentlemen or gentlemen farmers in their own right. Numerous lawyers acted as stewards, since much of the work was of a legal nature and disputes were relatively common. This caused certain agricultural writers to advise against such appointments as a lack of skill in husbandry would make them disinclined to introduce agricultural improvements. Such observations may have had some substance, but men like Thomas Gilbert had been raised on farms and through their own estates maintained an interest in agriculture.

It was not always easy for an outsider to break into these appointments and family connection was a vital recommendation, sometimes almost a prerequisite. John Coyney was the 'baylife' to the Earl of Shrewsbury at Alton in the late seventeenth century,[13] and another member of the family held the same post some fifty years later.[14] In the intervening period, it was held by the Bill family, passing on the death of Richard Bill in 1716, to his son Robert; who was the father-in-law of John Gilbert.[15] By the end of the century, a Charles Bill was acting as agent to the Earl, at the time when the Uttoxeter Canal was under construction.[16] The Bills were also closely connected with Earl Gower's Trentham estates, William Bill (John Gilbert's brother-in-law) being agent there from the 1760s until 1774.[17] Interestingly, Charles Bill (William's elder brother) qualified as a barrister like Thomas Gilbert; whilst their two younger brothers, William Bill and John Gilbert, became agents or stewards to noble houses.[18]

The family connections went even further than this. Elizabeth Bill (John Gilbert's sister-in-law) married a Michael Barbor in 1754,[19]

John Gilbert, 1724-1795.   *(Dr Hugh Malet)*

possibly the 'Ensign Barbor' who served in Earl Gower's Regiment.[20] One of their sons, Robert Barbor also appears to have taken up the law and he was working as an agent for the Marquis of Stafford (previously the second, Earl Gower) by 1797.[21] In 1803, he wrote to the Marquis seeking a position again and the letter reveals a great deal about the hereditary nature of such positions and the inter-relationship between agencies in the two estates:—

'The acquaintance your Lordship has had with my family and connections and the friendship and patronage which both my father and myself have in succession been honoured with . . . The favourable notice of my late, most respected Patron, the Duke of Bridgewater, which was continued to me for near twenty years to the time of his death, was originally issued to me from the same source, your Lordship's Patronage.'[22]

The presence of Michael Barbor in London, by 1760[23] and the address 'Charterhouse' on the above letter, suggest that both father and son undertook work in the capital for both Earl Gower and the Duke of Bridgewater.

Mary Gilbert, a younger sister to Thomas and John, married Thomas Birds of Bakewell and although he did not take up an agency, his sons did.[24] David Birds was making payments in respect of legacies and debts for the trustees of the Duke of Bridgewater, between 1804-1805; and it seems reasonable to suppose that he had enjoyed some sort of agency during the Duke's lifetime.[25] Another son, or possibly grandson, William Birds was acting as an agent to the Earl of Shrewsbury at the time that he began the redevelopment of his Alton estate.[26]

Abraham Rees identified the need for another stratum of agents: 'on large estates, especially where they lie in detached and scattered parts, it is considered necessary to have other assistants, as a woodward, land-reeve or ground officer, a clerk or under-steward, a law assistant or solicitor, and a surveyor. As the under-steward, a tenant's son who has been properly educated, and is fully acquainted with farming, is the most suitable and proper person that can be found for the business.'[27]

Here again family connections appear as being of paramount importance. John Gilbert's eldest son, Thomas, assisted his father with the management of the Worsley estate, as well as with the construction of the Bridgewater Canal to Runcorn.[28] By 1776, he was negotiating with the Mayor of Liverpool over proposals to extend the duke's dock at that place.[29] The younger Thomas does not appear to have been the Duke's agent there, for in 1778, Thomas Gilbert sent instructions to John to 'discharge the 2 Mr Banks's... as he (the Duke) is very sensible how much his affairs suffer under their present management at Liverpool.' John Gilbert may have been trying to obtain an agency or stewardship for his son, Thomas; as this same letter continues: 'as to obtaining a Land place for the young man, that is not an easy thing to get—it would require both time and good Interests to accomplish—he (the Duke) will talk with you upon it when he sees you.'[30] In 1789, this same Thomas was described as a 'Merchant' of Duke Street, Liverpool.[31]

Robert Gilbert, John Gilbert's second son, was 'educated for the church' and as the Reverend Robert Gilbert, he was given the Duke's 'second best preferment at his disposal to the amount of about £1200 per annum,[32] the living at Settrington, near Malton in Yorkshire, which he held from 1775 until his death in 1820.[33] The appointment was not merely a clerical one as he was involved with some agent's work and improvements to the estate.[34] Possibly, Thomas Gilbert's eldest son's appointment to the living at Little Gaddesden, near the Duke's main seat at Ashridge, also involved him in certain work of the same nature.[35] The family involvement was completed by the younger John Gilbert, who like his father was employed mainly on the Worsley estate. After his father's death in August 1795, the younger John Gilbert left the Duke's employment and with his mother moved 'to Barton House... early in 1796.'[36] Unlike most of the family, he appears to have been of a too independent nature and his relationship with the Duke deteriorated rapidly.[37]

A great estate in the eighteenth century was really a complex of enterprises which in addition to agricultural pursuits also embraced mining, quarrying, timber production, transport undertakings, housing developments and a host of miscellaneous industrial undertakings. They represented, consequently, one of the largest concentrations of capital and productive capacity that was known, and its control, administration, and development called for someone with managerial capacity and a wide range of technical knowledge and experience. The Duke of Bridgewater had an annual income of £106,000 in 1802; of which some £75,400 was derived from his estates and passed through the hands of various agents. The chief portion of this, a figure of £49,000 came from the: 'Canal, Lancashire Estates & Cheshire Estates & Dock at Liverpool.'[38] John Gilbert, towards the end of his employment with the Duke, was responsible for the collection of a figure approaching £50,000, and for collective properties worth in excess of a million pounds.[39] Thomas Gilbert had oversight of all the Duke's affairs, despite the

REPORT

OF A

CAUSE,

The Reverend *ROBERT GILBERT*

VERSUS

Sir M. M. SYKES, Bart. M.P.

TRIED AT THE

YORK LENT ASSIZES, 1812,

Before the Honourable Sir ALEXANDER THOMSON, Knight,

And a SPECIAL JURY,

Being an ACTION brought by the Plaintiff to recover a SUM of MONEY

WON ON

The LIFE of BONAPARTE.

————

This Cause created considerable interest, the nature of which was, One Hundred Guineas being paid by the Plaintiff in 1802, to receive One Guinea per day during the Life of Napoleon.

————

SECOND EDITION.

————

York:

Printed by and for J. SPENCE and T. DEIGHTON, Herald-Office;
And Sold by the Booksellers of York, Malton, Scarborough, Whitby,
Bridlington, Ripon, Hull, Beverley, Leeds, Howden, Richmond,
Driffield, Doncaster, Northallerton, &c. &c,

Price—One Shilling.

Despite his religious calling and duties as a land agent, Robert Gilbert still found time to engage in this curious lawsuit. *(Author's Collection)*

muddled statement made by Robert Lansdale in 1843, that he was merely the land agent for six out of the twelve. Bridgewater estates—'his grace's Shropshire, Northampton, Bucks, Herts, Durham and Yorkshire estates.'[40]

One less obvious aspect of an agent's duties could be the management of parliamentary seats for their aristocratic masters. The earliest known involvement that Thomas Gilbert had in the world of politics was as the manager of the Lichfield interest for the Leveson-Gower family. The Lichfield interest was in fact shared between the Leveson-Gowers and the Ansons of Shugborough Hall, who after a ruinously expensive contest in 1747, concentrated their efforts on the burgage vote.[41] Vast sums of money were spent in buying up burgage property which was conveyed to their supporters before elections, and this was combined with attempts to purchase freehold and freeman votes. The process was a slow one because of the complicated franchise and the stubborn independence of the Freeman voters. Much of the work was initially the responsibility of Thomas Cobb, a Lichfield mercer, who bought up most of the burgage property, whenever possible. Following the election of Viscount Trentham (later the second Earl Gower) and Thomas Anson in 1754, Thomas Gilbert was brought in to examine the interest. His brief was to put it in order and to find ways of avoiding wasteful expenditure in future elections; and his report describes how he found it to be a:—

'tedious and very disagreeable task, but as I have seen the disadvantage that you and my Lord Anson have laboured under for want of knowing the state of your affairs at Lichfield, I have long wished for an opportunity of representing the whole to you in such a light, that upon every occasion when anything is proposed you may be able to judge for yourselves, and not depend entirely upon representations from one person or other; I see your interest now in such a view, that with a tolerable degree of management for the future no opposition can hurt you or put you to much expense.'[42]

Gilbert approved of Cobb's purchases, but had several suggestions to make for the future management of the property. His main concern was to prevent any future repetition of the huge sums paid out to ale-house keepers during the two previous elections. The exact cost of free food and drink for voters is not known, but Thomas Gilbert managed to save the interest £1,073 10s 4d by reducing by 3d a gallon some of the bills for ale for the 1753 and 1754 elections. Three days after his report was submitted to the first Earl Gower, Thomas Gilbert was writing to Granville Leveson-Gower (later to be the second Earl Gower), one of the sitting members for Lichfield about the arrangements for yet another election at Lichfield. Henry Vernon was to be the Gower candidate for the vacancy caused by Granville Leveson-Gower's elevation to the peerage.

Thomas Gilbert, 1720-1798.   *(William Salt Library)*

Thomas Gilbert's careful preparations were to prove extremely valuable, for despite his optimism there was an opposition to be overcome at the election of 1755, just as there was to be in the election of 1761. Polling at the next general election took place in March 1768 when Thomas Anson and Thomas Gilbert were elected unopposed.[43] Thomas Gilbert was to sit as one of the members for Lichfield until December 1794 (five months after Earl Gower's retirement) but he never had to fight an election.[44] The Ansons and Leveson-Gowers in coalition continued to nominate the members for Lichfield for a further thirty years; and the only other election contest before the end of the century, that in 1799, only served to confirm the strength of the interest consolidated by Thomas Gilbert. This control continued until the 1820s when it was realised that 'boroughs were becoming too large and politically conscious to control.' The Leveson-Gowers gave up Lichfield, Stafford and Newcastle at this time, 'while sheer force of opinion drove them from the county seat.' The defeat of the Leveson-Gower interest was a clear indication of the disintegration of the old political systems in the 1820s. James Loch's examination of the various estates after his appointment in 1812 were to reveal another reason for this withdrawal from the local political scene.[45] George Granville Leveson-Gower, first Duke of Sutherland (1758-1833) was an immensely wealthy man, but he was also a careful one and he was made aware that his father's (the second Earl Gower) political activities had caused:

'The Staffordshire and Shropshire estates (to be) burdened under a system of leases for lives, to meet the election expenses incurred by the late Marquis, a system which, by destroying the enterprise of the tenant and crippling the landlord, had reduced the tenantry to considerable penury and backwardness.'[46]

Rees's *Cyclohaedia* contains a very full account of the duties of the eighteenth century 'land steward'.[47] This is so detailed that it almost reads like a job specification for what a contemporary, J. Lawrence, termed 'the modern land steward.'[48] The match between the requirements outlined by Rees and the qualities, skills and knowledge possessed by John Gilbert is very striking; and this must mark him out as one of the first, if not the first, of the new breed of professional land agents that developed during the eighteenth century. Thomas Gilbert, on the other hand was cast in a more traditional role, that of the lawyer who also dealt with accounts, but at a higher level than the mere bookkeeper, or embryonic accountant.[49] In as much as the early methods of industrial management were borrowed from the great estates, he should be seen more in the role of legal adviser and financial director. The major difference being that employers like the Duke of Bridgewater had the overriding say in policy formation, as Dr. Malet has demonstrated.[50]

Age was considered a primary qualification, for as Rees points out: 'stewards should have attained that thorough and correct knowledge of the business of life. . . which ought not to be expected earlier than the middle age.'[51] The eighteenth century view of 'middle age', however, was different from the contemporary one; for John Gilbert was thirty-five on appointment and John Farey was only twenty-six.[52] Employers were sometimes concerned that 'no material part' of their steward's time, or 'attention should be engrossed by their own private concerns';[53] but in practice many stewards developed other enterprises and frequently enlisted their employers as partners.

The main concern of any eighteenth century land steward, provided that he was a 'resident manager',[54] was agriculture. John Gilbert coming from stock that could be best described as 'Gentlemen farmers,' had been brought up on a farm.[55] When he returned from Birmingham to run the Cotton estate, he was to have control of a considerable holding at the young age of seventeen. 'Agriculture', wrote Rees 'is considered as the only firm foundation on which the other acquired attainments can be securely reposed. It is not more essentially valuable in the superintendence, than in the improvement of an estate.'[56] John Gilbert was responsible for a number of improvements on the Worsley estate, but his attitude to improvement is perhaps best seen through the interests of his son. The younger John worked with his father at Worsley and this clearly shaped his outlook when it came to agricultural practices. He was to be an early vice-president of the Newcastle-under-Lyme and Potteries Agricultural Society,[57] whose aims were to encourage a:—

'spirit of industry, emulation and improvement in husbandry; as well as by affording an easy opportunity for the communication of rural facts, observation and experiments, together with the most useful modes and practice.'[58]

His father may not have belonged to such a society, but he was certainly interested in 'experiments' and 'practices', as his work at Worsley demonstrated.

The most remarkable of these improvements was the draining of the Duke's portion of Chat Moss, 'a peat bog of immenze size . . . by computation 6000 acres.'[59] This operation was linked with the construction of the Duke's Canal which was extended gradually into the very heart of the Duke's holding, the first 'gutters' being cut in 1760 or 1761.[60] Problems were encountered with these drains as the soft, spongy peat was so mobile that it soon closed up again; and 'large bodies of peat' sometimes rose from the bottom of the branch canal to block the channel.[61] Such problems were overcome by patience and a systematic policy of dumping around the banks of the branch canal, the sole purpose of which had been to facilitate the dumping of 'all the rubbish which was necessarily brought out of the suff and coal pitts.'[62] If the Worsley Canal scheme is seen as the answer to a number of civil engineering problems (they will be described in Chapter Three,) then this scheme of John Gilbert's must be seen as an extension of the same kind of logic. Not only was he able to dispose of the 'spoil' from the mines, but at the same time he employed the 'spoil' to act 'much like marl' and so many acres of previously unusable land could be gradually brought into production.[63] Gilbert was to use the same tactic on Earl Gower's Lilleshall estate, although it was the overburden from the limestone that was dumped in this instance.[64] The idea may have come from his father, Thomas Gilbert, who, when working the Clough Head Colliery with Robert Bill, had dumped 'Pitt Lowes and Stone' to form an access road known as 'the Causey'.[65]

Dr Aikin mentions earlier schemes of drainage in the moss areas of Lancashire in the late seventeenth and early eighteenth century, but he adds that they had limited success.[66] The presence of a canal added a whole new dimension to such improvements, as demonstrated by the case of Trafford Moss which was 'manured' with marl and 'compost brought from Manchester.'[67] John Gilbert's steady progress at Chat Moss appears to have attracted the attention of other landowners and one of these, Thomas Eccleston, enlisted his help with another scheme in 1778.[68] Eccleston, incidentally was the first person to pay public tribute to John Gilbert's achievement at Worsley, for he wrote that he 'had judiciously planned, and happily executed the astonishing works of his grace, the Duke of Bridgewater.'[69] His project involved the drainage of Martin-Mere, a large pool and area of bogland, near to what is now Southport. Gilbert surveyed the area, drew up a plan and assisted Eccleston with the direction of the undertaking, including the legal element of obtaining leases. He also designed a series of 'flushing-gates' and encouraged Eccleston to use 'a draining or guttering plough.'[70] In all these respects, he was fulfilling the role of a good agent or steward, except that in this instance he was acting in a freelance capacity. Gilbert was acting as a consulting land-agent and engineer, for as will be seen later these two emergent professions were often combined in eighteenth-century land stewards.

Rees believed that 'land surveying' was another requisite qualification needed by a land steward.[71] By this he meant surveying for the purpose of measuring and mapping estate, although by the eighteenth century there was a growing body of professional surveyors to undertake such tasks.[72] The possession of such skills by John Gilbert is indicated by his statement before a House of Commons Committee in 1758, that he 'attended at the Levelling and Measuring of the ground for the first Bridgewater Canal.[73] Thomas Gilbert (John's son) also studied with 'Mr Wyatt' during his 'studies' with Matthew Boulton in Birmingham.[74] The Wyatts of Lichfield and Burton-on-Trent were the most famous family of eighteenth century surveyors, but found time to engage in other pursuits ranging from architecture to the invention of a spinning machine.[75]

Rees does not list aknowledge of geology amongst the desirable attributes of a land steward, perhaps because he considered it to be a too specialised branch of knowledge. John Farey after leaving his agent's post at Woburn, set up as a consulting surveyor and geologist in London adding the principles laid down by William Smith.[76] Smith was one of the most outstanding practical British geologists, whose achievements were all the more remarkable as he was self-taught and received little professional or financial support from others. He was the first to recognise the importance of fossils in identifying the chronology of rock-strata on his country-wide travels as a surveyor for the construction of canals and bridges.[77] The sciences of surveying and prospecting were closely related, and the Worsley scheme could not have been conceived by anyone who did not have a detailed knowledge of the geological structure of the area. Such information could have obtained in part from old outcrop workings, but John Gilbert also had borings made before finalising his plan.[78] Unlike William Smith, he attached no importance to fossils and declared 'Fosils I make no point of a collection of them. If any uncommon fall in my way that is not in the Hands of the Curious, I generally secure it for my curious friends.'[79] The inspection of mines could prove dangerous as John Gilbert knew from his close escape from death during a fire-damp explosion in one of the Lilleshall levels. The collier accompanying him was permanently disabled by the blast whilst John Gilbert was burnt around the head.[80]

The Woburn estate had an important functionary in Robert Salmon, who was variously described as 'Resident Surveyor' and 'resident architect and mechanist.'[81] Though his post was variously described his

A map of 1794 showing the extensive drainage system engineered at Martin Mere by John Gilbert. *(Author's Collection)*

role was clear as he was the 'inventor of many useful and valuable surgical instruments, implements of agriculture, hydraulics, etc.'[82] Rees argued that stewards ought to have 'some knowledge of mechanics, and the other sciences that are requisite to the business of an engineer and may be highly useful in prosecuting the improvements incidental to landed property.'[83] John Gilbert certainly had this type of knowledge and it developed as he became more advanced in years and experience. At Worsley, he called in Brindley, to assist in the work there utilising his experience as a practical millwright.[84] Twenty years later at Martin Mere, John Gilbert was able to exhibit an understanding of the total range of skills possessed by any accomplished millwright.

Likewise, in the Boulton and Watt papers, there are engine drawings accredited to John Gilbert, which show that he took an early interest in parallel motions and beams.[85] The drawings could have been made in connection with the rotative, sun and planet engine that was installed at Marston rockpits, under an agreement dated 1st January 1789.[86] The younger Matthew Boulton was a childhood friend of John Gilbert and the brothers had bought their first engine from him some ten years earlier.[87] The younger John Gilbert may also have spent some time at the Soho factory, but this did not prevent him from gleefully pointing out that some of the components sent for repairs to the Marston engine, lacked fixing holes and were thus useless.[88]

John Gilbert employed a number of what would be termed consulting engineers at Worsley. James Brindley is the best known, but at the time of his arrival at Worsley he was still calling himself a 'millwright'.[89] Indeed most of the 'other ingenious persons' employed by the Duke were millwrights, including Ashton Tonge who designed and constructed the impressive water-engine, seen by Sir Joseph Banks during his visit to the works in 1767.[90] James Brindley had erected a water-engine at Trentham Hall for Earl Gower in 1758[91] and another at Cheadle for the Gilbert brothers in 1759.[92] Aiken describes Gilbert as meriting 'a distinguished place (among the) other ingenious persons' employed by the Duke, a statement that confirms his knowledge of mechanics, if not his practical skill as a mechanic.[93] The Gilbert brothers introduced Brindley to the Duke as part of an on-going policy of recruiting talent and evaluating new ideas. Rees relates how:

'Mr. G., who, being acquainted with Mr Brindley as a neighbour, and knowing him to be a very ingenious and excellent millwright, engaged his assistance in the conduct and completion of the arduous undertaking, and introduced him to the Duke for this purpose.'[94]

Earl Gower (later Marquis of Stafford)   *(William Salt Library)*

Thomas was also very actively involved in this process as illustrated by his interest in the work of William Symington and more indirectly that of William Murdock. These men were early experimenters with model steam carriages. Both seem to have used non-condensing engines to propel their models; both came from South-West Scotland and both were involved with the building of steam engines at the Wanlockhead lead mines, these were operated by Ronald Crauford and Co. (the Countess of Dumfries, Sir Peter Crauford, and Gilbert Meason); who had ordered an engine from Boulton and Watt in 1777.[95] The Countess of Dumfries had until her marriage been Margaret, daughter of Ronald Crauford of Restalrig; and significantly Mary Crauford had become Thomas Gilbert's second wife in 1777. Through this family link, John Taylor, the mine overseer at Wanlockhead and Symington's informal business partner, was introduced:

'At Lady Dumfries's desire, [to] a Mr Gilbert as he passed to England. He is a member of Parliament. He comes from a mining county, and was desirous to have a few specimens of the different kinds of white ore, which I carried down. He gave me some account of the mines in his county, and made inquiry concerning the nature of the mines here. He likewise wanted much to be informed concerning the steam carriage, and from what I told him of its power, he said it would be a great affair for the Duke of Bridgewater on his canals, and desired me to inform you that if he could (end)'[96]

This incomplete letter was written in 1786 and is clearly concerned with a steam powered road carriage, but Thomas Gilbert apparently envisaged it being used on the Duke's Canals to tow boats and barges. Such a notion was a logical extension of the work of the Frenchman, Nicholas Cugnot, who in 1769 had developed a working steam carriage to pull artillery pieces onto the battlefield. As it was the first experiment in locomotive towing was not held until 1888 on the Middlewhich branch of the Ellesmere and Chester Canal.[97]

Thomas Gilbert's meeting with John Taylor in 1786 was probably not the first occasion on which he had heard of the potential of steam carriages. William Murdock is said to have experimented with model mechanical carriages in company with his millwright father in Old Cumnock, circa. 1776; just prior to him taking up employment with Boulton and Watt in the following year.[98] After working as a pattern maker at their Soho factory, Murdock was sent to help commission the engine on the Margaret Mine at Wanlockhead in 1779.[99] William Symington and Murdock met for the first time during this visit and it seems unlikely that their conversations did not take in the topic of steam carriages.[100] After completing his work at Wanlockhead, Murdock was sent to Shropshire to complete the Donnington Wood engine for the Gilbert brothers. In September 1779 Murdock went to work for Boulton and Watt in Cornwall and it was there in 1786 that Murdock demonstrated his working model of a steam carriage to Matthew Boulton. Both Boulton and James Watt discouraged Murdock as they wished to see him employed to their benefit and the idea lay dormant until taken up by Richard Trevithick.[101] Matthew Boulton may like Murdock have had the opportunity to discuss steam carriages with the Gilbert brothers, although their correspondence remains silent on this point. James Watt undertook to build a model to silence Murdock, or as he put it: 'to prevent as much as possible more fruitless argument about it, I have one of some size under hand and am resolved to try if God will work a miracle in favour of these carriages.'[102] He felt that Symington was also wasting his time 'chasing shadows', so Thomas Gilbert's continuing interest is even the more remarkable in the light of Watt's short sighted opinion.[103]

William Symington built an engine to power Patrick Miller's steamboat for the trial on Dalswinton Loch on 14th October 1788, probably encouraged by James Taylor; and he did the same for the steamboat tried on the canal at Falkirk the following year. Neither trial proved convincing although an observer felt that 'the invention bids fair to be of the greatest utility.'[104] This could have well been written by Thomas Gilbert himself and this enthusiasm seems to have been caught by the 'Canal Duke', for having observed a steamboat that sailed from Runcorn to Castlefield in 1797 he commissioned his own steamboat trials at Worsley. During 1798/99 a boat was specially built with a paddle wheel at the stern, to be driven by a steam engine built by the North Staffordshire engineer, William Sherratt at Salford.[105] The steamboat hauled a train of coal boats on its trial but no more quickly than if horses had been used and there was a real fear that the wash would damage the canal banks. At this point, the Duke abandoned the experiment but not his faith in the potential of steamboats. Following the commissioning of William Symington's *Charlotte Dundas* in 1801, the potential of steamboats was at last realised and the Duke subsequently ordered eight tugs along the lines of Symington's boat.[106] By this time both John and Thomas Gilbert were dead, but even in their last years they never lost their interest in new inventions and innovations as will be also shown in their dealings with Robert Weldon and his Caisson Lock.

The employment of such skilled workmen, who by the end of the century would be known as engineers, could create certain problems of a management nature. Brindley was frequently tetchy and he disliked working under John Gilbert's supervision, but there could be even more threatening problems.[107] Josiah Wedgwood records a 'mutiny' among the canal-cutters on the Bridgewater Canal in 1773, which John Gilbert had to deal with.[108] Before 1765, a group of Earl Gower's miners were 'proceeding to Trentham to pull down the Hall', until confronted by the Reverend John Middleton who managed to convince them of the 'rashness and wickedness of their conduct', whereupon they dispersed.[109] Such incidents indicate that the control exercised by land stewards had to be firm, but tempered with an almost paternal compassion. During John Gilbert's lifetime tips given to the boatmen, by visitors to the underground workings at Worsley were paid into a fund that he drew on to make payments to miners' widows and from time to time for ale for the boatmen.[110] His son, John had a similar nature and made a generous donation to a provisions fund for poor potters,[111] as well as distributing 'among his poor work people, a fine fat cow.'[112] These measures were associated with periods of food shortage, when employers and agents assumed responsibility for their work people, often purchasing food to be sold at cost price or lower.[113] At the time of the younger John Gilbert's death in 1812, he is said to have 'devoted nearly one thousand pounds per annum to genuine acts of discriminate charity.'[114]

Above all, the agent or steward was responsible for keeping the estate accounts; or in the case of a large grouping of estates, a chief agent would check the accounts for individual estates and compile a general account. Between 1760 and 1788, Thomas Gilbert audited the Lilleshall accounts; and made payments in respect of rents, taxes, pensions and sums sent to Earl Gower and other members of the family.[115] He relinquished this responsibility to John Bishton, who after 1791 took over Thomas Gilbert's role as chief agent and auditor.[116] This pattern of accounting was also followed on Earl Gower's estates at Trentham (which for accounting purposes included Newcastle), Wolverhampton, Lichfield and on the smaller estates.[117] From these accounts a general account was compiled with the receipts analysed under: Rent receipts; profits from timber; profits from collieries; profits from farms; cash from his Lordship; and incidental receipts. Expenditure was broken down into: cash paid to my Lord; building and repairs; rents; annuities; charities; purchases and interest; tradesmen; servants wages; servants board; gardens; husbandry; draining and improvements; housekeeping;

lewns and taxes; travelling; barley, oats and straw (animal feed and bedding); rent day expenses; cattle bought; woods and contingent expenses.[118] Likewise, on the Bridgewater estates, each estate kept a separate set of accounts, which after auditing by Thomas Gilbert were used to draw up a general statement. The same practice was followed for the Bridgewater estates, for as Robert Lonsdale recalled: 'He came to Worsley every Xmas 'till 1795 to examine and state His Grace's accounts, staying about 10 days and taking the General Accounts with him for his Grace's eye.[119]

The many and varied nature of a steward's or agent's duties meant that he often needed help, especially of a clerical nature. John Gilbert's letter writing was a serious weakness and indicative of his limited formal education, so that he had an assistant in Robert Lansdale to help him 'examine vouchers, make up books, copy letters, &c.'[120] Lansdale also observed that he (John Gilbert) was 'by profession . . . a Collier Miner, Canal Navigator . . . a practical, persevering and industrious outdoor man, (who) loved mines and underground works.'[121] There were other assistants as well, people like Thomas Kent, who was chief cashier and accountant at Worsley.[122] Thomas Gilbert also employed men who helped him with his estate work and his private business. John Johnson and William Garrett were his two clerks at the time of his death in 1798, but it is clear that he employed more assistants during his active years.[123] One of these was Francis Adams, who was in Thomas Gilbert's employment by 1769,[124] but who at the time of his death had found a post with the Duke of Bridgewater.[125] These assistants did not become agents in the course of time, presumably because they did not have sufficient social status and experience at the relevant level.

Thomas Gilbert's practice as a steward or agent really came about because of his limited success as a barrister.[126] The writer of his obituary notice relates that he never 'made any very conspicious figure, either in the courts at Westminster, or on the circuit.'[127] This meant that his prospects of making a really successful career in the law were limited, as 'seldom, if ever, were men raised to the Woolsack or the Bench who had not distinguished themselves at the Bar.'[128] So the other way of improving his 'fortune' was to attach himself 'to a noble family, that possessed great influence in his neighbourhood'.[129] There was nothing novel in this strategy and a number of lawyers had employed it to their considerable advantage.

One lawyer, who had been very successful in this way, had bought lands in the manors of Cheadle and Kingsley in the late seventeenth

Francis Egerton, third Duke of Bridgewater.   *(The Manchester Ship Canal Company)*

century.[130] He was Joseph Banks, steward to the Dukes of Norfolk, Leeds and Newcastle; and a Member of Parliament. Banks also acquired estates in Lincolnshire, where he bought Revesby Abbey for his son.[131] This son, also called Joseph, became Lord of the Manor of both Cheadle and Kingsley;[132] and in 1721 he made an agreement with John Philips to mine coal at Kingsley. The document was witnessed by George Gilbert and his son Thomas (1688-1741/2),[133] who had married John's daughter, Elizabeth Philips. So the potential of a career in law and the benefits of obtaining a stewardship, may have been realised in the Gilbert family, even when the future agent, Thomas Gilbert, was still an infant. The first Joseph Banks had been successful in founding a genteel family and that was clearly the aim of the Gilberts at that time.[134]

The post of steward or agent could pay quite well. On smaller estates, a salary of £50, with a house and a small farm on the estate was the normal pattern of remuneration.[135] This was the exact package given to the steward at Worsley, before John Gilbert's arrival in 1757.[136] Gilbert was appointed with a salary of £200 per annum,[137] raised to £300 in 1762;[138] plus the tenancy of a demesne farm on very lenient terms.[139] In addition, he appears to have lived rent free in the Brick Hall at Worsley, which was still one of the Duke's residences.[140] The arrangement may have been the same as that worked out between the Earls of Shrewsbury and their agents at Alton. The agent leased Alveton Lodge, described as 'a comfortable homestead with farm buildings adjoining', from the Earl, who had rooms reserved for his private use within the lodge.[141] Whatever, the precise nature of the arrangement, the opportunity to run a farm must have been a profitable sideline.

Some agents received much higher salaries, like the £700 given to the Duke of Bedford's 'agent-in-chief' in 1732, and by the end of the century the Duke of Devonshire's agent was paid £1,000. But as Professor Mingay has noted: 'these two posts, of course, were at the very top of the profession, and the general run of steward's salaries was considerably more modest.'[142] Thomas Gilbert occupied a position that was equal to that of any steward in the land, especially since through him the estates of the Duke of Bridgewater and Earl Gower were run as a sort of loosely structured combination. But despite this, he does not seem to have been paid a salary as such. He was probably paid a small retainer as legal adviser and 'receiver-general', but in the main, he charged for the work that he actually did. This is confirmed by many of the estate papers being accompanied by Gilbert's own account for legal work completed during the year[143] and he appears to have had a monopoly of this kind of work.[144]

John Gilbert also received special payments for the additional work involved in obtaining the Acts of Parliament for the Bridgewater canals.[145]

Another source of income for agents was freelance work as either legal or technical consultants. John Gilbert's involvement with the draining of Martin Mere has already been mentioned, but it was his mining expertise that was in greatest demand. In 1768, he made an inspection of some of Earl Gower's collieries in the Longton area, and his report contains recommendations about improving the drainage and the need 'to get proper Articles Executed . . . to confirm the agreement.'[146] John Gilbert was also employed by Ralph Oakden and Partners of Stafford, to construct a boat level for them into their mine at Castleton, after the fashion of the Worsley one.[147] The Speedwell level was excavated between 1774 and 1781, and during its construction John Gilbert made extensive use of gunpowder to blast out the tunnels. The venture was not a success as there was insufficient lead ore to make it pay.[148] Earlier in 1766, John Gilbert had been drawn into a partnership to work a lead mine near Winster, which involved the construction of another boat level. This Hillcarr Sough mine had as its principal shareholders, the Barker family, agents to the Dukes of Rutland and Devonshire and it was their idea to bring in John Gilbert.[149]

Thomas Gilbert also did some estate work mainly of a legal nature, for Lord Waldegrave, Earl Gower's brother-in-law. He spent some days with the Duke of Bridgewater at Lord Waldegrave's house in 1778 and the next year coal was discovered on his estate at Radstock. This could imply that John Gilbert may have been called in to look over the estate, but there is no evidence to confirm this view. The colliery was worked by a partnership, who fell behind with the payment of royalties to Lord Waldegrave, so Thomas Gilbert was involved in writing a number of 'pretty smart letters' before the matter was settled. One of Gilbert's letters also refers to a farm and the need for 'a proper course of Husbandry, to prevent it being made impoverished;' a further indication of his agricultural knowledge.[150] Again, this work would have been paid for on a fee basis as would John Gilbert's work as a consulting, mining engineer.

Dr. Trinder has identified early examples of agents, who 'leased some of the enterprises on their masters' estates and worked them in their own right . . . ultimately (acquiring) sufficient capital to extend their operations elsewhere.'[151] This should not be taken simply as an indication of a generous master, for employers realised that the

The Speedwell Mine in 1895 showing the canal and canal tunnels.   *(Author's Collection)*

entrepreneurial flair of their agents could also benefit them through the development of their estates. Professor Richards has described Earl Gower as 'the eighteenth century aristocrat/industrialist *par excellence,*' but it was the Gilbert brothers who did so much to organize the large-scale capitalist enterprises on his estates.[152] The most striking example of this being the formation of the concern known as Earl Gower and Company in 1764, to work the various mineral resources on the Earl's

Lilleshall estate.[153] Earl Gower was to provide the capital and to allow the Gilbert's to organise the exploitation of the mineral wealth on the estate and in return he was to receive one half of all profits. They, for their part, were to receive equal shares in the other half of the profit. Earl Gower provided safeguards for his own income by leasing the workings to the Gilbert brothers whose obligation to him was confirmed by a signed bond.[154]

Once the Donnington Wood Canal was completed, then the coal, lime and ironstone resources could be exploited systematically and the whole concern could become profitable. But the purpose of investing so much capital in the canal was to attract further investment, so increasing the profit from the sale of minerals and the collection of ground-rent. This additional investment was introduced by Richard Reynolds, who aware of the potential of the site, erected iron furnaces near the canal in 1772.[155] Such developments increased the demand for raw materials, and so the profits drawn by Earl Gower and the Gilbert brothers. Thomas Gilbert's interest in Earl Gower and Company were left to his nephew, David Birds; and in 1800, Birds was made a handsome offer by the Duke of Bridgewater, who was renowned for knowing a good investment when he saw one.[156] Another example of the employer/employee partnership is provided by the Alston Moor enterprise, which will be discussed in a later chapter.

On a more modest level, there were the enterprises that were allowed on the estates with the employers involvement limited to that of landlord. Edward Coyney, agent to the Earl of Shrewsbury was a major shareholder in the partnership that operated the Alton lead smelting mill, under lease from the Earl.[157] On the Trentham estate, William Bill, Earl Gower's agent there, leased a flint mill as part of a partnership. He wrote in 1777 that 'our stonemill is likely to turn out very well, the Pottery trade is extremely good, and I believe we shall begin of another mill at Consall this summer.'[158] They were successful in establishing the Consall mill and this was run in conjunction with a third flint mill at Kibblestone, near Stone.[159] At Worsley, John Gilbert leased a mill which he converted into a mill for pounding black lead to make pencils.[160] But the Duke helped in other ways, including the use of his workshop and millwright at Worsley: 'to make an engine for pounding the Black lead.'[161] He also helped the firm of Worthington and Gilbert, canal carriers and in doing so sparked off an acrimonious dispute with the management committee of the Trent and Mersey Canal Company.[162]

Finally, there was a less tangible benefit to the Gilbert brothers being

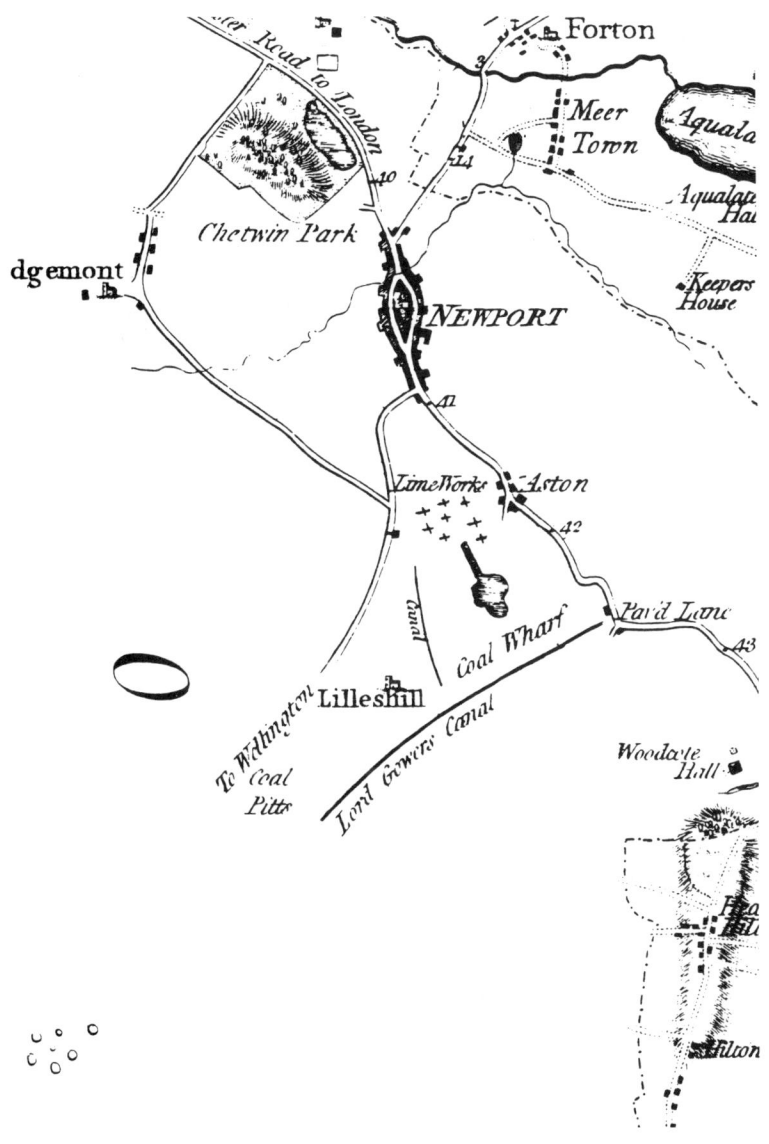

Lord (or Earl) Gower's canal system at Lilleshall as shown on a map of 1775.

(Author's Collection)

49

employed by Earl Gower and the Duke of Bridgewater. One writer said of James Brindley that he had unusual talents 'and under the patronage of his Grace the Duke of Bridgewater, they had an opportunity of being unfolded and exercised to their full extent.'[163] Afterwards, James Brindley liked to be known as the Duke of Bridgewater's engineer, even though the Duke had refused to offer him permanent employment.[164] Indeed, he built his second career as a canal engineer on his association and involvement with the Bridgewater canals. In a similar manner, John Gilbert had been given the opportunity at Worsley to demonstrate his talents and the practicality of his ideas. The success of his scheme was to ensure that he would be in demand as a consultant land-agent, mining engineer and canal engineer.[165]

III. THE DUKE'S AND EARL'S CANALS

Most of Britain's rivers were used for elementary transport purposes long before the start of recorded history, but little systematic improvement of river navigations took place until the fifteenth century when works were carried out on the Thames, the Lee and the Yorkshire Ouse. These improvements involved building artificial cuts or canals across the bends and it was an easy step from this to building a true canal to avoid a difficult section of a river. This step was taken for the first time in Britain between 1564 and 1566, when John Trew constructed the first Exeter Canal. Although it was only 1¾ miles long it incorporated Britain's first pound locks, fitted with vertically-rising gates.[1]

The art of improving and constructing navigations was much more advanced on the continent at this time. In Germany, the first waterway to cross a watershed was constructed between 1391 and 1398. The Duke of Milan's engineer, Bertola da Novate, built the first canal to overcome the problem of a rising gradient by the use of pound locks in 1452-8. A later successor to the same post, Leonardo da Vinci, further developed the Duke's waterway network through his invention of the mitre lock, about 1485.[2] Some indication of the gap between British and continental canal technology can be gauged from the fact that the mitre lock was not employed until the 1570s or 1580s in England.[3] The first French canal of note was the Briase Canal, built between 1604 and 1642. During the construction of this canal an even more ambitious scheme had been mooted to join the Mediterranean to the Atlantic Ocean. The vision of such a canal was the product of discussions between Francis I and Leonardo da Vinci, but it was too expensive a project and too technically difficult for the resources available to the King in 1516. By 1662 the scene was very different as Louis XIV now possessed the resources to see that the canal was built and the 150 mile long canal had been completed by 1681. Voltaire typified the reaction of all who saw this Languedoc canal (now called the Canal du Midi) when he wrote:

"Le monument le plus glorieux par son utilité, par sa grandeur, et par ses difficultés, fut ce canal de Languedoc qui joint deux mers."

In many ways Voltaire's words are reminiscent of the eulogistic descriptions of the early British canals that can be read in many eighteenth century newspapers.[4] The Languedoc Canal included numerous locks,

51

aqueducts and a 180 yard tunnel, meriting Hadfield's judgement that it was 'the first modern canal.'[5] It quickly became something of a tourist attraction for foreigners, especially the English engaged in the fashionable Grand Tour. One such visitor in 1754 was the seventeen year old Duke of Bridgewater, who had specifically sought the permission of his guardians for a visit to the region served by these remarkable engineering works.[6] No record of the Duke's impressions appear to have been recorded, but the subsequent hatching of the various canal systems around Worsley reflect the impact of what he saw. The subsequent adoption of the Dutch treckschuyts as the model for the Duke's passenger boats, suggests that as he passed through Holland he also took a keen and observant interest in the Dutch system of waterways.[7]

Francis, Third Duke of Bridgewater, is generally credited with the building of Britain's first modern canal and it is undeniable that his first canal caught the public imagination when it opened in 1761.[8] But two decades before, in March 1742, the eighteen miles long Newry Canal had been opened and the British Canal Age had begun. This canal was promoted so that the coal-mining area of Tyrone (south-west of Lough Neagh) could have a waterway link with the sea at Newry and thence to the rich markets of Dublin. The engineers were E. L. Pearce and his employee, Richard Castle, a French Huguenot refugee who had made a study of continental waterways, and was doubtless the more knowledgeable of the two. However, they were both dismissed and the role of engineer was undertaken by Thomas Steers from 1736 until the canal was completed.[9] Steers was a remarkable figure who had spent four years in Holland in the 1690s, before returning to undertake harbour work in London.[10] In 1715 he built Liverpool's first dock and then made the Mersey and Irwell Navigation under powers granted in an Act of 1720. Thomas Steers died in 1750 but he represents the link between the first British canal and what could be termed the first canal in England. His pupil, Henry Berry built this precursive waterway under powers granted in an Act of 1755; nominally this involved making the Sankey Brook navigable, but due to its small size it seems certain that a canal must have been envisaged from the inception of the scheme.[11]

The emergence of Liverpool as a great port and an increasing awareness amongst the merchant community of their Hinterland gave rise to the navigation schemes already mentioned. This awareness also encouraged the Douglas and Weaver Navigations, both of which were authorised by Acts of Parliament passed in 1720. Steers was involved in both of these undertakings and was probably the main motivating force.[12] These developments caused Daniel Defoe to remark:

'The situation of Liverpoole gives it a very great advantage to improve their commerce, and extend it in the northern inland counties of England, particularly into Cheshire and Staffordshire, by the new navigation of the Rivers Mersee, the Weaver, and the Dane, by the last of which they come so near the Trent with their goods, that they make no difficulty to carry them by land to Burton, and from thence correspond quite through the Kingdom, even to Hull, and they begin to be very sensible of the advantage of such a commerce.'[13]

So it is hardly surprising that the first survey in 1755 to determine 'the practicability of joining the river Trent with the Weaver or Mersey' was paid for by the Corporation of Liverpool.[14] The Duke of Bridgewater's schemes should also be seen against this background development and then the inevitability of his extending his system to the River Mersey (possibly through the Mersey and Irwell Navigation) becomes obvious. As will be demonstrated, the Duke of Bridgewater's achievement was not that of the original innovator, but more that of the entrepreneur who took existing ideas and combined them in a new way and with startling success. Although Charles Hadfield does not explore this idea in any great detail he provided a very neat summary when he wrote:

'Yet the credit for creating the heavy transport basis of the Industrial Revolution must go to the third Duke of Bridgewater, for it was his work that found time and place and need correct.'[15]

The influence of these local navigational works almost certainly exercised as much influence on the Duke of Bridgewater as had the impressive Languedoc Canal, but the Duke's canal could have met with only modest success had it not been for the central contribution of John Gilbert.

The myth that James Brindley was the genius behind the Bridgewater Canals has proved to be very durable, despite the findings of modern researchers.[16] Samuel Smiles took the already cherished Brindley myth, and bending it to his purpose, succeeded in introducing an element of almost universal appeal to distort the truth further.[17] Although accorded a limited importance by Smiles, the Duke of Bridgewater and John Gilbert (his Agent), sometimes take on the appearance of interested bystanders. One source which Samuel Smiles missed (or chose to ignore) was Abraham Rees' *Cyclopaedia*, (1819), which contains the only published biography of John Gilbert. The author of the actual article is not known for certain, although there are strong indications that it came from the pen of John Farey (Senior), a skilled engineer and noted writer on technical

The Barton Aqueduct in 1770.   *Author's Collection)*

matters.[18] In this detailed life, the following statements are particularly telling:

'Mr. Gilbert's name has seldom occurred in connection with this very important and lucrative undertaking; and as he preceded Mr. Brindley in this business, of which we have ample and satisfactory evidence, we thought that justice required a candid and impartial statement of the case.'

. . . 'The tunnel was entirely executed as well as planned, by Mr. Gilbert; who, being acquainted with Mr. Brindley as a neighbour, and knowing him to be a very ingenious and excellent mill-wright, engaged his assistance in the conduct and completion of this arduous undertaking, and introduced him to the Duke for this purpose.'

. . . 'Mr. Gilbert was probably so modest and unassuming, that he did not, during his life-time lay claim to the honour which belonged to him, with respect to the Duke of Bridgewater's canals and collieries; and we have introduced his name into the *Cyclopaedia,* in order to do him justice, without meaning to detract from the merit of his coadjutor and successor, Mr. Brindley, to whom we have already paid ample and deserved respect under this biographical article.'[19]

John Gilbert may have been 'modest and unassuming' as the author suggests, but a more likely reason is that more self-assertion would have offended the Duke of Bridgewater himself. Unlike Brindley, John Gilbert was a salaried permanent employee of the Duke and both he and his family greatly benefited from the Duke's bounty. Quite simply, John Gilbert stood to lose more than he stood to gain. James Brindley on the other hand was self-employed and dependent on his reputation to earn his new commissions. Although there is no proof that he claimed the credit for the Worsley plans for himself, there is also no evidence that he made any positive efforts to set the record straight. Brindley's widow petitioned the Duke after her husband's death for non payment of salary for the years 1765 to 1772, stating that Brindley's 'plans and undertakings have been beneficial to His Grace's interest.' The original appeals were made through John and Thomas Gilbert and in a letter she wrote that 'I conceive it owing to this channel of application that no settling ever took place.' She did, however, acknowledge that in 1774, 'the late Mr. John Gilbert paid my brother, Mr. Henshall, the trifling sum of £100 on account of Mr. Brindley's time.' She wrote directly to the Duke of Bridgewater in 1801, but he did not even bother to reply. Not to be deterred she made a claim against the Duke's estate, following his death in 1803 and she seems to have been under the general impression that the Worsley scheme had been devised by Brindley.[20] This belief may have been fostered by her brother, Hugh Henshall who supplied Thomas Bentley with some raw materials' which were worked up into—'The Life of Mr. Brindley', for *Biographica Britannica*.[21] Indeed as Hugh Henshall took over Brindley's mantle, it would have been in his interests to make the most of Brindley's achievements. As many of Mrs. Brindley's claims for compensation were sent through Thomas and John Gilbert, it must have been irksome for John Gilbert to read Mrs. Brindley's exaggerated accounts of her husband's achievements.[22]

The idea for a canal may have been that of the Duke or of John Gilbert, although credit for the novel scheme as an entity clearly rests with John Gilbert. One key question which remains unanswered is where John Gilbert obtained his knowledge of canal engineering. He and his family were still living at Cotton in 1755 and almost certainly remained there until their removal to Worsley.[23] However, it is unlikely that his activities were confined to that area but the period of his life from about 1745 to 1759 is at best sketchy. He may have followed his brother and worked on an *ad hoc* basis as an estate agent, but there is no evidence for this before he became involved with the Bridgewater estates, perhaps as early as 1753.[24] Two marriages point towards some sort of involvement with the Rochdale area, and if he was travelling that far afield it seems likely that he was aware, if not acquainted with the various navigational schemes around the River Mersey.[25] He may also have visited South Wales because of his involvement in the copper trade and seen for himself the navigational level at Clyn-du which was started in 1747. The idea may even have come from a secondary source as the Gilberts were involved in the Ecton mines and so was an individual called John Rotton. The name of Rotton also appears amongst the many firms who had copper smelting works at Swansea, although it has not proved possible as yet to link these with the Derbyshire Rottons.[26]

Entrance to the Worsley Mines in 1770.   *(Author's Collection)*

Thomas Gilbert, in his capacity as the Duke's steward directed his brother to examine the Worsley mines in 1757. John Gilbert was immediately struck by the possibilities of bringing the coal by water to the expanding market in Manchester;[27] and in this he was adopting an approach that was being implemented elsewhere in the area.[28] In a fashion reminiscent of James Brindley, John Gilbert is said to have 'secluded himself altogether from company for two days, at the Bull Inn at Manchester, to consider how this might be done by water-carriage.' The account goes on to state that the Duke was no less struck with the proposition suggested by Mr. G than the projector himself.[29] John Gilbert's scheme was brilliant in the sense that it solved three engineering problems in a very simple way. If a sough could be constructed that was big enough to take boats, coal could be taken directly from the coal face to a wharf in Manchester. The springs inside the hill would fill the canal but at the same time the canal could be used to drain excess water from the mines. Such a navigational level had been constructed in South Wales by 1757 and two more were nearing completion.[30] They all served to drain mines and could be used to convey coal to the mouth of the mines, but the idea of linking them to a surface canal was the essential difference and original component in John Gilbert's scheme. An alternate source of inspiration may have been the Scot, Michael Meinzies, who took out a patent in 1750 which proposed to remove coal from the mine by a navigational level. His patent also covered a self-acting incline and he proposed that boxes filled with coal could be drawn up shafts. This was an early suggestion of the container idea that was used in connection with the Bridgewater Canal and it lends weight to the notion that Meinzies provided some of the inspiration for the Worsley scheme.[31]

The first stage in implementing this scheme was to obtain an Act of Parliament and on 25th November 1758 'A Petition of the Most Noble Francis, Duke of Bridgewater' was laid before the House of Commons.[32] William Tomkinson, the Duke's Manchester agent and solicitor, presented further evidence to the House on 6th December of the same year. On this occasion he was supported by John Gilbert who exhibited the original canal plan, stating that he had 'attended at the levelling and measuring of the ground.'[33] Their combined evidence carried the day and the House agreed to bring in a Bill which was to be sent to a particularly large select committee and in due course the Bill was passed (23rd March 1759).[34] John Gilbert's contribution was that of Resident Engineer, but he was also clearly responsible for collecting the considerable body of evidence that supported the Duke's application. Now work could begin in earnest. John Gilbert was joined by his family at Worsley, as clearly he would not have the time repeatedly to make the long trip back to Cotton.[35] From this point in time, all his energies were needed to see the grand design through to completion. This first act enabled the Duke to build a canal from his Worsley mines to Salford with a branch to Hollin Ferry, but this project on its own was of doubtful financial viability because of the restrictive clauses concerning the price he was allowed to charge for his coal in Salford.[36]

The route of the main canal from Worsley to Salford was planned to run wholly to the north of the River Irwell, above the 82 foot contour and so avoid the need for locks. By the end of 1759 it appears that a decision had been made to alter the route and powers were sought. The Duke's second Act (Royal Assent granted 12th March 1760) allowed the canal to be carried across the River Irwell Navigation by an aqueduct at Barnton; thus laying the foundations for the realisation of the prime aim of connecting Liverpool and Manchester by canal.[37] John Gilbert was again involved in collecting evidence and generally administering the affair, but in the Parliamentary Committee stage, James Brindley appeared to present significant evidence.[38] Brindley had arrived at Worsley on 1st July 1759 with his small band of craftsmen, to find work already under way on the soughs and canal.[39] He had 'rare gifts when it came to machinery and water'[40] and these abilities were to be employed in a complementary way to those of John Gilbert. Brindley had erected a 'Mobile Water Engin' for the Gilbert brothers at their Woodhead Colliery in May 1759, so they were well aware of his skills.[41] Indeed, Dr Aikin describes Brindley as 'the author of a very ingenious improvement of the machine for drawing water out of mines by the contrivance of a losing and a gaining bucket.'[42] Gilbert as an experienced mining engineer knew about tunnelling techniques and as an estate agent he had the skills of the surveyor. However, he did not have any practical experience of making water work towards a particular end. He appears to have learnt from the Sankey Navigation and indeed he recruited men who had worked on that project for the Worsley canal.[43] Brindley as a practical millwright knew how to construct dams and leets, which provided him with the background knowledge and experience that could be scaled up and utilised around Worsley. Brindley, therefore, should be viewed as the consulting engineer and John Gilbert as the resident engineer, a point made by Sir Joseph Banks in 1767, when he wrote of the Duke of Bridgewater as 'author' and of his 'chief executor' as 'Mr. John Gilbert.'[44] Banks continued his description of the canal works with an evaluation of James Brindley's contribution:

'Many useful and ingenious inventions were thought of and executed by Mr. Brindley who also did most of the Engineering work of the canal. He is a man of no education but of extremely strong natural Parts. He was recommended to the Duke by Mr. Gilbert who found him in Staffordshire where he was only famous for being the Best Mill Wright in the Countrey.'[45]

Banks also relates how John Gilbert displayed 'most indefatigable industry himself overlooking every part and trusting scarce the smallest thing to be done except under his own eye (as) I myself have been witness of.'[46] This leads into a consideration of one important aspect of the two men's character and status. During the construction of the Bridgewater Canal, Josiah Wedgwood observed John Gilbert 'engaged amongst his men' who had 'mutinied'. This suggests a manager who stood above his workforce but at the same time one who could keep them at the job in hand.[47] Brindley lacked this necessary detachment and this is brought home by a tart reminder in the Oxford Canal Company's Minute Book expressing the requirement that: 'the Engineer, Surveyor (Brindley) and Clerks of this Company do not associate or drink with any of the Inferior Officers or Workmen.'[48]

A clear example of their relative roles is provided by the Barton

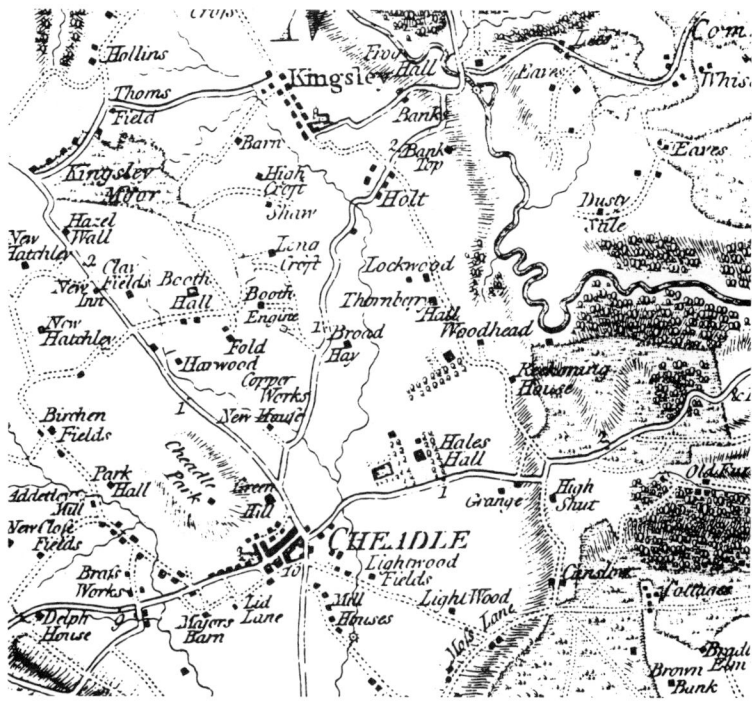

The Woodhead water-engine erected in 1759 by James Brindley for the Gilbert brothers. As shown on a map of 1775.   *(Author's Collection)*

aqueduct. John Gilbert designed the structure and James Brindley was entrusted with the job of constructing it. Brindley appeared to be up to the task, but when he adjudged the structure to be complete and flooded it, one of the arches showed signs of buckling. The whole affair proved to be too much for Brindley who promptly retired to his bed at a nearby inn, leaving John Gilbert to save the structure and with it the credibility of the whole scheme. Brindley had laid too much weight on the sides of the arch and so Gilbert had to remove the clay and puddle it again.[49] His efforts were successful and on 17th July 1761, the aqueduct was again flooded and a flat carrying fifty tons was towed across fulfilling 'the most sanguine expectations of everyone present.' More than any other early canal work it was the Barton aqueduct which symbolised the potential of canals; for as the reporter at the opening noted 'the canal is 38 feet above the navigable river under it.'[50] In the conception and construction of this aqueduct, John Gilbert added incalculable momentum to the slowly awakening interest in canals.[51]

The Barton aqueduct in 1794.

(Author's Collection)

60

Amid a blaze of national publicity, the Duke and his agent set about obtaining their third Act of Parliament, which would enable them to construct the canal between Manchester and Liverpool.[52] This bill met determined opposition from a body of Cheshire landowners, who protested that the canal would divide their land and even reduce its value by causing it to become waterlogged. The Duke's main opponents were Lord Strange and Sir Richard Brooke, but on the critical vote the canal lobby won by 127 votes to 98. The Duke's third Act received the royal assent on 24th March 1762, but the confrontation had not been finally settled. Brindley gave valuable evidence for the third Bill, but he was also supported by the authoritative submission of John Smeaton, whilst Brindley continued in his employment as consulting engineer.[53] Increasingly, he appears to have found it difficult to work under John Gilbert's direction and he found it particularly irksome when he was denied the use of particular workmen. The whole matter came to a head on 13th November 1763 when Gilbert sent an instruction to Brindley and received the curt reply 'no more society.' Brindley remained at his work but John Gilbert and his eldest son Tom called on Brindley a few days later and took him out for a night's drinking.[54] In the short term they seem to have placated him but increasingly Brindley only visited the canal works to advise on specific problems, so that the brunt of the work fell on John Gilbert and other consulting engineers who were employed (like Brindley) from time to time.

The canal was fraught with technical difficulties, including the building of an embankment across Sale Moor, the crossing of the Bollin Valley and problems connected with the building of the Manchester terminus. The Chat Moss line had been included to carry coal to the established markets in the Hollin Ferry area and to provide additional water. By September 1763 coal was being unloaded and sold at Cornbrook where the Cut linked the canal to the Irwell and Mersey Navigation, but it was 1764 before the canal reached Castlefield. The canal was opened as far as Preston Brook by 1771, but the connection with the tidal section of the Mersey estuary was not complete until the 25th March 1776.[55] The delay was caused by the opposition of Sir Richard Brooke of Norton Priory, near Runcorn, who placed every obstacle he possibly could in the path of the projected canal. Josiah Wedgwood visited Norton Priory in 1774 and at that time the canal had been constructed either side of Sir Richard's property.[56] The obstinate landowner finally gave way when public opinion was swayed in the Duke's favour, but the legal knowledge and parliamentary influence of Thomas Gilbert had also made its impact.[57] As with many canals a shortage of water had also proved to be a hindrance. Thomas, writing in 1773, related how the Duke: 'laboured under a disadvantage from the dryness of the season, but had found the means to raise water which I think will supply the locks at all times.'[58]

The final act in the realisation of the grand design of joining Manchester to Liverpool by means of a canal network, involved the construction of a dock in Liverpool that would always be open to the Duke's craft. He had purchased the land near Salthouse dock as early as January 1768;[59] and a newspaper report of 1776 announced that he had begun work on the dock and that he planned 'Wharehouses in the manner of those' he had built 'at Manchester.'[60] However, in the same year the Corporation of Liverpool refused to lease the Duke a further parcel of land so that he could extend his proposed dock. They seemed determined to limit this intrusion from a Manchester based interest and despite the efforts of John's son, Thomas, on the Duke's behalf, the matter was still unresolved in 1790.[61]

The developments at Worsley and the subsequent extension of the Duke's canal system grew out of the Duke's desire to develop his mineral resources. But unlike many great landowners of his day he did not seek to do this by leasing them to others, but instead sought to achieve this by direct exploitation organised by agents. The same involvement was a feature of the development of the Lilleshall estates by Earl Gower at the same time. The Duke and the Earl who were brothers-in-law, both worked in a partnership with the Gilberts, one formal and the other of a more informal nature. The original plan for the Worsley estate was to supply a single urban market, but as the scheme progressed the more widespread possibilities became more and more attractive and the Duke of Bridgewater had the nerve to grasp the opportunities that lay before him. He was favoured by the area in which he was operating with its rapidly expanding industries which desperately needed a cheap and reliable means of access to the port of Liverpool. Had this not been so the Worsley system would have remained as modest as the small network of canals engineered in east Shropshire by John Gilbert.

Sir Joseph Banks was shown over the Lilleshall works by Thomas and John Gilbert in 1767 and he recorded the following brief description of the Donnington Wood Canal: 'the navigation which Lord Gower has made for five miles (upon the same principle as the Duke of Bridgewater's) for the conveniency of his coal and lime with both (of) which it communicates and carries them to the turnpike roadside upon the canal'.[62] This waterway actually ran from Pave Lane on the Newport-Wolverhampton road to Donnington Wood and was authorised by an agreement between

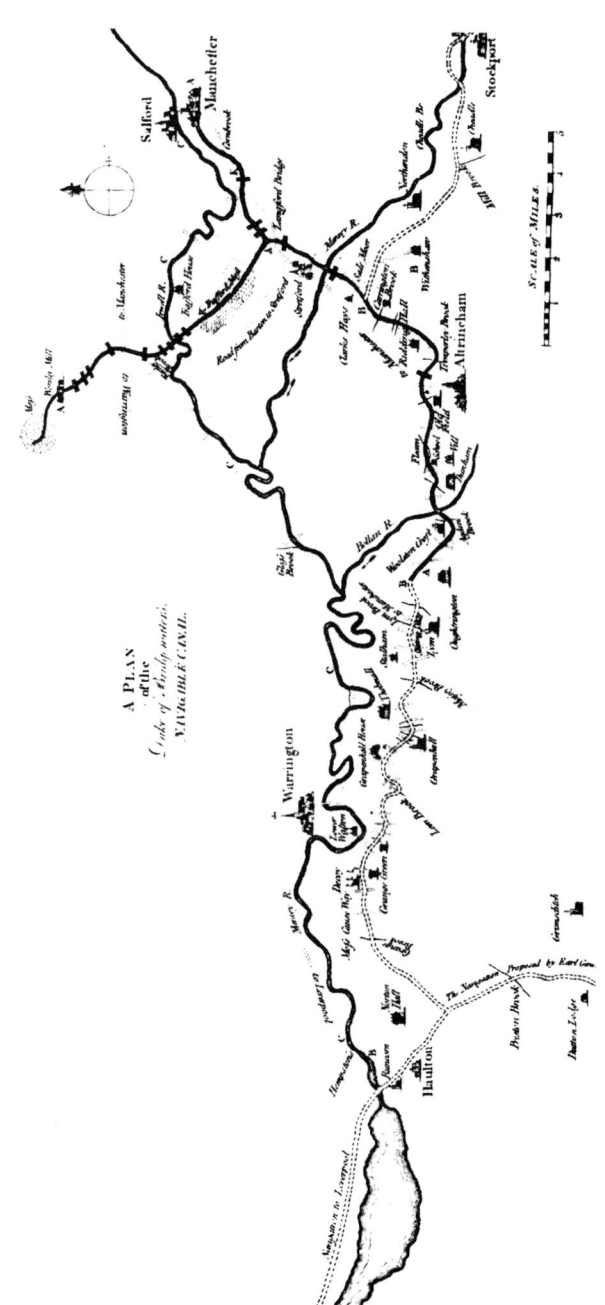

(Percy Marling)

Plan of the proposed Bridgewater Canal system.

Sir Joseph Banks in old age.   *(Author's Collection)*

Earl Gower and the two Gilbert brothers drawn up in 1765.[63] In just the
same way as he had done at Worsley, John Gilbert carried this canal into
an underground navigational level which ran to the coal faces and he was
simply repeating a proven solution to a particular set of problems. Soon
after this canal was completed a branch from Hugh's Bridge to the
limekilns at Lilleshall came into use. However, these two canals did not
form a junction with each other and there was a 43 foot difference in height
between the two levels.[64] Again, John Gilbert employed a tried and proven
solution. At the Castlefield terminus of the Bridgewater Canal, a tunnel
gave access to the base of a shaft and a crane lifted the containers full of coal

up the shaft to street level. The idea of winding up a shaft using containers is reminiscent of Meinzies, but the Castlefield winch was powered by a water-wheel and operated in an identical fashion to a miller's hoist. The credit for this refinement, confirmed by Sir Joseph Banks, belongs squarely with James Brindley.[65] The solution employed at Hugh's Bridge was a modification of the Castlefield idea. There were two shafts approached by a tunnel at the lower level, and as the hoisting gear was interconnected, the descending container helped the ascending one.[66] In this adoption of containers for use within the boats, John Gilbert had taken up the ideas expounded by Meinzies, but he was also using an idea that had been proven practical, for:—'Mr. Bridge, about the year 1759, upon the Stroudwater river before mentioned, where the cargoes of the boats were disposed in a number of boxes or frames, just adapted to the size of the boats; which boxes of goods were drawn up by cranes to be lodged in other boats on the higher level, and the reverse in descending; which method was afterwards more successfully tried on the Bridgewater Canal.'[67]

Once again, John Gilbert had demonstrated his talent for taking ideas and making them work. However, he was not without inventive powers and he must be accorded the credit for the design of the first Shropshire tub boats which appeared on the Lilleshall system. The boats were small, carrying only about 8 tons and measuring 19 ft. 8 ins. by 6 ft. 4 ins. These wooden boats were square at both ends and were chained together in short 'trains' for haulage by horse along the canal.[68] Their beauty lay in their simplicity of construction as they could be made by the average carpenter and so avoided the expense of employing a boat builder.[69] The later versions were made of iron plates riveted together and in this form they survived on Shropshire canals into the twentieth century.[70] The Lilleshall canal system remained isolated until the Shropshire Canal was completed in 1792, thus linking it by means of canals and inclined planes to the River Severn at Coalport.[71]

Both Earl Gower and the Duke of Bridgewater had been moved by 'economic' considerations. The Worsley Canal and the Donnington Wood Canal had brought remuneration through the increased volume and increased profitability of coal and lime sales. They were part of a general policy of estate development, although this was not always so regarded in the short term. The Bridgewater accounts for 1782 reveal a net profit of only £2,000 on coal sales in 1781, but a profit of £7,000 on the carrying trade.[72] This does not take account of the revenue received from associated ventures for the Duke had numerous other 'economic' interests, including the general prosperity of Manchester. The Donnington Wood and Worsley canals also played significant roles in the agricultural developments on the two estates, especially in terms of land reclamation and the increasing practice of "liming" the land.[73] The realisation of the profit to be made from the passage of other men's goods also introduced 'financial' motives to the Duke of Bridgewater's schemes and it was these motives which kept the Duke on course despite a debt that rose to £319,927.[74] Only in 1786 was Thomas Kent, the chief accountant at Worsley, able to enter in the ledger 'Debt decreased this year by £434 7s 7d.[75] When the Duke had a statement of his income drawn up in 1802; it revealed that the Canal, the Dock at Liverpool; and his Lancashire and Cheshire estates yielded £49,000 per annum, out of a total annual income of £106,000.[76] Such were the potential long term returns on his investment, although it should be remembered that he was still paying off his canal debt at the time of his death. By 1803 the gross income amounted to:—

On tonnage carried	£48,403
Colliery profits	£24,300
Lime	£ 91
Net profit after deductions	£65,952

and so in a single year he was able to reduce the canal debt by £57,832,[77] even though it still stood at £162,397.[78]

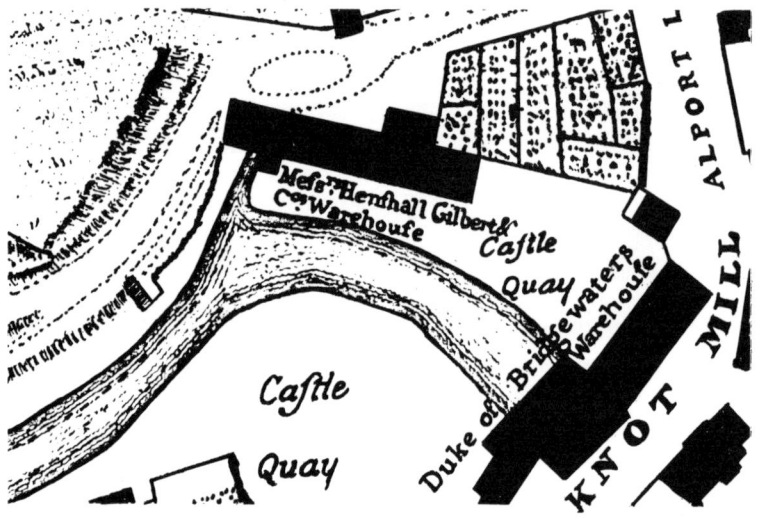

Map of Castlefield, Manchester, c. 1795.   (Percy Marling)

Rees felt that any person worthy of the name of land steward ought to be 'well versed' in 'the cutting of canals'; and that their 'intelligence (knowledge) ought also to extend to the valuable inventions and improvements of other countries.'[79] Rees was writing some sixty years after John Gilbert had begun work at Worsley and in view of this it is possible to see Gilbert as one of the first of a new breed of land steward that evolved during the Industrial Revolution. They needed a much wider range of knowledge and skills, plus the energy and determination to carry out a multiplicity of duties.

The development and improvement of their estates was a primary aim of aristocrats like Earl Gower and the Duke of Bridgewater, who were intelligent men with a real interest in such matters. The mineral wealth of their estates had long been known, but the problems of transport and a limited market meant that the rewards were frequently outweighed by the financial risks involved. One major contribution made by Thomas and John Gilbert was to convince their employers of the practicality of canal construction and of the profits to be made from the large scale and systematic exploitation of mineral resources. In the first instance, they were entering what was largely new ground for them, but in the case of mining, they could offer advice based on expertise derived from personal involvement over a number of years.

Messrs. Henshall and Gilbert's warehouse at Castle Quay, c. 1950.
(Manchester Ship Canal Company)

John Gilbert may not have always had actual experience of 'inventions and improvements', but he certainly had the necessary knowledge that enabled him to bring them together in an original way. Aware of his limitations, in such instances he was prepared to call in consulting 'engineers' like Smeaton and Brindley. The canal projects also called for a high degree of management skills as he had to recruit and control a sizeable workforce, which lacked the stability associated with the exisiting estate workers. There were also numerous legal problems to be overcome and this could be done more expediently due to the close co-operation between the two brothers. Thomas dealt with the bulk of the legal work, or directed other lawyers like Tomkinson, but John, as the Duke's steward, kept himself busy sorting out leases and the like. The additional payments made to John for work in obtaining the canal acts serve to demonstrate that he had also played a significant role in this essentially legal exercise.[80]

The canal work of both brothers was initially part of their role as diligent stewards, but there was also a financial slant to their interest. At Lilleshall, they were the Earl's partners in a business enterprise; and on the Worsley estate they were able to draw profit from a variety of enterprises associated with the canal as well as from the beneficence of a grateful Duke. The Duke of Bridgewater is frequently regarded as 'the father of canal navigations', but it would be more accurate to see him as 'the patron of canal navigations.' For his contribution to canal development in Britain hinged on the fact that he had provided the opportunity and resources for John Gilbert to try out his ideas. The soundness of Gilbert's logic was proved not only by the success of his scheme, but also by the fact that numerous landowners were keen to emulate his achievements at Worsley and Lilleshall. Sir Nigel Gresley and Sir John Glynne were two such landowners, who built short canals on their estates to carry coal from the mines to a place of sale.[81]

IV THE GRAND TRUNK

The River Trent was navigable as far as Nottingham throughout the seventeenth century, but efforts at improvements further upstream were blocked by determined landowners. An Act was passed in 1699 for improving the Trent Navigation from Wilden Ferry to Burton, but little seems to have been achieved and a further effort in 1714 appears to have shared the same fate.[1] Improvements were subsequently made, but even in 1766 Staffordshire merchants were complaining at the poor state of this river navigation and about the monopolists who controlled it.[2]

The potters of North Staffordshire made use of all three river navigations. China clay from Cornwall and Devon were brought by coaster to the Mersey, where it was transhipped to flats for its journey up the Weaver to Winsford and thence by waggons and packhorses to the Potteries. For the return trip the waggons and packhorses carried ware destined for Liverpool and the rapidly expanding export market. Waggons and packhorses also made regular trips to Willington on the Trent Navigation with loads of ware for the London market and carried back flintstones brought from the south coast through the ports of Gainsborough and Hull. Sir Richard Whitworth described the weekly traffic to Bridgnorth on the River Severn as amounting to 'about eight tons of pot ware to be conveyed to Bristol', with back loads of groceries, foreign iron and 'white clay for Burslem.'[3]

The high costs and delays involved in transporting ware was a terrible burden to the master-potters, who were doing their utmost to be competitive. Therefore it is hardly surprising to find them amongst the most fervent supporters of the plan for a 'Staffordshire Canal.' Sir Richard Whitworth expressed their hopes when he declared that 'inland navigation will encourage old manufacturers to work with fresh vigour, now their materials come cheap to them, and will give opportunity to set up new trades and manufactures as they can convey the produce or materials to any part whatsoever.'[4] Potters figure prominently among those who shared the expense of James Brindley's 1758 survey, along with landowners like Earl Gower who were equally aware of the possibilities created by a dependable navigation.[5] The subsequent act makes clear the consideration that was being given to the development of Staffordshire mines and industries as well as the untapped parts of the Cheshire Saltfields.[6]

James Brindley, 1716-1772.   (*Josiah Wedgwood and Sons Ltd.*)

The original impetus for the joining of the rivers Trent and Mersey came from John Hardman, MP for Liverpool; who was the 'intelligent merchant' responsible for organising a survey in 1755 on behalf of the port's merchant community.[7] The interest of this body came to nothing as the Liverpool merchants became involved with the less ambitious Sankey Brook project and so the initiative passed to the 'Staffordshire interest.' This consisted of a group of Staffordshire potters and landowners (including Earl Gower), who sponsored James Brindley to carry out a survey.[8] There is no basis for the myth that Brindley conceived the idea of joining the two rivers, and the involvement of John Smeaton in checking and revising the proposed route indicates that the 'Staffordshire interest' had reservations about his capacity to undertake such a major project.[9] Smeaton had viewed French waterways before working on various Yorkshire schemes, most notably the Calder and Hebble navigation, so unlike Brindley, he had practical experience of this type of engineering.[10]

John Smeaton, 1724-1792.   *(Author's Collection)*

The exact route took some time to settle, and in February 1758 the plan was for the canal to run from 'Longbridge' (now Longport) to the River Trent, near Wilden Ferry. A wharf at Longport would have served Burslem and Tunstall, and completed the link between the pottery towns and Hull.[11] Later it was proposed to extend the canal to the southern side of Harecastle Hill, so that the coal measures could be worked in the same fashion as was being pioneered at Worsley. This proposal was made in 1760, when a partnership made up of John Gilbert, Thomas Gilbert, Hugh Henshall, Robert Williamson and John Brindley (a younger brother of James) purchased the Goldenhill estate. Curiously, James Brindley does not appear to have been one of the principal partners in the purchase of this estate, although he probably had a financial interest[12] and he certainly played a part in the planned exploitation of the mineral resources.[13] The original plan involving the joining of the two rivers was not revived until 1765-6 with Josiah Wedgwood and Thomas Bentley as the principal activists. Josiah Wedgwood spent a great deal of his time between 1765-6 popularising the scheme and seeking the help of influential local figures, like Earl Gower.[14] He also succeeded in protecting the yet unborn canal from the monopolistic Gower-Bridgewater interest represented by the Gilbert brothers.

A romantic view of Longport and Burslem drawn during the 1840s. Longport was originally intended to be the northern terminal of the Trent and Mersey Canal.
(Author's Collection)

On his return from Liverpool in December 1764, Wedgwood was presented with a copy of a pamphlet[15] written by Thomas Gilbert which argued that the projected Trent and Mersey canal should be controlled by a group of proprietors. Such an arrangement would have provided both the Duke of Bridgewater and Earl Gower with extensive powers and a disproportionate financial return on their investment. Wedgwood was able to express his strong objections to such a plan to John Gilbert, who arranged a meeting with Earl Gower and Thomas Gilbert. According to Wedgwood's own account of the meeting, he clearly got the better of an unconvincing Thomas Gilbert, before asking Earl Gower bluntly:

'If it would not be very cruel, when a set of men had employed their time, talents & their purses for ten years together . . . in the execution of a design by which the public would gain 300% and when they have executed this laborious task—what is their reward? Why a new sett of Masters are raised up to controul both them & their works.'

Faced by a such a positive statement of the fears of the humbler promoters, it became obvious that the whole scheme would collapse if a committee system was not adopted as the mode of management for the projected canal, so Earl Gower gave ground and remarked that 'if the Proprietors can save so much to the Public as Mr. W. hath proposed I do not think their plan can be rejected by Parliament.'[16] It was a classic example of compromise brought about by mutual need as the Duke desperately needed a northern junction between his projected canal and the one to be built between the Trent and Mersey, whilst Wedgwood's friends needed the 'great and ministerial weight' of the Gower-Bridgewater interest.[17]

Even though the form of management had been agreed, the precise route and indeed the extent of the canal still remained unsettled. A meeting of the Burslem potters at the Leopard Inn, was addressed by James Brindley, in March 1765 and they discussed the original plan for a canal from Longport to the River Trent at Wilden Ferry.[18] Some weeks later, Josiah Wedgwood and Thomas Sparrow had 'prevailed upon' the Mayor of Newcastle-under-Lyme, 'to call a Hall in order to petition Lord Gower to take this Navigation under his patronage,' a further indication of the importance that was placed on Earl Gower's support.[19] The Duke of Bridgewater's interest in forming a junction between the two projected canals was conveyed to Wedgwood by John Gilbert who pointed out that it would 'be allmost as near a way to Liverpool, & much nearer to Manchester & save our locking down into the River, for which we might afford to give his Grace a small Tonnage.'[20] Evidently, the 'Burslemites' had taken up the idea favoured by the Liverpool and Cheshire interests, of building the northern section of the canal to the River Weaver. At the same meeting the rift between Wedgwood and Thomas Gilbert was healed, for Gilbert expressed his approval of the plan and afterwards Wedgwood wrote 'one might plainly see his heart was engaged along with his tongue in the scheme, so that I have no doubt of his being a steady friend.' Thomas Gilbert also suggested that they needed to 'get a Pamphlet well wrote upon the subject'[21] and this led to Thomas Bentley's famous *A View of the advantages of Inland Navigation.*[22]

When Wedgwood launched the subscription to cover the expense of obtaining an Act of Parliament, he once again expressed his concern that the less powerful promoters should not be ousted by 'one individual who

Thomas Bentley, 1731-1780.   *(Josiah Wedgwood and Sons Ltd.)*

hath no other connection with it.'[23] The subscription was arranged by
Thomas Whieldon and Josiah Wedgwood, and in line with Wedgwood's
wishes ninety-seven subscribers raised a total of £766, although the Duke
of Bridgewater and Earl Gower each gave £100.[24] The then current plan
for the northern junction was revealed to the Weaver Navigation Trustees
at Northwich in May 1765, by Josiah and Richard Wedgwood. This plan
envisaged a canal to the Weaver at Frodsham Bridge, which meant that the
canal would enter the part of the Weaver over which the Trustees had no

control and no power to levy tolls.[25] The Trustees were very anxious that the canal should join the Weaver, so a survey was ordered 'from Harecastle where Mr. Brindley's survey ended' to the Weaver at Winsford with an alternative route by Middlewich to Northwich. A further survey was also undertaken 'in order to discover the most convenient places and properest method of making a communication between the river Weaver' and the 'intended' Bridgewater canal.[26] In the light of such comprehensive plans, it becomes clear why Wedgwood felt there was 'but little danger of any powerfull opposition as I believe we shall be able to make both the Duke of Bridgewater & the Committee of the Weaver our friends.'[27] The Northwich meeting was followed by another in Newcastle and the result was a further example of Wedgwood's ability to bring together opposing factions.

In a document lodged with the Mayor of Liverpool in May 1765, Wedgwood outlines the full scale of the plan at that time:

'As this canal is proposed to be carried from Wilden in Derbyshire to the Duke of Bridgewater's navigation in Cheshire, with branches to Birmingham, Litchfield, Newcastle & the River Weaver, it will extend the inland navigation from this port (Liverpool) through a fertile & manufacturing country for upwards of a hundred miles.'[28]

The problems posed by the Gower-Bridgewater interest reappeared and by October 1765, both were said to have declared publicly that they would have nothing to do with the canal 'if it had any connection with the river Weaver.'[29] Wedgwood apparently heard the same report and both John Gilbert and James Brindley added that they doubted whether the Duke would fall in with the compromise plan.[30] John Stafford, a Weaver Navigation representative, provided a very sinister interpretation of the Duke's motives in pressurising the Burslemites, when he wrote that he aimed at becoming 'the largest dealer as a carrier in Europe.' He also thought that 'a monopoly in the hands of a peer of the realm' was like 'a monster, as I hope this land of liberty will never suffer to live.'[31] Wedgwood also had doubts about Earl Gower's motives, he commented that 'it grieves one to suspect such a Character should mean to serve himself only at the expense of what is most dear to a people by whom he is so much be loved.'[32]

By this time 'the Potters were determined to accept the best Navigation they could get if they could not get the best they wished for.'[33] Wedgwood suspected they would be 'humbug'd' and he employed the same sort of tactic that had brought him victory over the management issues. In a conversation with Thomas Gilbert he expressed the desire of the lesser promoters 'to put our intended Navigation under the protection of his Lordship and the Duke.' He also pressed Gilbert and so indirectly Earl Gower to come 'down into Staffordshire and PUBLICLY at a meeting of the Gentlemen of this County to be appointed for that purpose to put himself at the head of our design.'[34] This meant that if Earl Gower served his own interests, or those of the Duke, he would lay himself open to attack and he was too practiced as a politician to allow this. He had two choices open to him, he could take up the cause of the navigation on what were essentially Wedgwood's terms, or he could disassociate himself from the whole affair which would damage the interests of the Duke of Bridgewater. Faced as he was by a direct choice between the Gower-Bridgewater and the Weaver interests, Wedgwood and his associates had opted for the support of the most powerful potential ally. It did mean that the promoters would have to confront the Weaver trustees along with the proprietors of the Trent navigation, and as Wedgwood noted 'The Weaver will die hardest.'[35]

No notification of the changed plan was forwarded to the Weaver trustees, but they received their answer at the meeting of the canal promoters at Wolseley Bridge on 30th December 1765, secured by Wedgwood's campaign to pressure Earl Gower into acting as patron to the canal scheme. The Earl presided and Sir Richard Whitworth first outlined his rival scheme, to unite the ports of Liverpool, Hull and Bristol,[36] but this received little attention, other than that dictated by a sense of fair play and politeness.[37] When Thomas Gilbert introduced the plan for a canal from the Trent to the Duke's canal, near the Mersey, he was in fact introducing an already agreed plan to the general public. No mention was made of the plan earlier agreed with the Weaver Trustees and this caused John Stafford to remark: 'A glorious scheme it will be for him if he (The Duke of Bridgewater) can draw all the carriage between the two great ports of Liverpool and Hull and a great deal from the interior parts of the country into his canal.'[38] Stafford realised that the Duke had in fact won, although Wedgwood had incorporated enough safeguards to prevent him from dominating or even controlling the projected canal. Subscriptions were immediately opened for the construction of the canal and a further one towards the cost of obtaining an Act of Parliament. The first petition was presented in Parliament on 15th Jaunary 1766 and this requested leave to bring in a bill. After the second reading it was referred to a committee of which Thomas Gilbert, in his capacity as a Member of Parliament for Newcastle-under-Lyme, was Chairman.[39] The Duke of Bridgewater, true to his promise to 'exert all his talents and interests',[40] presented a petition against the proposed Macclesfield Canal and one to alter the line of his own canal to form a junction with the Trent and Mersey at Preston Brook.[41] The Act was passed on 14th May, authorising a line from the Trent near Wilden Ferry to Preston Brook.[42] The news was greeted with great enthusiasm in the Potteries, where they had long realised that 'nothing but an Inland Navigation can ever put their Manufactory on an Equality with their foreign competitors.'[43]

Josiah Wedgwood after a painting by George Stubbs, 1780.

(Josiah Wedgwood and Sons Ltd.)

The Act laid down that there were to be two bodies: the Company of the Proprietors of the Navigation from the Trent to the Mersey, and the Commissioners of the Navigation. There were 101 proprietors, all of whom were shareholders, and they included Earl Gower (10 shares), the Duke of Bridgewater (10), James Brindley (10), Thomas Gilbert (10), John Gilbert (5), Samuel Egerton (15), Josiah Wedgwood (10½), and the only person to take up a full quota of shares, a William McQuire (20).[44] The subscriptions do not appear to have been payable immediately, for in March 1769, John Gilbert asked Wedgwood to pay his 'subscription to the Navigation for a while.'[45] The function of the 816 commissioners named in the act was 'to settle, determine and adjust all questions, matters and differences,' which might arise between the Canal Company and individuals interested in land or water affected by the Act.[46]

The first Committee was appointed on 3rd June 1766, but no list survives of the original membership of this body. Four officers were appointed: James Brindley, Surveyor General; Hugh Henshall, Clerk of the Works; Thomas Sparrow, Clerk to the Proprietors and Josiah Wedgwood, Treasurer. Thomas Gilbert was present at this meeting and in view of his prominent role in the earlier Wolseley Bridge meeting, it would not be unreasonable to suppose that he took the chair.[47] The first list of the Committee members dates from 1776, by which time a powerful group based on the Gilberts existed within the Committee:

'Independent members'	'The Gilbert faction'	
Josiah Wedgwood	Edward Salmon	) Business
John Eld	Mr. Griffin	) Associates
Richard Morland	The Rev. J. Bill	) Related
The Rev. Dr. Falconer	Mr. W. Bill	) by
Mr. Boyer	Mr. Phillips	) Marriage
Mr. Hollinshead	John Gilbert	
Mr. Twemlow		

& Thomas Gilbert (Chairman)[48]

The balance between the two groups was even, until Thomas Gilbert's casting vote as Chairman is considered. In this way, the Gower-Bridgewater interest could be protected and eventually it was bound to lead to a serious dispute amongst what Earl Gower styled 'the Amicable society of Navigators.'[49] Such disputes, involving personal attacks on individuals do not seem to have been uncommon. Josiah Wedgwood laid himself open to attack in December 1767, when he spent two days 'at

NAVIGATION
from the *TRENT* to the *MERSEY*,

At a Meeting of the COMMITTEE *of the faid* NAVIGATION, *held at the* Crown *in* Stone, *in the County of* Stafford, *on* Thurfday *the* 13th. *day of* June, 1776.

Prefent, THOMAS GILBERT Efq; in the Chair.

John Eld	The Rev. Dr. *Falconer,*	Mr. *Twemlow*	Mr. *Boyer,*	Mr. *J. Gilbert.*
Edward Salmon } Efqrs.	The Rev. Mr. *Bill,*	Mr. *Phillips,*	Mr. *Griffin,*	
Richard Moland	Mr. *Wedgwood,*	Mr. *Hollinfhead,*	Mr. *W. Bill,*	

THE Act paffed the laft Seffion of Parliament, enabling the *Company* to make a navigable Canal, from the faid *Navigation* on the South fide of *Harecaflle,* to *Froghall,* and a Railway from thence to or near *Caldon,* by borrowing Money on the Credit of the Tolls thereby granted, (an abftract of which is hereto annexed) was taken into confideration ; and it appeared to the *Committee,* to be extremely well calculated for the accommodation of the Country, with the Articles of Lime, and Coal, on very reafonable Terms, and likely to conduce very much to the advantage of the *Proprietors* of the *Trunk Navigation,* not only by increafing their Tonnage, but alfo, producing a furplus of Tonnage, beyond the Payment of the Intereft of the Money to be borrowed, and the neceffary expences attending the making and keeping the fame in repair.

THE *Committee* alfo confidered the expences which are likely to attend the execution of the faid Act, which they apprehend will amount to about 23,000l. befides the Sum of 5000l. which was ftipulated (before the paffing the Act and which is confirmed by it) to be paid by the owners of fome Colleries, for part of the Tonnage upon the Article of Coals only, on the faid Railway and a fmall part of the faid intended *Navigation.*

THE *Committee* likewife confidered the means which appeared to them moft proper and eligible, for procuring the faid Sum of 23,000l. and were of opinion, That a Subfcription fhould be opened for a Loan of Money, upon the Credit of the Tolls to arife from the faid intended *Navigation* and Railway, with Intereft at the rate of 4l. 10s. per Cent, per Annum. which Tolls, upon Calculations made of the probable quantities of Lime-ftone, and Coal, to be carried annually upon the faid *Navigation* and *Railway,* (without taking into their Calculation a confiderable number of other Articles which muft neceffarily come upon the fame) appeared greatly to exceed the amount of the Intereft, and other annual expences.

'THEY were alfo of opinion, That a Subfcription Paper fhould be prefented, to the moft confiderable Land Owners who will be benefited by this new *Navigation,* and alfo to the *Proprietors* of the *Trunk Navigation;* but as thofe *Proprietors* have already made very large contributions, in refpect of their feveral Shares, it was thought an application to them for the Loan of further Sums, though apparently for their advantage, might be difagreeable or inconvenient, and as many of thofe *Proprietors,* have befides the Money advanced in refpect of their Shares, lent feveral Sums of Money, on the Credit and Security of the Tolls of that *Navigation,* (which Sums may eafily be procured from Perfons who have no connection with the *Navigation,* on the Affignment of fuch Securities) it was thought proper for the eafe of fuch *Proprietors* as are inclined to encourage the execution of the new *Navigation,* that they fhould be requefted to fubfcribe, fuch Sums as they fhall think fit to transfer from their Securities, to fuch Perfons as will advance the Money thereupon, and to accept new Securities for the like Sums at the fame rate of Intereft, upon the Tolls to arife from the faid new *Navigation* : by which means they will give an effectual fupport to this intended branch of the *Trunk Navigation,* without advancing any Money, or (as is apprehended) fuftaining any lofs or diminution of their Property.

THE *Committee,* being fully convinced of the Propriety of this meafure, have declared their readinefs to exchange their Securities for a confiderable part of the Money fo advanced by them, on the Terms here fubmitted.

IN order to collect the Sentiments of the *Proprietors* at large upon this bufinefs, fo important, and likely to be fo beneficial to their property, the *Committee* have thought fit to appoint a *General Affembly,* to be held at the *Crown* in Stone, on *Tuefday,* the 23d. day of *July* next, which the feveral Proprietors are defired to attend in Perfon, or to fignify by a Letter, directed to the *Navigation Office* at *Stone,* the Sum they will be pleafed to transfer, or lend, on the Terms aforefaid, upon the Tolls of this new *Navigation.*

By order of the COMMITTEE,

J. *S P A R R O W,*

Clerk to the COMPANY.

Report on a meeting to consider the Caldon Canal, 1776.   *(County Record Office, Stafford.)*

Hetruria, in seting out the canal' and trying to persuade Hugh Henshall to alter the line of the canal so it would run through his estate. Henshall, who Wedgwood described as an 'inflexible vandal', would not alter the line of the canal, claiming that he had to take the most direct route or Brindley would be furious.[50] Three months later Wedgwood's problems were made worse when John Brindley and a group of other potters objected to any deviation to the proposed route that would be to his advantage. Wedgwood tackled them at a committee meeting and clearly got his way.[51] Work started on the Etruria factory in 1768 and it was practicallly completed towards the end of the same year.

A more serious charge was made against Wedgwood by 'a junta of our Proprietors', concerning the purchase of a piece of land at Etruria for the Canal Company in 1773. This 'junta', according to Wedgwood 'represented the transaction as a fraud upon the Company by myself, the Deputy Treasurer and many of our Proprietors.' The whole matter was taken to a Committee meeting presided over by Earl Gower, who 'summed up the evidence by which it appeared to the entire satisfaction of all present,' that 'the transaction was a fair one.' Thomas Gilbert observed, 'that he and the Proprietors had ever unlimited confidence in me,'[52] but despite this Wedgwood shortly afterwards gave up his post as Treasurer, although he apparently remained on the Committee.[53] The next quarrel was to bring Wedgwood and both the Gilbert brothers into direct conflict with one another, and to cause Thomas Gilbert to relinquish the position of Chairman.[54]

The apparent cause was the new carrying firm of Worthington and Gilbert, which intended to compete for the carriage of goods between Manchester and Stourport with Hugh Henshall & Co. (a carrying firm owned by the Canal Company itself).[55] Not unnaturally, the Duke's traffic went to his Head Steward's firm, and 'His Grace's people' were said to be 'very partial to Worthington'; his boats being unloaded in two hours, whilst those of Hugh Henshall and company had to wait up to two days to be unloaded.[56] The whole affair took on a more sinister aspect when a rumour was spread that Hugh Henshall & Co. intended to give up the carriage of goods between Manchester and Stourport.[57] By the end of 1782, the two factions of the Committee were at each others throats and it became clear that the group centred around Wedgwood were determined to prove to the Duke of Bridgewater that they would not tolerate him treating the canal as a branch of his own. The Trent and Mersey Company's chief agent at Manchester provided Wedgwood with ample examples of the partiality shown to Worthington and Gilbert, so that when his evidence was shown to the Duke he was furious. He demanded the agent's dismissal and threatened to part with his shares if his demand was not met.[58] Meanwhile, Thomas Gilbert was circulating shareholders about the Committee, 'representing their affairs as totally derang'd' due to 'constant Quarrelling'; a strange admission from the Chairman.[59] Thomas Gilbert was desperate as he realised that Wedgwood was determined to break the dominance of the Gower-Bridgewater interest.

By March 1785, the Committee had changed considerably from that of 1776, most significantly due to the absence of Josiah Wedgwood. Messrs. Hollinshead, Twemlow, Salmon, Thomas Gilbert and the two Bill brothers remained; with the additions of Lord Gower, the Earl of Harrowby and Thomas Whieldon. Twenty individuals sat on the Committee but the centre of power had been shifted by Wedgwood and decisions were now being made by votes taken among the proprietors at numerous General Meetings. So that when Josiah Wedgwood moved for the discharge of Mr. Price (possibly the Company's Chief Agent), a majority of the committee were for retaining him but he was dismissed by a majority of 63 on the proprietors voting. In this way, Josiah Wedgwood was leading the fight against the Gower-Bridgewater interest without even being on the Committee.[60]

William Jessop reported that by April 1785, a large proportion of the shareholders were 'in favour of a proposition to give up trading as a Company', despite pressure brought to bear by both Earl Gower and the Duke of Bridgewater.[61] Whether Wedgwood and his faction were bluffing is not known, but he did succeed in breaking up the faction centred around the Gilberts and the new Committee wrung certain undertakings from the Duke. In the absence of the Committee's Minute books it is difficult to piece together the developing story of the dispute, but the accounts for the Canal Company for the year ending 25th June 1785 include an item: 'Paid for a Silver Tureen presented to Thomas Gilbert, Esq.'[62] Surely marking the end of Thomas Gilbert's nineteen year 'rule' as Chairman of the Company and Wedgwood's reaffirmation as the most influential member of the committee (possibly chairman) and as such he brought in many reforms prompted by the 'problems of late.'[63] Thomas and John Gilbert retained their shares in the canal but ceased to play any active part in its management. Thomas at least was reconciled to the interests of the company following Wedgwood's death in January 1795.[64]

Even before the main line of the Trent and Mersey had been completed in 1777, plans were being advanced for the further development and intensification of the company's system. The Caldon Canal was the second important canal development in North Staffordshire; and most of the credit for its promotion must go to the Gilbert brothers and their associates in the Caldon Low quarries.[65] James Brindley had made his final survey for this canal in 1772, but as he was taken ill during the work he never had the opportunity to report his findings.[66] However, on 9th January 1773, John Sneyd was able to write to Sir Joseph Banks (who owned an estate at Kingsley), providing him with a detailed description of the plan:

'We are going to petition Parliament for a navigable canal from ye Potteries beyond Leek principally for coal and lime carriages wch. be executed at a very moderate Expence by means of an Invention one of our Moorlanders has hit off for drawing loaded Barges 7 or 8 ton up an inclined plane wch. rises 13 inches in year yard instead of Locks. This has been tryed at large and a Boy of 12 years old draws them up with ye greatest Case by a common capstan. The boat swims over a 4 wheel'd carriage wch. sinks to ye bottom of ye canal it is then fastened upon it and so drawn over.'[67]

Some weeks later, Josiah Wedgwood wrote to Bentley outlining the same scheme, but adding that 'The Canal 12 feet wide only and the boats to carry five tons burthen.'[68] Essentially, the scheme was to build a canal like that constructed at Donnington Wood by John Gilbert which would employ tub boats. The only refinement was the use of inclined planes instead of locks, a technique used extensively on the Shropshire canals after 1788. Despite Sneyd's statement, the idea was not new as it grew out of an idea that had been imported from Flanders by Davies Dukart, who began building an ill-fated canal from the Drumglass Colliery to the Tyrone Navigation in 1757. The canal consisted of a series of level pounds connected by inclines which the boats were to be let down on rollers. John Smeaton inspected the completed canal and unfinished inclines in 1774 and subsequently recommended the replacement of the whole system by a waggonway. But it was too late to change and Dukart adopted the method proposed in connection with the Caldon Canal, that of laying rails on the inclines, with wheeled cradles for carrying the boats.[69] Apart from the similarities between the two systems, further evidence of John Gilbert's involvement comes from a record of a visit to the 'Duke's works' at Worsley in August/September 1768 by Davies Dukart.[70] Subsequently, John Gilbert was to relate his interest and knowledge to Richard and William Reynolds in Shropshire.

Josiah Wedgwood viewed the proposed route of the canal in October 1775, a month after saying that 'We (the Company) are begun upon it in earnest.' In a letter to his nine-year old son John, he describes how the course of the canal was to run 'parallel with the road from Leek to Ashbourne for some miles' until it reached the western side of Caldon Low.[71] By November of the same year this plan had been finally approved and an estimate prepared. Then for some reason the Company had a change of mind and decided on a route which would follow the Churnet Valley down to Froghall. A possible explanation for this sudden change can be found in the Act which refers to a group of colliery owners, in Kingsley and Cheadle, agreeing to advance £5,000 towards the cost of building the canal.[72] The Gilbert brothers had collieries near Cheadle and there is sufficient evidence to show that they were instrumental in raising this sum, which was to be a definite incentive to their fellow proprietors to undertake the construction of the canal.[73] Clearly it was in the best interests of those colliery owners in that area to have the canal follow the route that it finally did; and it was also of advantage to the Company who were short of funds and faced with estimated costs of £23,000.[74] Another factor contributing to the change of plan was the acquisition of Consall Forge and slitting mill by William Bill and Thomas Griffin.[75] They were both members of the Canal Company's Committee and without their support, it is doubtful whether a Parliament jealous of guarding water supplies would have accepted the plan that brought the canal to within ten yards of the mill buildings. The motives of both men were not as unselfish as it might seem for they were able to redevelop the site into a highly successful and profitable flint mill.

The Canal Company made agreements with the owners of the various limestone quarries around Caldon Low. These proprietors fell into two groups; those who held leases from the Earl of Shrewsbury and those who owned quarries in their own right. The first group consisted of John Gilbert, Richard Hill, George Smith and Sampson Whieldon; and the second of Thomas Gilbert, Henry Copestake, Robert Bill, Sampson Whieldon and William Wooliscroft. The proprietors also bound themselves to supply the Canal Company with limestone, the various proprietors to supply a proportion of the required quantity.[76] When the canal and railway opened in 1778, it had an immediate effect on the income derived from the quarries which had previously only supplied limestone for a restricted local market.[77] The canal enabled a string of limekilns to operate throughout North Staffordshire and it must have provided a tremendous stimulus to improving landowners. John Gilbert derived particular benefit from the canal through his creation of the Cheddleton Lime Company. This concern started trading in 1778, using

Consall Flint Mills, 1923.   *(Caldon Canal Society)*

limekilns at Cheddleton and Horsebridge on the Caldon Canal and supplied lime to the area around Leek. Coal was supplied to these kilns from the adjacent Shafferlong Coalfield by the Reverend Edward Powys, who was under contract to the Company.[78] All of John Gilbert's partners in the Company (except his son John) were quarry proprietors, these being Sampson Whieldon, Richard Hill and George Smith.[79]

The outline plan for the Caldon Canal was with little doubt the work of John Gilbert, although there are indications that the more detailed surveying work was undertaken by Hugh Henshall.[80] The two Gilbert brothers were also the main movers in the campaign to get the branch adopted by the Canal Company, moves which led to the passing of the authorising Act in May 1776.[81] John Gilbert was also responsible for the final link in the system linking the quarries to the main line of the canal, namely the railway from Froghall to Caldon Low. The problem was to transport the limestone through the 700 feet which separated the wharf and the quarries; and again John Gilbert drew on his Shropshire experience. He was very familiar with the Coalbrookdale railway system and as M. J. T. Lewis points out 'the track (was) pure Shropshire.'[82] The railway opened in December 1778, but within a year Edward Ball (a Canal Company employee) wrote that: 'The Railway has been repaired but in Frost the Waggons slide so much that it is almost Impossible to carry

84

anything upon it.'[83] John Farey expressed the problem more precisely and when he wrote of:

'The railway branch to Mr. Gilbert's Caldon lime-works, made about the year 1777 or 1778, was composed of cast-iron bars pinned down upon the rails of wood fixed across wooden sleepers . . . it appears to have been set out before the true principles of this excellent mode of conveyance were so well understood as at present (c. 1805), being very crooked and with frequent variations in the angle of its ascent.'[84]

This was obviously one of John Gilbert's less successful projects, but perhaps it is excusable when it is considered that it represents a pioneer effort. When claiming railway 'firsts' great care needs to be taken to qualify what is actually being asserted. It has long been known that the Middleton Colliery Railway was the first railway to be built using powers granted by an Act of Parliament in 1758. However, it is still not widely known that the Caldon Low Railway was the first railway using iron rails to be constructed (1776-1778) with an authority derived from a legislative enactment, albeit a mainly canal Act. The situation was not irretrievable and the most expedient solution was to partially rebuild the railway, abandoning the worst sections and attempting to create a more workable line with easier gradients. A new Act was obtained in 1783 and this gave the Company power to carry out the necessary improvements.[85] The bulk of the work was carried out in 1785 at a total cost of £2,697 13s. 8½d,[86] and so considering that the original line cost about £1760 per mile,[87] it seems that much of this expenditure was on expensive embankments and cuttings. A desire to avoid such expensive earthworks, which is also reflected in canal engineering at this time, may have in fact been the root cause of the unsatisfactory construction of the original 1778 railway. The Gilberts maintained their interest in the reconstructed railway and in 1787 Thomas Gilbert agreed to organise the transport 'down the Railway.'[88]

The growing significance of canal projects during the 1760s explains why Thomas Gilbert was brought into Parliament by the Leveson-Gower interest when the Newcastle-under-Lyme seat was vacated by John Waldegrave in December 1763.[89] Thomas Gilbert sat as member for this borough from 1763 to 1768, taking his seat when the discussions about the projected Trent and Mersey Canal were reaching their climax. He had previously been instrumental in obtaining canal Acts for the Duke of Bridgewater in 1759, 1760 and 1762, so he was already familiar with the relevant parliamentary procedures. His presence in the House of Commons, and more especially on the committees that met to consider

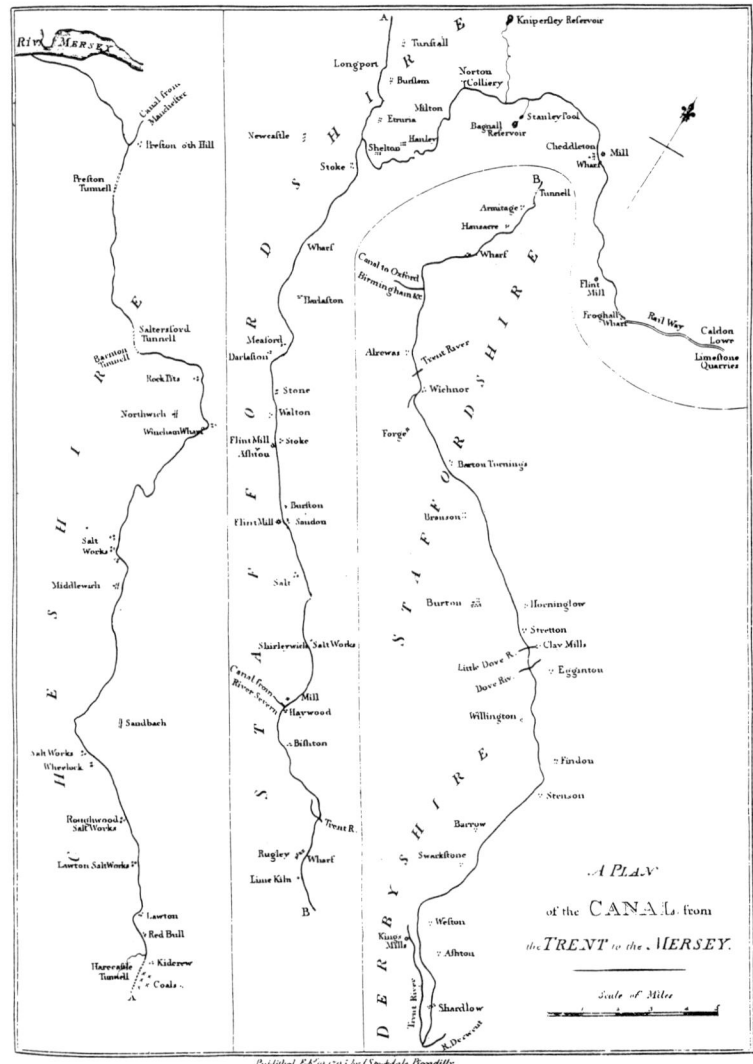

Map showing the Trent and Mersey Canal system, 1795.　　　　(Author's Collection)

such Bills, would have greatly facilitated their passage.[90] For as Sir Lewis Namier pointed out: 'in the eighteenth century, parliamentary politics were transacted to a disastrous extent in terms of jurisprudence.'[91] The rapidity with which Gilbert was able to establish himself in the promotion of these aims is indicated by his Chairing the parliamentary committee, to which the Trent and Mersey Canal Bill was referred in 1766.[92] His role as member for Newcastle-under-Lyme may also have been significant, as the Corporation were anxious to see the canal built; especially since the first proposals had included a branch canal from the main line at Stoke to Newcastle.[93]

The significance of canals to estate development has been discussed in previous chapters, but Thomas Gilbert was also active in the promotion of turnpike roads. His obituary writer noted that he knew that:—'the best interests of commerce, manufacturers, and agriculture, are intimately connected with an easy and speedy communication, he zealously applied himself to the amendment of the roads, and although he did not succeed in his original plan of procuring a general Act for their improvement yet he carried through the House many provincial bills which tended to make travelling in the counties of Northampton, Warwick, Stafford and Derby, the places to which he particularly directed his attention, infinitely more commodious and agreeable: indeed it is well known, that before his time, the highways were the worst in the Kingdom.'[94]

These improvements obviously took time, as the Lord Chancellor Thurlow was able to remark, after a visit to Cotton in 1782, that he found:—'Dangerous roads, ill made and worst kept; and that within so few miles of Cotton, and in so few hours after I had been learning how to make and keep roads.'[95]

Earlier in 1773, Gilbert had been successful in framing an Act, which consolidated the law relating to turnpikes and has subsequently come to be considered as 'a landmark in the history of English highway administration.'[96] The prime motivation for this work can be deduced from the fact that most of his provincial bills for highway improvements concerned with counties where his employers had estates. Earl Gower had extensive estates in Staffordshire and the Duke of Bridgewater in Northamptonshire; and in the other counties they had lesser estates.

V FURTHER CANAL SCHEMES

Following the committee crisis of the 1780s, both John and Thomas Gilbert had little to do with the affairs of the Trent and Mersey Canal, apart from being interested to the same extent as any active shareholders. Instead their energies were directed towards promoting developments that were taking place on the Shropshire Coalfield. Twenty years had elapsed since the building of the Donnington Wood Canal, when in 1787-88, William Reynolds built two short private canals on the coalfield. One ran from a junction with the southern terminus of the Donnington Wood Canal to a colliery at Wombridge, hence its name of the Wombridge Canal. The other was the Ketley Canal, just over a mile in length from Ketley ironworks to Oakengates. This was significant chiefly because of the inclined plane, which conveyed boats from the ironworks in the valley floor to the summit level above. It was the first practical inclined plane on a canal in Britain, although John Gilbert had put forward the same idea for the Caldon Canal, some fifteen years earlier. The boats used on the Ketley Canal were also similar to those employed on the Donnington Wood Canal.[1] The credit for the Ketley incline is generally given to William Reynolds, the Shropshire ironmaster. His father, Richard Reynolds, was a tenant of Earl Gower and the 'very respectful and obliged friend' of Thomas Gilbert.[2] He was almost certainly on friendly terms with John Gilbert as he had visited Worsley in 1769, a year after the visit to the 'the Duke's works' by Davies Dukart who had already built inclined planes in Ireland.[3] Worsley and the Bridgewater Canal appears to have made a lasting impression on Richard Reynolds:

'We went to the Duke of Bridgewater's coalworks, and came along the side of the navigation as far as it extends towards Warrington, which is, I think, within two or three miles. There have been frequently published in the newspapers descriptions of the works and navigations, but I shall only say, I never read one which gave me an adequate idea of the performances: they are really amazing, and greater, I believe, than were ever before attempted, much less achieved by an individual and a subject.'[4]

To what extent Richard and William Reynolds were prompted or encouraged by the Gilberts may never be known for sure, but they must

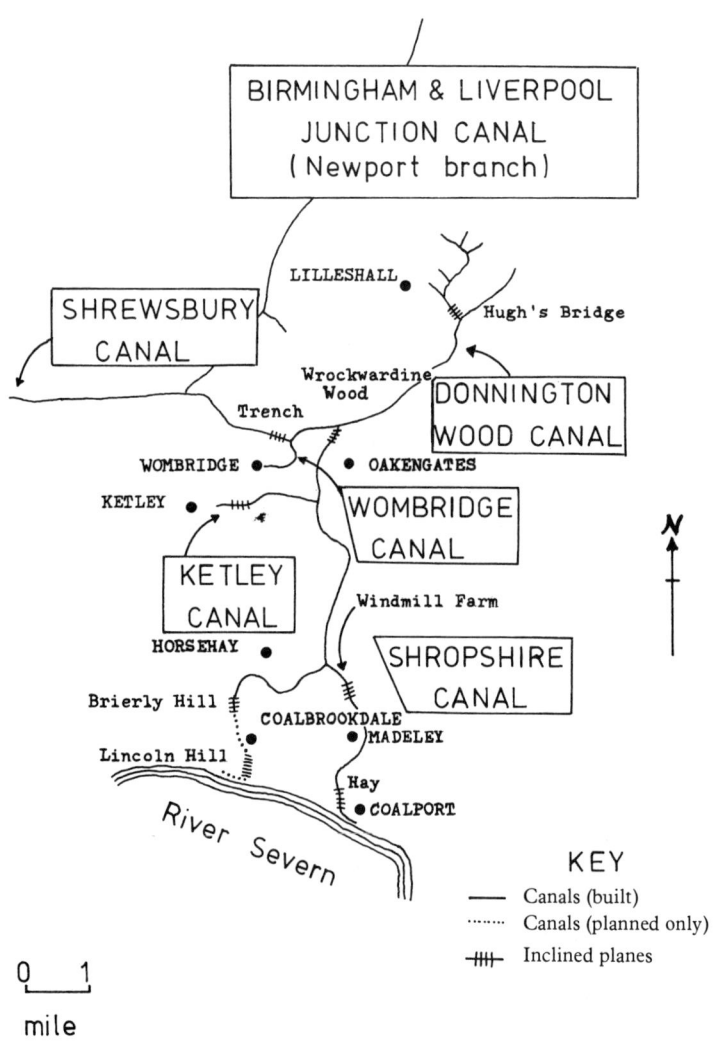

BIRMINGHAM & LIVERPOOL
JUNCTION CANAL
(Newport branch)

LILLESHALL
Hugh's Bridge

SHREWSBURY
CANAL

Wrockwardine
Wood

Trench

DONNINGTON
WOOD CANAL

WOMBRIDGE ● ● OAKENGATES

KETLEY ●

WOMBRIDGE
CANAL

N

KETLEY
CANAL

Windmill Farm

HORSEHAY ●

SHROPSHIRE
CANAL

Brierly Hill

COALBROOKDALE
● MADELEY

Lincoln Hill

Hay
● COALPORT

River Severn

KEY

—— Canals (built)
········ Canals (planned only)
-⊞⊞- Inclined planes

0   1

mile

The Canals of East Shropshire.

have often discussed such matters with the Gilberts during their frequent
business visits to Shropshire. William Reynolds certainly did take up
another of John Gilbert's favourite strategies, when in 1787 he began to
cut an underground canal from a point near the banks of the Severn in
Madeley towards the Blists Hill collieries. Dr. Trinder has noted that

newspaper reports of the time 'reported that a level had been driven'. . . 'partly as a drain (to the collieries) and as a navigable waterway'. After being driven for about 300 yards, the tunnellers struck natural bitumen or mineral oil, although to the people of that time it was known as 'natural tar', hence 'the tar tunnel.'[5]

This initial burst of private enterprise was followed by the promotion of the Shropshire Canal. In 1788 Richard Reynolds took a leading part in obtaining an Act of Parliament to allow the construction of a canal from major ironworks to the River Severn.[6] The Act received the Royal Assent on 11th June 1788 and the next day, Thomas Gilbert was elected Chairman of the Committee at the first General Assembly, held at the Tontine Inn, Madeley Wood. Thomas held 10 shares of £100 in the company and he continued to play a very active part in their affairs until the construction phase was concluded.[7] The fact that they were able to hold their first General Assembly so soon after the Act was passed, suggests that Thomas Gilbert helped to guide the Bill through the various parliamentary stages. John Gilbert also held shares in the company and like his brother, he sat for a while on the Committee of Management.[8]

The Shropshire Canal was confined to the coalfield and it linked together the three earlier and private canals. From its junction with the Donnington Wood and Wombridge Canals, it ran southwards to a junction with the Ketley Canal and then to Southall Bank where it split into two branches. One branch was to go to the River Severn near Dale End, Coalbrookdale, but it was never completed beyond Brierley Hill, above Coalbrookdale. The other branch terminated by the River Severn in what is now Coalport, a settlement that grew up around the canal-river interchange. The canal included three inclined planes, all built to the design of Henry Williams and John Lowdon; but obviously inspired by the Ketley incline.[9] The construction of the canal was carried out to a design prepared by William Reynolds, who was wrongly accorded the credit for the tub boat designs by Thomas Telford: 'It is proper to observe that Mr. Reynolds reduced the size of his canal boats, for instead of making use of boats of 70 feet in length, each carrying from 25 to 30 tons, he made them only 20 feet in length, 6 feet four inches in width, and 3 feet 10 inches deep; each capable of carrying eight tons.'[10]

In 1793 an Act of Parliament was obtained for the Shrewsbury Canal, which extended the tub boat canal system to Shrewsbury.[11] This canal joined the Wombridge Canal at Trench, where another inclined plane formed the junction. The canal then descended by means of eleven locks

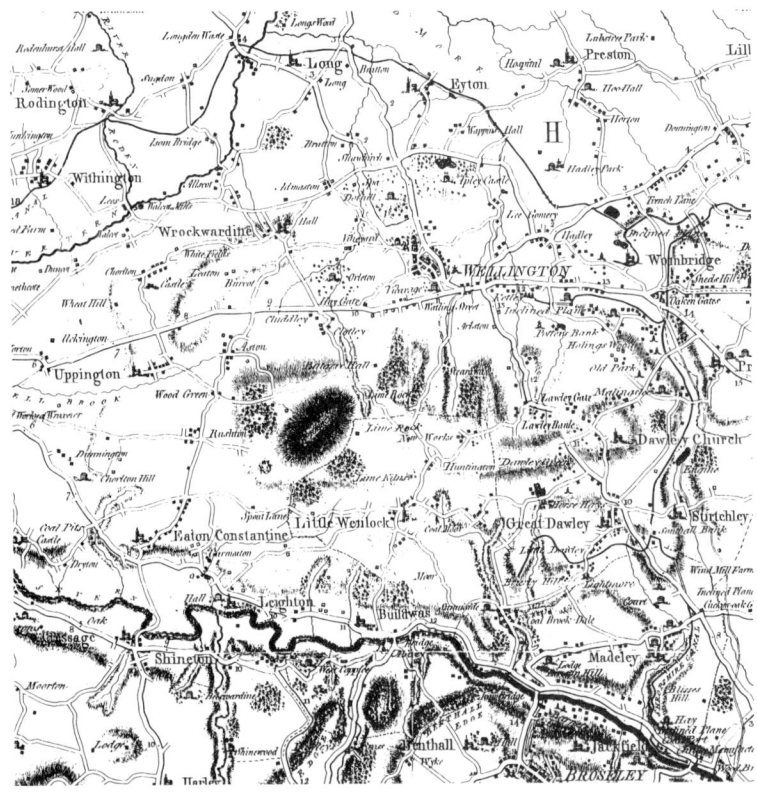

A map of 1808 showing the canals of East Shropshire.   (Percy Marling)

to Eyton, from where it followed a contoured path to Shrewsbury. A major engineering feature was the aqueduct over the River Tern at Longdon, which was begun by the first engineer, Josiah Clowes as a conventional masonry structure; and completed by Thomas Telford as the world's second iron aqueduct.[12] Clowes was a North Staffordshire engineer, who had previously been resident engineer to the Thames and Severn Canal Company and he had renewed his acquaintance with John

Gilbert in 1785, when Gilbert was called in as an arbitrator by that Company.[13] John and Thomas Gilbert also held shares in the Shrewsbury Canal and sat on the management committee.[14]

Despite their advancing years both brothers were still intrigued by new ways of doing things on the canals. They had interested themselves in the early experimental use of inclined planes and in Symington's designs for steam carriages and steamboats; and so it is hardly surprising to find them promoting the use of the first working caisson lock. Erasmus Darwin can be regarded as the innovator of the vertical canal lift and entered in his common place book (1777) a description of the principle on which it worked:

'Let a wooden box be constructed so large as to receive a loaded boat. Let the box be joined [to] the end of the upper canal and then the boat is admitted, and the doors of the admission secured again. Then the box with the boat in it, being balanced on wheels, or levers, is let down and becomes part of the inferior lock.'[15]

Until 1781, Darwin lived in Lichfield and was on friendly terms with Thomas Gilbert who was one of the Members of Parliament representing the city between 1768-1794. Lichfield was also the home of Robert Weldon who patented a canal lift in 1792, which was sufficiently similar in outline to Darwin's ideas so as to suggest some contact between the two.[16] Darwin's line of design envisaged the use of counterweights rather like the Anderton lift opened in 1875, whereas Weldon's concept involved complete submersion in a water filled cistern. Abraham Rees described how the caisson lock consisted of a:

'Long covered and close cassoon or trunk, with close shutting doors at its ends, in which water enough is contained for a boat to float into it, when it coincides with the surface of the water of the upper canal; when being shut in, this cassoon or dining trunk containing the boat, is to be sunk through a deep pit to a door or valve opening to the lower canal, and the end of the cassoon being fixed closely and exactly against the opening of the same, it, as well as the door of the cassoon, is opened and the boat passes out into the lower canal, and the apparatus is then ready for another boat to enter and ascend in like manner.'[17]

To the modern mind the whole operation suggests the working of a submarine and it would be of interest to determine whether Robert Fulton knew anything of Weldon's work. Certainly, contact was made between Weldon and the Gilbert brothers at an early stage of development when he was demonstrating the practicality of his plan by means of a model.[18] They facilitated the construction of a half-size lock 'for an experiment, by the side of the canal at Oaken Gates, in Shropshire', on land that belonged to the Lilleshall partnership.[19] Thomas Gilbert also sought to interest John Ward who was involved in the planning of the Kennet and Avon Canal, due to his role as land steward to the Earl of Aylesbury and because of his family links with earlier canals. (John Ward's mother had been Margaret Bill, which made John, William and Charles Bill his uncles as was John Gilbert through his marriage to Lydia Bill.)[20]

June 1794 Ward wrote from Leeds:

'I saw Mr. [T] Gilbert at Cotton on Tuesday night. He was very earnest in recommending it to our committee to send Rennie into Shropshire to see a cassoon which is calculated to raise and sink boats from one level to another without waste of water. Weldon is the patentee and the cassoon is at [W] Rockwardine near Lilleshall in Shropshire. If it would save a tunnel and a steam engine at Crofton or Wolfhall I should be very glad for I do not know but a steam engine (which will be necessary if a tunnel is not adopted) will be a greater nuisance than a tunnel and deep cutting on account of the smoke it will send up.'[21]

Subsequently, in December of the same year, John Rennie received a note from Charles Dundas (a Berkshire landowner and supporter of the canal), informing him that 'I have had a letter from Mr. T. Gilbert strongly recommending the cassoon'.[22] This was a direct result of a successful trial held near Oaken Gates:

'Weldon's Patent Cassoon

As many impediments arise in the Progress of Canals, from a want of water to supply the lock's in dry seasons, and elevated situations, Mr. Weldon has formed a CASSOON for conveying Boats on Canals, from higher to lower levels, and so vice versa, with great expedition, without locks, and with very little loss of water.

This Cassoon is now completed on the side of the Shropshire Canal, between Colebrook Dale, and Donnington Wood, near the Oaken Gates, where the turnpike road from London to Holyhead crosses the said canal, and was yesterday exhibited to several persons of distinction, and others conversant in that business who expressed very great satisfaction in feeling so useful an invention brought to perfection.

It will be shown at the same place every Monday, Wednesday, and Saturday, at twelve o'clock for six weeks next, when and where proper persons will attend to explain the machine, and deliver proposals to such persons as shall be desirous of introducing it upon their Canals. Ketley, Shropshire, Sept, 26, 1794.'[23]

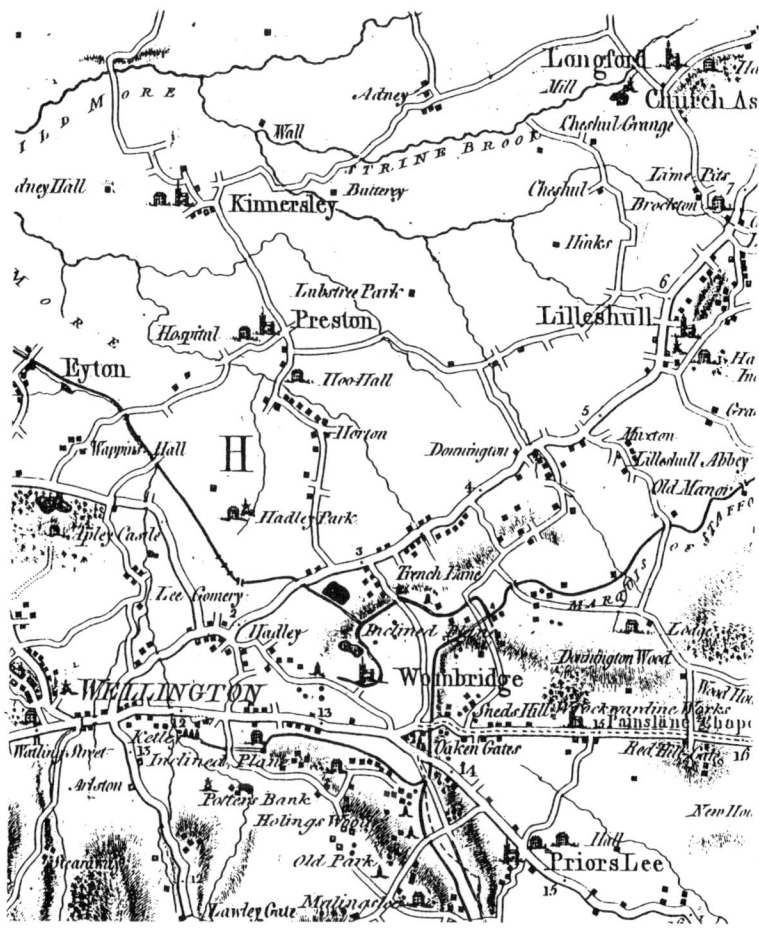

A map of 1808 showing the Shrewsbury, Wombridge, Ketley and Shropshire Canals; along with that belonging to the Marquis of Stafford (Earl Gower.) Robert Weldon built his prototype caisson lock by the side of the Shropshire Canal at Okengates where the London-Holyhead road (Watling Street) crossed the canal. *(Percy Marling)*

Thomas Gilbert (who was now nearly seventy five) attended these trials and related how 'the cassoon [was] so nicely balanced in the water that he could push it down with his cane and it would rise up again.'[24] The choice of Shropshire as the site for the earliest trial of a cassoon lock was not solely a product of the Gilbert brothers interests and influence in the area. William and Richard Reynold's had constructed the Ketley inclined plane as part of the Ketley Canal in 1788, the first such incline to be built on a canal in Great Britain. But despite this, the committee of the Shropshire Canal Company in the same year decided 'That a Reward of Fifty Guineas be offered by an advertisement to that person who shall discover and communicate to the committee . . . the best means of raising and lowering heavy weights from one Navigation to another.' It was in this sort of climate that the Weldon caisson experiment was arranged, although the 'banks of slipping loam . . . and old coal mines' might have rendered Weldon's lock inoperable as happened later at Combe Hay.[25]

If it was hoped that the Shropshire Canal would take up his caisson lock, then Weldon and his supporters were disappointed. John Ward was interested and organised a visit by Weldon to Devizes in January 1795 where he saw both Ward and Charles Dundas. This visit caused Ward to express concerns about the proposed use of the caisson, in February he wrote:

'Weldon's cassoon is for boats of only 8 tons—besides it is so great a concern that it will be highly proper for us to see a large one or two erected and used where it can be changed for locks, if not answering as between Crofton and Wootton Rivers, before we trust to having a wholeset made at Devizes, which in case of failure would stop our trade for several years.'[26]

Ward's view that the caisson had to be demonstrated as reliable was shared by the committee of the Kennet and Avon Canal and following a meeting on 8th June 1795 when Weldon demonstrated his model, but it was reported that they were afraid to adopt it 'as of the danger of its getting out of order and the difficulty of putting it to rights again.'[27]

Weldon was also demonstrating his model to the proprietors of the Somersetshire Coal Canal in the same month with a view to it being employed at Combe Hay, near Bath.[28] Despite their hesitation to use the caisson lock on the Kennet and Avon Canal, the committee was not averse to making a contribution to the one being erected at Combe Hay. The first trial of the Combe Hay lock was held in February 1798 and, as Dudley Clarke (resident engineer to the Kennet and Avon) observed, all did not go well; for when the water was admitted to the chamber the caisson itself broke loose and ended up wedged diagonally from the top to the bottom of approximately 30° to the chamber floor. Clarke ventured the opinion that

'the cassoon had sprung a leak and by one end being a little lower than the other gave the water within the cassoon an opportunity of getting to that end, and consequently created the weight to make the cassoon descend in the above manner to the great surprise of all present.'[29]

Such shortcomings in the construction of the cassoon were soon overcome and a successful trial was held in June 1798. A 'scientific correspondent' reported that:

'It is a great pleasure to reflect that the hydrostatical contrivance for conveying boats from upper to lower levels and vice versa, is completed, and may now be esteemed one of the greatest discoveries of the age; every scrupulous objection to the practability of its operation being removed.

On the 4th of June, in the presence of a large body of spectators, this stupendous machine underwent a complete trial.... We can scarcely describe the satisfaction this trial afforded; the facility and exactness of its ascent and descent were such as to encourage several gentlemen of this city (Bath), some of whom are officially engaged in the canal, with others who volunteered, entered the boat, and descended to the bottom of the cistern, (an immersion of 60 feet) which was particularly gratifying to the committee, and the ingenious inventor, Mr. Weldon.'[30]

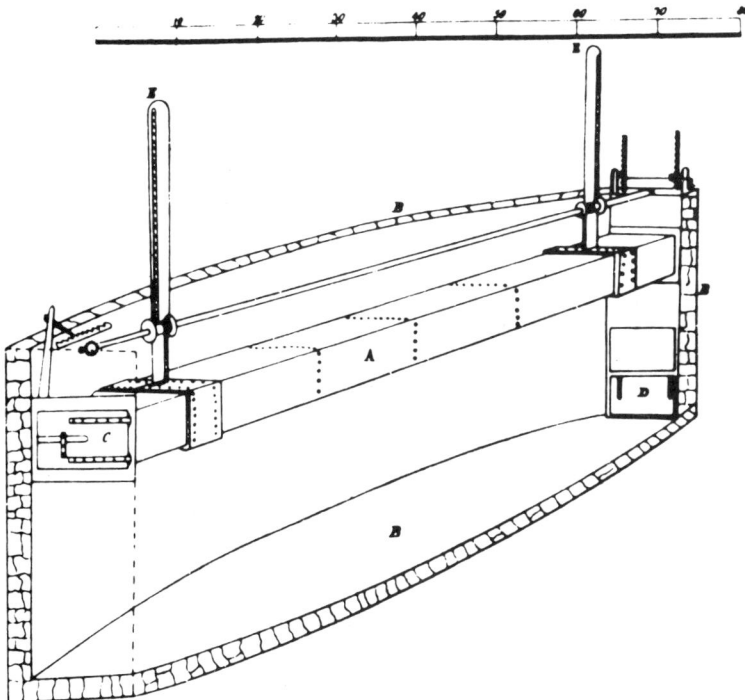

A drawing of Weldon's caisson lock from Billingsley's *General View of the Agriculture of the County of Somerset*, 1798.   *(Hugh Torrens)*

One of these officials was William Smith, the resident engineer, who acquired greater fame for his work in establishing the principles of geology. The trials were continued through 1798-99, but 'It was discovered, that, the walls of the lock-pit (chamber) had not been constructed with the requisite care . . . [so] the water had got behind them, and on draining off the water to make some alterations, they bulged so much, that the whole was rendered unsafe and useless.'[31] Most of the blame was directed at the Masons who built the chamber, but recently Hugh Torrens has shown that the real cause of the malfunction was the Lower Fullers Earth Clay in which the Chamber was excavated as:

'This is composed of clays which have a varying capacity to change volume, sometimes considerably, by absorbing water. Wet periods would cause the clay to exert alarming pressure on the cistern walls which would bulge, destroying the critical geometry of the cistern and causing the cassoon to jam in transit as in fact happened. The distorted cistern wall would be almost incapable of remaining water tight under these conditions.'[32]

William Smith may have recognised the problem but he was dismissed after a meeting of the canal committee held on 5th June 1799, at which it was decided to persevere a little longer with Weldon's experiments.[33] Weldon was ultimately frustrated by a decision to build his caisson lock in an unsuitable geological setting and not by any inherent flaws in his design (a similar fate might have awaited any lock built to his design on the Shropshire Canal for the reasons Telford outlined.) Rennie and the Trent and Mersey Canal Company were still considering either Weldon's caisson or a rival one as late as September 1798 for use on the projected Hanley Branch Canal.[34]

By the time that the canal reached Shrewsbury in February 1797, John Gilbert was dead and Thomas Gilbert was living out the last few months of his life in retirement at Cotton.[35] The respect felt for Thomas Gilbert and his usefulness as an ally had brought representatives from the Trent and Mersey Canal Company to seek his aid in 1796.[36] At this time, the Trent and Mersey Canal was threatened by a rival scheme for a Commercial Canal, prepared from a survey by Robert Whitworth and later re-surveyed by William Jessop. The promoters of this scheme seem to have been Sir Nigel Bowyer Gresley, a canal and colliery owner, the Burton Navigation, representatives of the Ashby and Chester Canals and certain pottery manufacturers anxious to promote transport competition. The proposal was for a barge canal from the Chester Canal at Nantwich (a broad canal providing a connection to the Dee at Chester and the

Mersey via the Wirral line) through a tunnel to join Sir Nigel Bowyer Gresley's canal in Apedale, then across the Trent and Mersey Canal near Burslem and the Caldon Canal near Bucknall, and by the Cheadle Coalfield to Uttoxeter and then down the Dove Valley to join the broad section of the Trent and Mersey below Horninglow. A further section would take it across the Trent below Burton and form a junction with the Ashby Canal.[37]

This canal offered the Potteries an alternative route to both the west and east, avoiding the Duke of Bridgewater's canal altogether. The use of barges would also have brought economies of bulk and it would have been impossible for the Trent and Mersey to compete. The Duke of Bridgewater recognised a common enemy in the scheme and pledged his support for the Trent and Mersey's Uttoxeter Canal plan. However, the Canal Company's main agent, William Robinson, did not pursue his intention to secure Thomas Gilbert's aid, for as he wrote to Charles Bill: 'I should have waited on Mr. Gilbert on Monday in hopes of prevailing on him to sign some letters to his friends which would no doubt be very useful, but the account Mr. Yeoman's gave me of his declining state induced me to think such application improper.'[38]

As was common in such matters, the controversy became heated and the tactics positively underhanded. An anonymous hand-bill was circulated entitled *Observations upon the Committee of Subscribers to the proposed Commercial Canal Scheme;* and later John Gilbert's son, John, signed a declaration with forty-two other pottery owners disassociating himself from a declaration supposed to have been made by a meeting of pottery manufacturers in support of the Commercial Canal scheme.[39] Thomas Gilbert seems to have been sufficiently recovered to sign an answer to the Commercial Canal scheme in June 1796[40] and he attended a proprietors' meeting in October of the same year.[41] A lack of funds and the powerful alliance formed against them, ensured that the Commercial Canal scheme failed but not before the Trent and Mersey Canal Company had been forced into an undertaking to build the Leek and Uttoxeter Canals.[42]

John Gilbert's involvement as resident engineer on all the various parts of the Duke of Bridgewater's canal system led to his sons, Thomas and John, receiving a training in canal construction techniques. The two brothers were certainly involved in the work on the Manchester—Runcorn line of the Bridgewater Canal and later John (Junior) was to embark on contract work for the Rochdale Canal. The early canals were not usually built by a single contractor as contracting firms of sufficient size did not appear until the 1820s. Instead, the principal engineer would authorise a number of contracts to separate contractors for cutting a few miles of canal, at about 3d to 6d per cubic yard. Puddling and lining were also calculated on the same basis, but separate contracts were normally arranged for the construction of locks, bridges, tunnels and canalside buildings. Before the Napoleonic Wars, there was still not sufficient public works contracting to promote the development of a class of professional construction workers and generally the men were recruited from the immediate neighbourhood.[43] This did not mean that labour was not moving from one canal construction site to another, but the workforce cannot be compared with the professional railway navvies of the nineteenth century. Possibly, advertisements were placed in local newspapers like the advertisement placed for 'Sober (and) Diligent Colliers' in 1762.[44]

The first plans for what eventually became known as the Rochdale Canal were laid in 1766, but the time was clearly not ripe for such a scheme and the plans were abandoned.[45] One of the subscribers to this first preliminary survey was John Royds, a merchant of Rochdale, who had married Ann Gilbert in 1754 and so was brother-in-law to both Thomas and John Gilbert.[46] He had a son, also called John Royds and it is not clear whether it was the father or the son who took such an active role in promoting the canal during the 1790s.[47] However, it is clear that it was John Gilbert (Junior) who took an active interest in the promotion of the canal, as well as having an interest in its construction. In 1791, the survey work was offered to both William Jessop and Robert Whitworth, but these two established canal engineers were fully engaged elsewhere and had to turn the offer down.[48] John Gilbert (Junior), by then a committee member, wrote to Matthew Boulton (Junior) 'to enquire the character of a Mr. Rennie as a Navigation Surveyor.'[49] In view of Rennie's reputation as a civil engineer this enquiry might be regarded as churlish, but it should be remembered that at that time Rennie had not been involved in any canal building projects. A vital requirement to the success of this canal was a junction with the Duke of Bridgewater's Canal in Castlefield, Manchester. The first approach was made to the Duke in September of the same year but he turned the request down as he feared a loss of revenue, for goods came to his canal by road and he could charge for wharfage and warehousing. The dejected promoters were to return to him with a request for his permission to build their canal 'so near his Navigation, that the Goods Etc transported on those Canals might be unloaded from the Vessels on the One, into those on the other by means of a crane.'[50]

The main intermediary between the canal committee and the Duke was John Royds, who presumably would expect a more cordial reception as he was related by marriage to the Duke's Head Steward. The interviews with the Duke went badly and in his dealings with the Rochdale Company, he is once again revealed as the monopolistic figure who had loomed over the infant Trent and Mersey Canal. He only appears to have relented when threatened by a rival canal scheme, but he demanded an enormous compensation toll of 3s 8d a ton on all traffic except flagstones from the Rochdale Canal Company.[51] The Rochdale Canal was also threatened by the Bury and Sladen Canal project and so in desperation they accepted his terms as 'reasonable', despatching John Royds to the Duke to thank 'his Grace for his good intentions.'[52] By the time the Act passed in 1794, this compensation toll had been reduced to 1s 2d per ton on all goods except flagstones that passed either way through the junction lock.[53] The elder John Gilbert had no direct involvement in the Rochdale Canal and it seems likely that his son's involvement was the initial cause of his dispute with the Duke.[54]

Many of the enterprises that the Gilberts were involved in were very dependent on the availability of transport by canal. The cases of the Donnington Wood Collieries and the Caldon Low quarries provide two prime examples. Likewise, the land purchasers at Goldenhill in 1760 and Clough Hall (Kidsgrove) in 1781 were the beginnings of large-scale coal-mining operations, adjacent to the Trent and Mersey Canal.[55] In both these instances lateral tunnels were driven from Brindley's Harecastle tunnel into the various collieries and the coal was brought out by means of small boats. This practice seems to have still been going on in the 1880s or 1890s, for one boatman recalled that his father 'said the coal was brought down in a little boat to be loaded in the big boats and he had seen the men coming on the big boats.'[56] His story can be substantiated by reference to a photograph of one of these small boats which survived until the late 1940s at Kidsgrove.[57] At first the practice was simply to knock a hole in the tunnel lining and construct a lateral boat level, so the colliery undertakers were constantly making payments to the Canal Company for repair work.[58] One major branch canal ran under the Goldenhill ironworks and its functions were described as follows in 1826: 'The Harecastle Tunnel of the Grand Trunk Canal Runs under this Estate; by which means, as well as by a cross canal which has been driven at an immense Expence beyond the Furnace, the mines are not only laid dry to a depth of from 45 to 75 yards but Coals, Ironstone and Lime-stone are

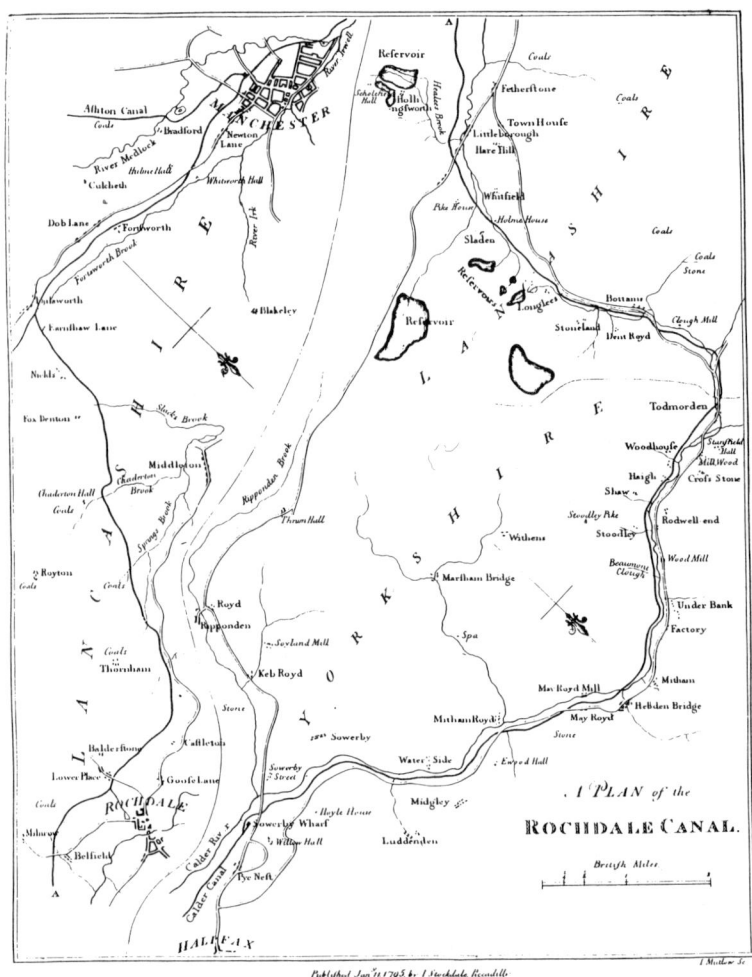

A plan of the Rochdale Canal, 1795.   (Author's Collection)

conveyed to the Furnace, and manufactured Iron carried to Market at very light expence.'[59]

The local legend that the original section of this lateral tunnel was built by John Gilbert appears to be confirmed by the name of Gilbert's Hole. The ironworks were probably commissioned after John Gilbert's death and apart from his involvement with the Donnington Wood furnace of 1783, there is no evidence of his direct involvement with ironmaking

The entrance to Brindley's Harecastle Tunnel in the late 1940s. The tub-shaped boat was a work flat, but the other boat is of considerable interest. Smaller boats were used in the side tunnels to reach the coal workings, in the same way that the 'starvationers' were used at Worsley, and a local source stated that the Harecastle boats were not unlike the one shown in this photograph. *(Evening Sentinel)*

elsewhere.[60] John Gilbert (Junior) had a foundry at Middlewich which was on the banks of the Trent and Mersey Canal, but like his father, he does not appear to have had any interest in the Goldenhill ironworks.[61] There was a small ironworks on the Clough Hall estate which was operated by John Luckcock, at the time of the 1812 sale.[62]

Following the completion of the Trent and Mersey Canal, John and John (Junior) soon established a steady trade in supplying broken limestone to the various kilns that sprung up at various points along the canalside. They supplied their own kilns at Cheddleton and Horsebridge on the Caldon Canal; and by 1781 they were making regular deliveries to the Etruria and Longport kilns.[63] John Gilbert (Junior) extended this interest when he erected limekilns and a coalyard at Stonefield, near Stone in 1796.[64] Burnt lime was reaching Acton Bridge (in Cheshire) before 1808 having been 'brought by the Staffordshire Canal, in *iron* boats, from the neighbourhood of Leek.' [65] The trade may have been even more widespread as the Forebridge kilns at Stafford were burning 'Froghall stone' (limestone from Caldon Low), as well as Dudley limestone by 1812.[66] The younger John Gilbert was able to maximise the return from his carrying operations between Froghall and Kidsgrove in 1806, when he 'contracted with the Lime burners for all (slack) I now get.' This is revealed in a letter to Josiah Wedgwood (Junior), written in June of that year, but the seasonal nature of such a trade is underlined by the comment 'in about two months that Trade will decrease.'[67] John Farey noted this same trade, when he wrote 'I saw the Caldon and Froghall Limeworks in 1808 (and) the Coals used thereat, were brought 22 miles along the Canal, from Mr Gilbert's Kidcrew Collieries.'[68]

The Gilberts involvement in carrying concerns was very widespread. The Cheddleton Lime Company were said to have seven boats in July 1795,[69] a number that had decreased to four boats and 'two old boats past work' by 1804. They also had a dockyard at Cheddleton and they appear to have built their own boats there, as well as using it for more general maintenance purposes.[70] Sometimes these boats operating into Cheshire, brought back a load of salt from 'Gilbert and Company, of Marston.'[71] The salt-mining operation at Marston seems to have provided the original incentive for John Gilbert to become involved in the carrying trade. John Gilbert had formed a partnership to work this salt mine, and owned seven boats in partnership with Cornelius Bourne, a Liverpool merchant, and Edward Mason, also of Liverpool, to take salt along the Trent and Mersey Canal to Runcorn.[72] These boats also operated to Anderton by 1799, where salt was transhipped from the Trent and

Cheddleton Wharf in 1905. The boatyard operated by the Gilberts stood to the left of this picture and their limekilns were situated directly opposite on the other side of the canal.
(Caldon Canal Society)

Mersey Canal to the Weaver Navigation.[73] This would have reduced the revenue on the Bridgewater Canal and may have further contributed to the friction between the younger John Gilbert and the Duke of Bridgewater. At Anderton, the Trent and Mersey lies just over 50 feet above the River Weaver and salt was transferred from the canal to river craft, by means of wheelbarrows, which ran along wheeling stages to chutes which discharged into Weaver flats.[74] In 1799, the Weaver Trustees were prepared to construct a "railed way" to facilitate a more varied interchange of goods, provided that Gilbert and Co. entered into a bond to carry their rock salt and other goods on the Weaver.[75] The "railed way" was built, but there is no evidence that the younger John Gilbert agreed to such a restrictive bond, he was too shrewd a businessman to bind himself to such a restrictive practice and he was unlikely to give the Duke so positive an indication of his intentions.

Before 1800, the emphasis at Anderton had been almost entirely on salt, but on 11th September of that year, a party of gentlemen 'concerned in the pottery trade' approached the Trustees 'and proposed to carry, flint, and crates down and up the canal and to reship the same to and from vessels navigating on the river Weaver.'[76] The younger John Gilbert as a Burslem potter, may have been amongst this deputation and he was certainly involved in this sort of traffic two years later. In January 1802, Wedgwood and Byerley paid him £133 for 'Freight and Tonnage on clay from Anderton'.[77] A list of boat-owners drawn up in 1795 shows that

'John Gilbert, of Clough Hall, Merchant'[78] had 16 boats and the role of merchant is emphasised by his offer to sell Wedgwood and Byerley '32 tons of Flint, then at Clough Hall.'[79] This demonstrates that the operation based at Kidsgrove was not simply a carrying concern and it should be remembered that the chief cargo leaving Kidsgrove was coal and coke from the four kilns on the Clough Hall estate. The life of a merchant and carrier was not without its upsets, as David Birds the younger, John Gilbert's chief clerk and agent at Clough Hall, noted in a letter to Wedgwood and Byerley in April 1802:
'Sirs,
The continuation of the Excise Law upon salt by which Mr. Gilbert already had three Boats seized and condemned obliges him to advance the price of Coals conveyed by his Boats.'[80]

The elder John Gilbert's involvement in the firm of Worthington and Gilbert had precipitated the Trent and Mersey Canal Company's management crisis in the 1780s, but it also represented his second venture into canal carrying and his first into warehousing. The exact date when the partnership was established is not known, but it seems likely that it was formed just before the first complaints were made by the Trent and Mersey Canal Company as these complaints were brought on by the appearance of this new competitor. John Gilbert's partner was Jonathan Worthington, a carrier on the Bristol route, who like Pickfords was originally a road-waggon proprietor.[81] To make matters worse, Worthington and Gilbert shared a warehouse at Castlefields with Hugh Henshall and Company (the Trent and Mersey Canal Company's carrying concern), so any preferential treatment given to Worthington and Gilbert could hardly be expected to go unnoticed.[82] The Duke of Bridgewater also allowed the firm to use his clerks and in 1791, he made a charge of £40 for work undertaken by his clerks at Preston Brook.[83] Warehousing and wharfage could be quite profitable. John Gilbert (Junior) made £45 each year from the small Newton Wharf at Middlewich,[84] on the Trent and Mersey Canal; and presumably this accounts for his purchase of a wharf at Berkhampstead (on the Grand Junction Canal) worth an estimated £30 per annum.[85]

Worthington and Gilbert were operating 23 boats by 1795, quite independently of the other carrying concerns which involved the Gilberts.[86] The younger John Gilbert does not appear to have been included in the partnership and after the death of his father in 1795, Johnathan Worthington carried on the business on his own account. According to one writer on the pottery industry, he lived at Moorhill

The rear of Messrs. Henshall and Gilbert's warehouse at Castlefield, Manchester, c.1950.
(Manchester Ship Canal Company)

Hall, Worcestershire and his granddaughter married William Adams (1833-1905), of Greenfield, Stoke-on-Trent.[87] A directory of 1820 refers to 'Worthington & Co, Liverpool and Manchester, Carriers' and the same work indicates that the Company's activities were very widespread at that time:—

'Worthington & Co's Fly Boats . . . to Birmingham, Wolverhampton, Stafford, the Potteries, Congleton, Warrington, Liverpool, Manchester, and intermediate places, from whence goods are forwarded by respectable carriers, to all parts of Cheshire, North Wales, Westmorland, Cumberland and parts of Scotland adjacent.'[88]

As land stewards to major landowners, the two Gilbert brothers were bound to become involved in any canal scheme which envisaged a route through or near, the extensive and widespread estates of their aristocratic employers. In the first instance, the rights of their employers as landowners had to be safeguarded, but they were also aware of the value of canals in the development of their estates. They were the principal activists in obtaining a junction of the projected Trent and Mersey Canal with the Duke of Bridgewater's Canal, which was to ensure that the Duke received increased revenue from his own canal and access to new markets for his coal.[89] There was also the awareness of how public canals could help in the development of Earl Gower's estates in both Staffordshire and

Shropshire. In the case of the Earl's estates in North Staffordshire, any stimulus to the growth of the pottery industry would in turn increase the demand for coal and so boost the Earl's income from his collieries. The canal would also act as an encouragement to the employment of more progressive agricultural practices, such as 'liming' the land. Before the construction of the Trent and Mersey Canal, small amounts of poor quality lime were obtained from Clayton and Madeley, but with the construction of the canal vast quantities were processed through the limekilns at Hemheath.[90]

Traffic on the Bridgewater Canal near Worsley.   *(Author's Collection)*

The two brothers were also aware of the value of a canal network as a means of further developing their own estates; and in creating the opportunities where they could exercise their entrepreneurial flair. The motivation behind their involvement in the promotion of the Caldon Canal was the prospect of increased sales from their quarries at Caldon Low. Always alert and quick to seize opportunities, they launched operations like the limekilns at Cheddleton and Horsebridge at the precise time that the canal was opened. Other interests like the carrying company and the Marston Saltworks were all dependent on the existence of the Trent and Mersey Canal. John Gilbert's purchase of the Clough Hall estate (near Kidsgrove) in 1781, again demonstrates how closely he identified canal transport with estate development.[91] He had clearly been aware of the great mineral wealth of the Kidsgrove area, even before 1760 when he was one of the partnership who purchased the Goldenhill estate. At Clough Hall, he intended to build a new hall and to develop the estate which would be the most profitable part of his business empire.

To safeguard the interests of their employers and to promote their own interests, it was crucial that the brothers became involved in the management of the Trent and Mersey Canal Company. This was easily achieved, as the other promoters needed the support of influential figures like Earl Gower and the Duke of Bridgewater, both in a local sense and in Parliament. Josiah Wedgwood would have preferred to have been able to do without this support as it did give the Duke of Bridgewater the impression that he was capable of arranging the affairs of the Company. This unbearable situation brought about the 'management struggle' of 1782-85, which ended with the 'independent' promoters asserting the autonomy of the Canal Committee. Following on from this crisis, Thomas Gilbert, who had done so much to guide the Company's various Bills through Parliament, was ousted due to his leadership of the Gower-Bridgewater group within the Committee. This whole episode is a fascinating example of how rising industrialists were able to exercise their new-found power in a rapidly changing society.

There was another important aspect to the involvement of the two brothers in canal promotion and management. John Phillips recognised that the Bridgewater Canal had 'shewn the great advantage to be derived from such works', and in this sense, the Gilberts had helped to perform a national service.[92] For at that time, it was widely recognised that such enterprise was in the Nation's best interest, even if this was not always recognised by the 'landed interests'. Wedgwood's memorial in Stoke parish church records how he 'converted a rude and inconsiderable Manufacture into an elegant Art and an important part of National Commerce.' The same kind of national service is also mentioned in a comment on his Etruria Factory, described as being for 'thirty years and upwards, all the efficacy of a public work of experiment.'[93] No writer described the Worsley Canal System in such terms, but it is undeniable that it merited the same sort of notice.

To the modern mind, the idea of patriotism and personal profit often seem incompatible, but to the eighteenth century mind no such division existed. The Duke of Bridgewater was praised for creating new jobs and for providing a stimulus to the growth of Manchester, but these were by-products of his schemes which were 'like in a Merchant's Counting House' calculated on 'profit and loss, and individual interest.'[94] The same is true of the Gilbert brothers as their primary concern was to promote the interests of their employers and themselves through their involvement with various canal schemes. It would be unjust to suggest that someone like Thomas Gilbert, who expended so much energy on the improvement of the Poor Laws, was not aware of the benefits that canals could bring to the Nation as a whole. He richly deserved the accolade of 'worthy senator' as he had not:

'confined his exertions for the good of his country to the House of Commons. (Instead) he had a very considerable share in promoting the execution of the second canal in point of consequence in this Kingdom, that of the Grand Trunk (Trent and Mersey), to the promotion of which he dedicated a considerable portion of his time.'[95]

In their involvement with the Shropshire and Shrewsbury Canals, the Gilberts should be seen in less active roles but nevertheless important ones. In the first instance they both had considerable status in the world of canal companies and promoters, so that any scheme they were associated with acquired additional credibility through their involvement. Thomas still retained his seat in Parliament until 1795, and the standing of John can be seen from his role as an arbitrator for the Thames and Severn Canal Company, in which he had no personal interest. They were also keen to promote the interests of Earl Gower and Company, the partnership made up of the two Gilbert brothers and Earl Gower. Initially, their Donnington Wood Canal had existed in isolation and the two Shropshire Canals brought the vital link with the River Severn, as well as with the local ironworks. From Earl Gower's point of view, a number of the local ironmasters were his tenants and so his investment in these canals was again an indirect means of stimulating the development of his estate in a very wide sense.

During their initial involvement with the Trent and Mersey Canal, the incentive of the interest paid on canal shares was limited. Returns were modest during the period of construction and consolidation, although there was the long-term prospect of a healthy return on the initial investment. The test of the financial success of any canal was the dividend paid on the capital and the price of the shares when sold in the open market. Thomas Gilbert's shares in the Trent and Mersey Canal, purchased for £2,000, were yielding a mere £130 (6½ per cent), in 1790. These shares were bequeathed to his nephew, David Birds, who in 1810, was drawing a princely £800 (40 per cent) per annum from this source. Likewise, one £200 share had a market value of £1,000 in 1790, which rose to £2,100 by 1810.[96] As John and Thomas Gilbert were both dead before their shares began to pay really handsome dividends, the benefit of their canal investments were enjoyed by their beneficiaries. It seems certain that they never really expected considerable returns, except in the sense that the canal network ensured the prosperity of their many other enterprises.

VI ENTERPRISE AND INNOVATION

At the time of the elder Thomas's death in January 1741/42, the Gilbert family were already embarked on a programme of entrepreneurial endeavour. He was aware of the untapped resources that existed in the neighbourhood and the growing market demand for these reserves. To his two sons he bequeathed his interests in the Cloughhead Colliery; the Cauldon Low quarries; two smelting mills and a collection of lead and copper mines.[1]

The capital requirements for such enterprises were not large, although sometimes they must have seemed so, considering the numerous small enterprises in which Thomas Gilbert was involved. External supplies of capital were not as important as personal or family funds, which could be scraped together to finance another enterprise. The Gilbert-Bill partnership in the Cloughhead Colliery depended on inter-family co-operation, and this was to be continued by John and Thomas Gilbert, after their father's death in 1741/42.[2] The elder Thomas also mortgaged his land to finance his industrial enterprises and then used the profit to both redeem the mortgage and to buy more land. In his will it mentions 'the Land wch. was purchased of Barnets at £400 now in the possession of Tunicliff,' which was willed to his son, John.[3] The same method of raising working capital was employed by John Gilbert, and with equal success. Matthew Boulton financed his Soho works in a very similar way.[4] He sold some of the property that he had inherited from his father, mortgaged the rest, and then did the same with the £28,000 worth of property that came to him through his marriage to an heiress, Anne Robinson.[5]

The example of previous enterprise by the forebears of entrepreneurs is worth stressing. John Wilkinson, the famous eighteenth-century ironmaster was the son of Isaac Wilkinson, a potfounder, who exhibited a considerable degree of the entrepreneurial flair that was the hallmark of his son.[6] George Stothert, the founder of the Bath firm that later became Stothert and Pitt, was himself the son of an ironmonger. His father, also called George Stothert, had worked as book keeper to a Manchester ironmonger called Bateman, better known because of his partnership with the North Staffordshire engineer, William Sherratt, in the firm of Bateman and Sherratt.[7] Heaton also made this point when he remarked that:

'Josiah Wedgwood was at least the fifth generation of potters; the Midland ironmasters looked back on an ancestry of nail or lock makers, smelters or founders, brassworkers or ironmongers; and the builder of one of Yorkshire's early large factories was the eleventh generation of clothmakers.'[8]

The enterprise of forebears was often crucial in moulding the interests and character of the entrepreneurs who emerged during the Industrial Revolution, but this observation needs qualification. For example, John and Nathaniel Philips, the sons of the John Philips, who had leased coalmines at Kingsley in 1721, embarked on linen tape weaving at Upper Tean in 1747. They were showing the same entrepreneurial inclination as their father had done, but they were more astute in choosing an enterprise where the competition was limited, and the capital outlay more modest. The 'old loom house' cost them a mere £160, although there was also the cost of employing a Dutchman to show them how to construct 'swivel looms' and later he was consulted on the best way in which to improve them.[9]

In view of these opening statements, Professor Mathias's comments on the role of entrepreneurs seem particularly enlightening:—

'The entrepreneurs... were not the long-lost cause of the industrial revolution. They sprang from economic opportunity as much as they created it. They depended everywhere upon a necessary creative environment. They joined the circle of other factors in economic growth as part cause and part effect, a dependent attribute and a creative part of industrial progress. But they are important. Latent resources can lie unused until "men of wit and resource" organize them for a market they have promoted.'[10]

Entrepreneurs had long been present in British society, but in many instances they were of such limited stature as to go almost unnoticed. Also, they were so intent on improving their social status through the purchase of land that they soon disappeared among the ranks of the so called 'landed classes.' If John and Thomas Gilbert are compared with their father as entrepreneurs, then the differences that emerge are not ones of instinct or ability, but more of time, place and opportunity. For they began to work in the pattern of enterprise that he laid down and then through their involvement with the Gower-Bridgewater interest, they became aware of the greater opportunities that existed for the exercise of their talents.

The family involvement with lead smelting was being developed by the elder Thomas Gilbert at the time of his death.[11] The lead ore that was raised from the mines could either go 'to the merchant or (the) smelter', so the obvious way of making more money was to assume one of these roles.[12] That of the merchant was less attractive, for it depended upon a network of contacts and also it might mean holding considerable stocks of ore or metal, which would tie up capital that could be employed elsewhere. On the other hand, a smelting mill could be set up at comparatively little cost. The site would be chosen as near to the mines as possible, bearing in mind: transport costs, the availability of a water-power site, and the ease of superintendence made possible by a spatially compact holding.

As Aikin stated: 'smelting furnaces are of two kinds, the hearth and the cupola.'[13] The cupola was in fact a low-arched reverberatory furnace with a fire at one end fuelled by coal and a low curved roof sloping down towards the other. A low wall separated the fire from the ore and the draught caused the flame to pass over the ore towards a flue at the far end which led to a chimney. This was the most efficient way of smelting, but it represented the most expensive option. Aikin wrote a description of the alternative:

'The hearth consists of large rough stones placed so as to form an oblong cavity about two feet wide and deep, and 14 long, into which fuel and ore are put in alternate layers; the heat is raised by means of a large pair of bellows worked by a water wheel. The fuel is wood and coal. The lead procured this way is very soft, pure and ductile, but a considerable quantity of metal remains in the slags. These are, therefore smelted over again with a more intense fire of coke: but the metal produced is inferior in quality to the former.'[14]

The smelting mill at Greenlowfield (near Alstonfield) was of the hearth type and work on building the mill had started sometime before October 1739. The principal partner was William Hall Walton, another 'yeoman', but one who was later to style himself 'gentleman'.[15] His son, Hall Walton, 'gentleman', had been involved in leases of the Ribden, Thorswood and Ecton mines, but his involvement with the construction of the costly Apes Tor Sough at Ecton had contributed to his serious financial difficulties.[16] This caused him to sell his interest in the smelting mill to Paul Nightingale, a Derby grocer.[17] The Gilberts were already involved by this stage[18] and six months after the mill was conveyed to Nightingale, 'Thomas Gilbert of the Inner Temple' took it over for the remainder of the lease for £200.[19] This meant that the ore being produced on the Burgoyne royalty at Ecton, by the Gilberts, Robert Bill and others, could now be smelted in their own mill and so another source of income became available to the family.[20] The degree of integration becomes more marked, when it is realised that the coal used in the smelting mill came from the Cloughhead colliery, worked jointly by the Gilberts and the Bills.

The second smelting mill at Dimmings Dale, near Alton was also a venture that the elder Thomas Gilbert had been instrumental in launching.[21] The Earl of Shrewsbury built the mill at his own expense, then leased it to the younger Thomas Gilbert and his father's partners in the Thorswood and Ribden mines, at a peppercorn rent of 1 shilling per annum.[22] Presumably, the Earl's motive for this action was connected with his general desire to develop his estate.[23] The other partners were Anthony and Edward Hill, but on the death of Anthony Hill, John Gilbert increased his holding in the mill.[24] It was described as a 'smelting mill refinery and slag harth', so it was of the same type as the Greenlowfield mill.[25] The lead ore came from the mines in which the Gilberts had interests, but the relative locations would suggest that the Alton mill would have primarily served the Thorswood and Ribden mines.

John and Thomas Gilbert enlarged the partnership which was running the mill in 1760.[26] At the same time certain changes had been made in the mining partnership operating the Ecton mine. The brothers agreed to divide their shares in the mill between their mining partners, namely: the Duke of Devonshire; four members of the Bill family; and almost certainly, Edward Coyney.[27] Before 1760, the Gilberts had only worked the Burgoyne mineral field at Ecton, in partnership with the Bills, Edward Coyney and probably others.[28] The new partnership was established to work the Chadwick mine, owned by the Duke of Devonshire. The Chadwick mine was worked for lead between 1761-1773, but the amount raised seems to have been modest. The Burgoyne mine also appears to have been still working in 1772, but accounts for both mines are missing.[29] The earlier operations at the Burgoyne mine, between 1737-44, made an estimated profit of at least £726, but this would be divided amongst the partners.[30]

After 1773, the Gilbert brothers and their partners seem to have withdrawn from mining operations at Ecton. This meant that the smelting mill at Alton was no longer an economic proposition and it was abandoned. The mines at Thorswood and Ribden may also have become less profitable during this period, and this would also have had an adverse effect on the fortunes of the Alton smelting mill. Another factor was the spread of the more efficient cupola furnace, including one erected at

Ecton before 1767.[31]

The Gilberts' involvement with the Ecton mines are of interest on two other counts. Firstly, within the mines worked by the Duke of Devonshire at Ecton, there was a boat level by the time of Sir Joseph Banks's visit in 1767.[32] The link has already been mentioned between the Barker family, agents to the Duke of Devonshire, and John Gilbert in the Hillcar Sough project of 1766.[33] Therefore, it seems almost certain that John Gilbert advised on the Ecton boat level, a further example of his work as a consultant mining engineer. John Gilbert also brought James Brindley to Ecton, in March 1759 or 1760; and the most logical reason for this would be to advise on some form of pumping machinery.[34] In 1769, the mines were drained by 'a common Wem or engine', a horse-powered machine that raised water in barrels.[35] These were replaced in 1783 by a massive water-engine, like those employed at the Gilbert's Woodhead colliery and at Worsley.[36]

By 1747, John and Thomas Gilbert had gained complete control of the Thorswood and Ribden mines, under a lease from the Earl of Shrewsbury.[37] They issued a prospectus in order to attract partners and this provides a valuable insight into the way capital was raised. The Gilbert brothers proposed to keep one half of the shares (12 in number) and to sell the rest at 25 Guineas for one twenty-fourth share. This would give them an authorised share capital of £630, although it is clear that the capital was subscribed in yearly instalments. The partners were required to forward sums of money to get the mines operational and this amounted to £5-5s-0d, £10-10s-0d, £7-0s-0d, and £10-0s-0d in 1747, 1748, 1749 and 1754 respectively. The only figures available suggest that the mines were not profitable.[38]

During 1748-49, the cost of working the mines came to £461 and the ore produced was valued at £402. From 1754 to 1757, the costs were £515 resulting in the production of lead and copper worth £321.[39] It seems unlikely that these losses were typical for the brothers surrendered the lease in 1763 and immediately took out a new lease, which bound them to spend £1,000 over seven years on trials for fresh deposits of ore. The mine was productive in the 1760s and 1770s, but again no figures are available.[40]

A lease of the Thorswood mine in 1793 shows that the Gilberts had abandoned their interest in this mine, but in the same year, John Gilbert took out a lease of the Ribden mines. Following John Gilbert's death, his son, John, formed a partnership to run the mines. Again, twenty-four shares were to be offered, and the concern was to be run on the usual cost-book system, deposits being made (on request) to cover operating costs. The Shareholders were: Thomas Patten of the Alton Wire Company (10 shares); John Gilbert, Junior (2 shares); Thomas Gilbert (2 shares); Charles Bill (2 shares); the Reverend John Bill (2 shares); Henry Yeoman (2 shares); George Smith (2 shares); William Bird (1 share); and Matthew Brindley (1 share). The family connections emerge once again in this partnership, but in a more limited way, as only nine of the twenty-four shares were held by John Gilbert, Junior, or his relatives.[41]

The Cloughead colliery appears to have been reaching the end of its useful life by 1755 and the two Gilbert brothers began to look for another colliery in which to invest. On the 18th May, 1759, they secured a lease of Mr Whitehall's mines 'on the south west side of the Churnet', in the Woodhead coal seam.[42] The previous day, James Brindley had visited the colliery to advise on the construction of a water engine for pumping out the mines.[43] The Gilberts were to pay Whitehall a duty of an eighth on all coal raised and on this basis they worked the mine for three years.[44] Then in 1762, the brothers sub-let the mines to John Leigh, Thomas Hurst and John Bill, requiring a duty of a sixth on all coal raised. This meant in effect, that John and Thomas Gilbert received the profit on the sale of just over four tons, out of every one hundred tons, their return being equal to four and a quarter per cent, with no expenses.[45]

A meeting of coal leaseholders and those actively concerned with mining in lands adjacent to the Gilberts, was held at Cheadle on 2nd November 1762.[46] From this meeting a very large partnership was formed, made up of members of the Hurst, Leigh, Bill and Gilbert family. As all leases were to be submitted to Thomas Gilbert for scrutiny, it seems likely that he was the moving force behind the formation of this partnership. Three days after the meeting, John and Thomas Gilbert sub-leased their colliery within the partnership, of which Robert Hurst and Edward Leigh were to be the chief executives.[47] Such an arrangement would have suited the Gilberts very well, as at this time John was preoccupied with the Worsley project and Thomas was about to embark on his parliamentary career.

The arrangement worked well until 1777, when John Gilbert protested that he was not satisfied with the statement of accounts. He objected to a payment of £150 made between two of the partners, and insisted that the matter be submitted to counsel for an opinion.[48] The matter was eventually sent to a barrister, J. Mansfield, who found in favour of John Gilbert's partners.[49] Three years later, another meeting was held at the Star Inn and John Gilbert raised the matter again. He told the meeting that 'if they do not produce the books and accounts, a Bill of Equity ought to be filed for that purpose to oblige Mr. Hurst, Mr. Rupert Leigh and Mr. Ed. Leigh to produce upon oath or give the best account they can of the transactions.'[50] In such a climate of distrust, the partnership collapsed, which was probably not such a disaster for the Gilbert brothers as their original lease had only five years to run. The episode does serve to illustrste the intransigent side to John Gilbert's character; a weakness inherited by his son, John, who showed the same blind determination in his dispute with Sir John Edensor Heathcote.[51]

John Gilbert also obtained a lease of all the coal mines in Farley and Cotton, from the Earl of Shrewsbury in 1767.[52] His purpose in obtaining control of the small mines in this area and of opening others, was to secure a supply of cheap fuel for the limekilns at Caldon Low, that he and Thomas were operating. By this time, the mine at Cloughead was worked out and an alternative supply of slack or poor quality coal was needed. Six years earlier, John Gilbert had obtained a lease from the Earl of Shrewsbury of all the limestone in 'Ribden Stones or Ribden flats', which he held in addition to his share in the Caldon Low quarries.[53]

Breaking and loading limestone at Froghall Wharf, 1910.   *(B.H.Snow)*

The Act for the Caldon Canal reveals the names of the owners of the various limestone quarries. Thomas Gilbert, Henry Copestake, Robert

Bill and William Wooliscroft were what might be termed 'semi-independent' operators, as they did not co-operate closely. On the other hand, John Gilbert, Richard Hill, George Smith and Sampson Whieldon, were all part of a concern known as the Caldon Lime Company. All of the quarry operators made an agreement with the Trent and Mersey Canal Company, to deliver to the Canal Company (on request) 'good and merchantable Limestone... at 7d per Ton.'[54] The same proprietors were operating the quarries in 1794, when the Canal Company took between 2,000 to 5,000 tons per month.[55]

The tonnage required for the year 1795 was estimated at about 40,000 tons.[56] This allows an estimate to be made of the figure, paid by the Canal Company to the proprietors, the amount being about £1,166. The quantity of stone taken from the individual quarries, to fulfil this order was left to the owners to decide amongst themselves. John Gilbert and his partners in the Caldon Lime Company usually supplied two-fifths; Thomas Gilbert one-fifth; and the other owners the remaining two-fifths.[57] The quarry owners also sold limestone that was carted away for use in the surrounding area, much as it had always been.

The Caldon Lime Company took over John Gilbert's lease of the coal mines in Farley and Cotton, concentrating especially on the poor, shaly coals mined near Froghall.[58] But the Company's interests were more extensive than this, for at the time that John Gilbert established the Caldon Lime Company, he was also organising another Company based at Cheddleton to burn the broken limestone. John Gilbert and 'others' bought land at Cheddleton in 1778,[59] and subsequently his partners in the Cheddleton Lime Company are revealed to be the same people who comprised the Caldon Lime Company.[60] The Cheddleton Lime Company erected kilns at Cheddleton and Horsebridge, on the banks of the Caldon Canal.[61] The company purchased slack from the nearby Shafferlong coalfield and until 1786, they controlled the only limekilns between Cauldon Low and the Potteries.[62] They also operated a boatyard at Cheddleton which constructed and maintained their own narrow boats, and offered the same facility to other boat-owners.[63] The concern remained profitable for many years, John Gilbert's place being taken by his son, John, whose executors drew £300 from the concern in 1815.[64]

In all the enterprises so far mentioned, John and Thomas Gilbert were either continuing, or extending a pattern of activity that their father had laid down. He had been concerned to increase the family's land holding, and the quickest way to achieve this was by investment in extractive industries. The first extensions of the brothers' interests came about through their involvement with Earl Gower and the Duke of Bridgewater. Their activities, with the exception of the pencil factory at Worsley, were not new in nature, but they did take the Gilbert brothers from the familiar surroundings of the Staffordshire moorlands.

The major venture within this category was Earl Gower and Company, a concern that was intended to develop the Earl's Lilleshall estate and as such was described an earlier chapter. The financing of this enterprise was mainly left to Earl Gower, although the Gilbert brothers did provide a small proportion of the capital. The Earl safeguarded his income by leasing the workings to the brothers and by requiring them to sign a bond. Thomas does not seem to have been short of working capital; for he had the residue of his £10,000 windfall; the income from the Cotton estate; and an income from the fees he charged for his work as a solicitor and land agent.

John's income on the other hand was more modest and he had extensive commitments to a number of enterprises. Therefore, it is not surprising to find that John Gilbert's share of the working capital needed at Lilleshall was provided by Thomas, who required that:—

'Mr John Gilbert's 4th share in the . . . works and also £2,000 capital stock in the Navigation from the Trent to the Mersey . . . be assigned to (him) as Collateral security.'[65]

The intricacies and shoestring nature of John's finances were stressed some five years later, when he requested Josiah Wedgwood to pay his 'Subscription to the Navigation for a while'; his canal shares forming part of the collateral security for his Lilleshall investment.[66]

At Worsley, the underground canal network also served certain coal mines at Farnworth, which John Gilbert purchased in 1774 and 1793.[67] These seem to have been a particularly good investment as in 1812, the younger John Gilbert received an annual income of £144 from this source.[68] The other enterprise established in the Worsley area was the pencil factory, which in itself was a natural extension from John Gilbert's interest in black lead mining.[69] Curiously it is only one of two ventures that the elder John Gilbert made into the manufacturing sector of industry, the other being Gilbert and Wind, Fustian Manufacturers established in Manchester by 1789.[70] The Gilberts were trying to put a partnership together to work the black lead (graphite) mines near Seathwaite in Borrowdale as early as June 1765, when John Gilbert was tempting Matthew Boulton to take a share in a partnership to work and sell the black lead; 'You [will] make a Fortune in the Black Lead' predicted Gilbert.[71]

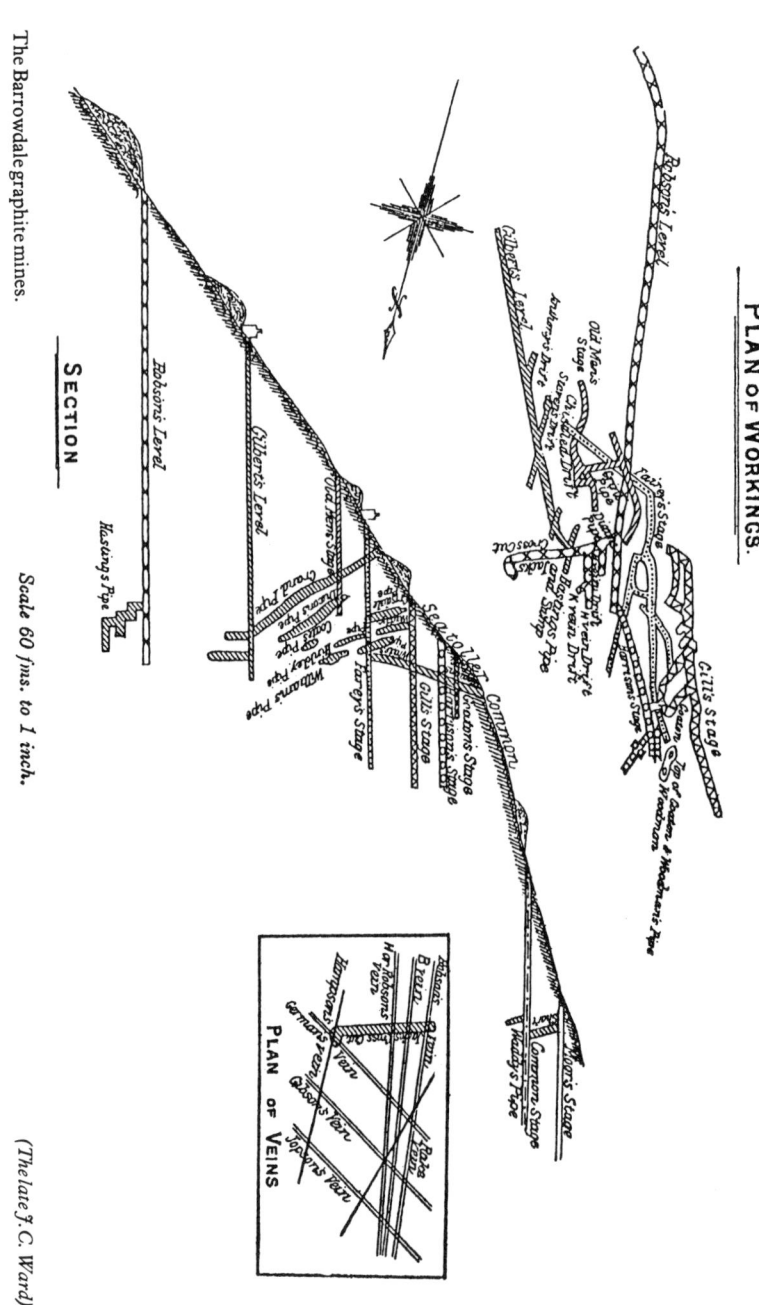

PLAN OF WORKINGS.

PLAN OF VEINS

SECTION

Scale 60 fms. to 1 inch.

The Barrowdale graphite mines.

(The late J. C. Ward)

122

Later in the same year, John Gilbert proposed that Boulton accompany him to inspect the mines, possibly bringing his son, Thomas Gilbert, with him from Birmingham where he was serving some sort of 'apprenticeship.'[72] Boulton was unable to make the journey to the mines in September of the same year, but John Gilbert went along with his brothers-in-law—Charles and John Bill, plus a Mr. Fox 'One of their London partners.'[73] John Gilbert was in favour of obtaining an effective monopoly for the partnership both in terms of production and sales, for output depended on the richness of the lode and that was mainly a matter of luck.[74]

Not that the methods of working the mines were left to chance and the investment made by the partnership was to pay handsome but not fabulous dividends. A gift made to Josiah Wedgwood in 1767 prompted him to write to Thomas Bentley: 'Mr. John Gilbert . . . has promised to get me a doz. of good black lead pencils, and a lump of the same for shading with, you are to share in this valuable acquisition.'[75]

Despite this largesse, the partnership does not appear to have started active mining until 1769 and even then only prompted by another mine in the immediate vicinity having failed.'[76] At this opening the 'old mines' Day level. . . had been widened and heightened so as to admit wheel barrows.'[77] Originally, the mine had only been opened once in six or seven years, but as demand increased and the size of the lode diminished, the partners opened up the mine for six or seven weeks every year.[78] Further trials were carried out in 1778, 1788-89 with limited success; the rubbish heaps left behind by previous workings, however, were picked over and yielded much valuable graphite. The resident agent seems to have exercised a dominant influence as to the way mining operations were carried on, which perhaps accounts for a strange practice described by John Farey:

'At another period (1778), some conjurer, in the interest of mill-wright, I suppose, recommended the erection of a mill, and one James Morris came from Lancashire, as "the blue miller" as he was called, and was actually employed in grinding the mine rubbish to coarse powder, to destroy the many valuable pieces of wad, left in it, for preventing their being stolen.'[79]

This sounds totally incomprehensible and in view of the fact that in 1778, the Duke of Bridgewater allowed his carpenters at Worsley to make 'an engine for pounding the Black Lead' the present author is left wondering whether any of this 'destroyed' wad (graphite) found its way to Worsley. Thomes Gilbert was a partner in the concern and in the same year he proclaimed that he was 'glad to hear so good an account of our Black Lead'.[80] The Duke of Bridgewater and the two Bill brothers may also have held shares although precise details of the partnership are missing. The only indication comes from Samuel Parkes writing in 1815:

'The propriety of this valuable mine is divided, as I understand, into two equal parts, one of which belongs to Henry Bankes, Esq., representative in parliament for Corfe Castle in the county of Dorset; and the other moiety is divided into ten or twelve shares belonging to Sir Joseph Banks, Sir John Mifford, the Executives of the late Mr. John Gilbert and others. In some years net produce of the black lead has amounted to thirty or forty thousand pounds.'[81]

Farey also relates how the whole concern was placed on a more systematic footing:

'From about the year 1790, the late John Gilbert Esq., one of the Owners, recommended that a new level should be driven, from the surface to the bottom of the Low Mine . . . and levellings with this view were separately taken with great care by two of his miners, Thomas Timperley and Thomas Kent sent from Lancashire, yet this important measure seems not to have been determined on, until 1798 (owing to Mr. Harrison preferring and adopting his day level). . . . it was driven entirely in hard rock, until it was finished, in June 1800.'[82]

John Wilson Harrison was the resident agent at that time, but his paramountcy disappeared as the completeness of Gilbert's proposals were recognised and rapidly implemented. Farey noted:

'An excellent Iron Rail-way was, as its driving proceeded, laid along the floor of this Gilbert's Day Level, which is itself quite straight, and the passage of ample width and height; and over its south east-end, a House was built since called Gilbert's mine-house; having therein, various rooms for the dressing, sorting and barrelling up of the wad (graphite); and also, for the workmen and miners, to undress and dress and be searched, before leaving the House at all such times, as any wad is accessible to pilferers; a smith cellar, for sharpening the miners tools; and a room for the mine agent to keep his accounts, and settle with his workmen; and for him to sleep in, as a security whenever a sop of wad is in work and until all its most valuable contents may be safely barrelled up, if not also sent off for the London warehouse.'[83]

The traditional way of making black lead pencils was to cut slips from blocks of graphite, which were then fitted into 'a groove made of the softest wood, as cedar, and another slip of wood glued over them.' Sometimes the pencils were not always what they seemed, for 'different

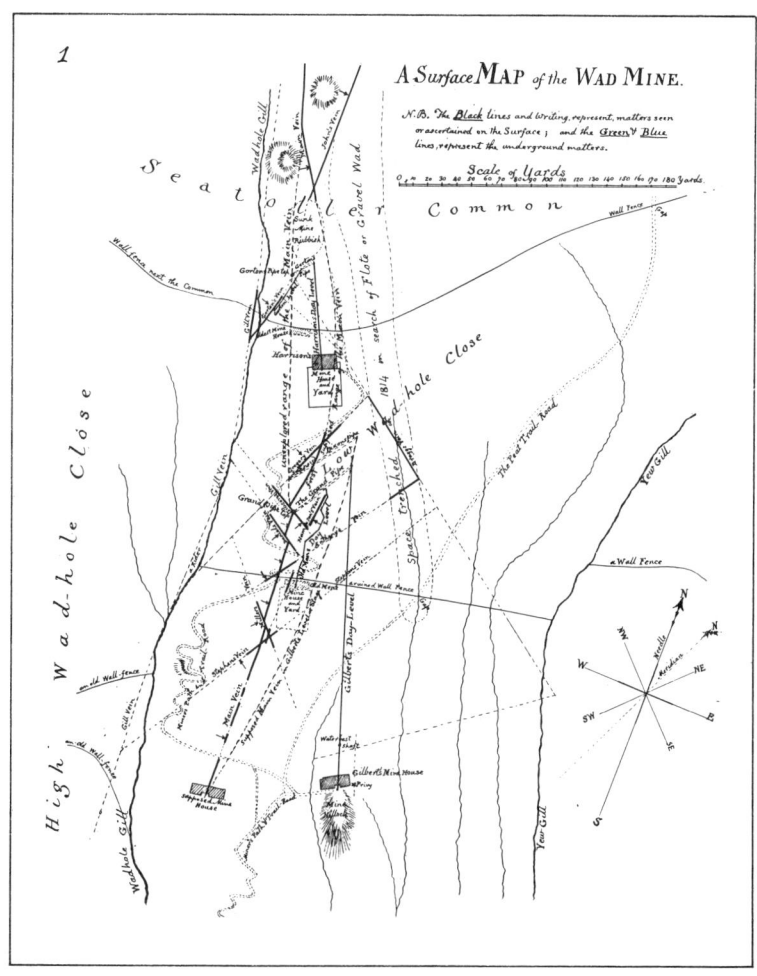

A Surface MAP of the WAD MINE.

N.B. The Black lines and writing, represent, matters seen or ascertained on the Surface; and the Green & Blue lines, represent the underground matters.

Scale of Yards

John Farey's map of the Borrowdale graphite mines 1818.   *(Dorset Record Office)*

sorts of the mineral (could be) fraudulently joined together in one pencil, the fore-part being commonly pretty good, and the rest of an inferior kind.' This was the traditional English way of producing pencils, but imported German pencils were made of finely powdered black lead blended with other substances, according to the hardness of the pencil required.[84] John Gilbert adopted the German method of production, which allowed pencils to be produced at competitive prices, but of a lower quality. The factory was in production by 1782.[85] An advertisement of 1815 gives quite a detailed picture of the scope of this enterprise at Worsley:—

'To Clean & Polish Stoves, Ovens, Grates &c.

JOHN GILBERT & Co., Worsley, prepare BLACK LEAD POWDER, for cleaning & polishing stoves, ovens, grates &c, which with very little trouble, gives a higher polish than anything yet offered for the purpose.

N.B. Thin Black Lead Pencils are made from the purest genuine LEAD only and School Slates from the best materials.

Sold by Mr. CHESTER and Mrs. SMITH in Newcastle and in most other towns by STATIONERS, SILVERSMITHS &c. The powder in packets at 1s. 3d. and 2s. 6d. each.'[86]

BLACK-LEAD PENCIL Manufactory at WORSLEY.

J. GILBERT and Co. refpectfully ac-quaint the public, that they now make that valuable and ufeful article, and that they will ufe their utmoft endeavours to retrieve the reputation of them, which has been fo much injured by perfons who have impofed on the public by felling Pencils of little or no value. This impofition has prevented much the fale of good lead, which is a great difappointment to the public; and a great lofs to the proprietors of the Lead Mine, of which J. Gilbert has a fhare, and has induced him to begin this Manufactory in which the public may be affured none but the beft Lead will be ufed. As the Manufactory is fo far fituated from the Metropolis J. Gilbert and Co. have appointed them to be fold wholefale (only) by William Champante, No. 4, Minories, from whom they may be had on the fame terms as from the Manufactory. They are to be had retail of moft Stationers in London; alfo of T. Wood, Printer, Salop; and by all the Bookfellers in Birmingham, Glofter, Bath, Briftol, Hereford, and moft principal Towns through Great-Britain; to prevent Impofition they are marked on each Pencil I. G. Worfley.

Newspaper advertisement for John Gilbert's pencils, 1785.   *(Hugh Torrens)*

The Earl of Carlisle and Company was an enterprise inspired by Earl Gower and Company, although the form of the partnership was by no means novel. The company was formed to work the lead mines on Alston Moor, in Cumberland, the first application for the lease being made in 1771.[87] In that same year, John Gilbert had been involved in another mining enterprise, under the adjacent, Middle Fell.[88] He also acted as adviser on the proposed sough, even before the Earl of Carlisle and Company obtained a lease of the mining field on 30th May 1778.[89] The previous year, John Gilbert had recommended that the sough:

126

'may serve as a navigable Canal, in order that it may be seen whether the expense of making the said canal will not . . . be greatly different from that of making the said level of the size already begun.'[90] The main sough became known as the Nent Force level, but as it soon struck basalt, progress was slow and expensive. After twenty years of heavy investment and little return, the surviving partners sold their interests to the London Lead Company.[91]

John Taylor, mining entrepreneur and engineer[92] visited Alston Moor in 1823, to report on the mines. His report vindicates John Gilbert's scheme, stating that:—

'there were fair reasons to expect a different result, the intersection of so large a tract of Mineral Country, and the exploring of deep beds of Lime Stone similar in many respects to that which has produced so large a proportion of the Lead raised at Aldstone Moor, appear to me to have warranted the undertaking, and to justify those who so long ago recommended it.'[93]

The entrance to Gilbert's Level, Borrowdale, 1989. (Ann Lead)

Taylor's view would have been little consolation for the partners, who paid nearly £12 for every foot of the level cut through the basalt.[94] The Earl of Carlisle's partners in the enterprise were: the Duke of Bridgewater, Earl Gower (his father-in-law); John Gilbert; John Royds (John Gilbert's brother-in-law); Thomas, Robert and John Gilbert,

Junior, (John's sons); Jonathan Hilton; Joseph Hilton; and John Cleaver.[95]

All of the brothers' other enterprises were linked with the Trent and Mersey Canal, and in the case of the firm of Worthington and Gilbert with the Duke of Bridgewater's canal.[96] This is hardly surprising, as they fitted in with the 'new range of economic opportunity... (that depended) on transporting heavy raw materials across country.'[97] The first of these enterprises was tied up with the purchase of the Goldenhill estate in 1760, which highlights another involvement in the establishment of the various enterprises. This is the role played by the attorney as a financial intermediary, in touch with the hidden capital market which existed outside London.

Already, Thomas Gilbert's role in bringing together the Cheadle coalmaster's partnership has been mentioned, and in the case of the Goldenhill purchase it is possible to see similar processes at work. Thomas Gilbert was in fact, a 'money-scrivening attorney, characterised as much by his familiarity with business practice and local affairs as by his knowledge of the law.'[98] Land sales at that time were mainly the concern of attorneys in much the same way as property and land are still sold in Scotland today.[99] Therefore, the attorney was amongst the first to know of properties and land coming onto the market, and indeed they were in a position to arrange private sales. But attorneys also dominated the 'county mortgage market in the eighteenth century through their intimate knowledge of local society and their ability to tap reservoirs of savings in order to accommodate an increasing demand for loanable funds.'[100] This connection was to be of particular use to John Gilbert in financing his numerous enterprises. As Samuel Johnson said of these attorneys: 'What is their reputation but an instrument of getting money.'[101]

The Goldenhill estate was purchased in four equal shares by: Hugh Henshall; John Brindley; Robert Williamson; and John and Thomas Gilbert. It was then conveyed to Robert Hurst of Cheadle, who held it in trust for the four partners in the purchase.[102] The whole concern was then operated as a kind of partnership with the partners receiving shares of the rents received and the income from the coal mines. The lands were not in fact partitioned until 1786, when John Gilbert was consolidating the Clough Hall estate; but the coal mines were not divided and remained within the partnership arrangement.[103] James Brindley was not one of the partners in the purchase, although he might have contributed to his brother's share.[104] Samuel Smiles bases his statement that James Brindley was a partner, on an entry in Brindley's notebook. The entry is of most interest as it shows how the partnership raised some of the necessary capital through local connections:—

'Mr. Joh. Gilbert	£ 81-0-0
Mr. Joh. Gilbert	£ 20-0-0
Mr. Joh. Gilbert	£ 8-5-0
	£109-5-0
Mr. Lanslet, Leek	£400-0-0
Mr. Robert Barks, Ginders Ash.	£ 17-1-8
Mr. William Allen	£ 20-0-0
Totall is	£543-6-8

31st March 1769.'[105]

Smiles uses the above entry to show that 'amongst his townsmen and neighbours . . . (Brindley) . . . stood in good credit and repute.'[106] But as Robert Barks and William Allen were residents of the Cheadle area, the entry probably says more about Thomas Gilbert's reputation as an attorney. The conveyance of the Goldenhill estate to Robert Hurst, in practice the chief executive of the Cheadle coalmasters partnership, and John Gilbert's wife's uncle, points towards the partnership being the brainchild of the Gilbert brothers.

Thomas Bentley in his pamphlet on *Inland Navigation*, drew the attention of the general public to an area of mineral wealth that was largely untouched:—

'From Northwich to Lawton there is a vast bed of rocksalt about forty yards thick, which (besides being purified and crystallized for home consumption and exportation as will be mentioned in its proper place) might be made great use of in agriculture, and probably in Metallurgy, and several of the mechanic arts; if any method could be discovered of granting the liberty of using it with safety to the revenue.'[107]

This saltfield was intersected by the Trent and Mersey Canal and this roused certain entrepreneurs to begin the search for salt and brine. The first successful borings were made at Lawton, just after the canal had opened, and these revealed the presence of the normal rock salt deposit at 120 feet, and a lower one at a depth of 150 feet.[108] This discovery stimulated the Northwich proprietors to bore deeper, something they had been reluctant to do in the past, due to the danger of flooding. John Gilbert organised a boring through 'the sole of the Marston Top mine', near Northwich, in 1780 or 1781, and he hit the lower bed some 30 feet down.[109] After this discovery, all the new mines in the Winsford and Northwich area were sunk to the lower bed.[110]

When Sir Joseph banks visited the Northwich rockpits in 1768, the workmen brought the salt down with 'Picks made very strong and Heavy . . . sometimes in peices 2 or 3 tons weight.'[111] John Gilbert is credited with an innovation which must have speeded production as he is 'said to have been the first person who suggested the use of gun-powder in obtaining rock-salt.'[112] Although he was not the first person to commission a Boulton and Watt engine on the saltfield, he did realise the benefits that could be obtained from the employment of an engine. The partners in the Lawton saltworks erected a small engine, to pump brine in 1778,[113] and this could have been the engine that was later used to pump water on the Trent and Mersey Canal.[114] The Boulton and Watt engine erected at Marston for 'John Gilbert of Worsley and partners', was used for winding rock salt and for pumping brine.[115] Significantly, Edward Salmon of Hassall Hall, one of the partners in the Lawton saltworks,[116] also sat on the management committee of the Trent and Mersey Canal with John Gilbert.[117]

In order to operate the Marston mine, John Gilbert brought together another partnership. The identity of his fellow partners is not known for sure, but this concern also owned seven narrow boats 'to take salt along the Trent and Mersey Canal to Runcorn'.[118] John Gilbert, Cornelius Bourne (a Liverpool merchant), and Edward Mason (also of Liverpool), are recorded as the owners of these boats, and it is likely that they also comprised the partnership that ran the Marston mine. As a considerable quantity of the salt was refined in Liverpool, and a vast quantity exported through this port; it seems likely that John Gilbert would turn to the merchant community there, in search of partners.[119] He obtained his working capital for this venture by purchasing a number of houses and twenty-two acres of land at Marston, which he mortgaged to Lady Leicester, in 1782, for £1,000.[120]

In describing entrepreneurs, Phyllis Deane observed that:— 'It was natural enough for successful industrialists to build up the social prestige and creditworthiness, which they needed to help them finance their industrial ventures, by putting some of the profits into landed property.'[121] These motives certainly ring true for John Gilbert, when he bought a moiety of the Clough Hall estate in 1782.[122] But at the same time, he was well aware of the great mineral wealth underneath the estate; and at fifty-eight years of age he was also looking for an estate to which he could retire.' As it was, the yeoman's farmhouse called Clough Hall was still standing when John Gilbert died, and it was left to his son to build the mansion that was also known as Clough Hall.[123] The Duke of Bridgewater is supposed to have lent John Gilbert the remainder of the sum needed to buy the estate,[124] and this could have been one of the debts outstanding at the time of the Duke's death.[125]

Kidsgrove was also to be the scene of a dispute that was marked by the ruthless determination, which characterised some of the eighteenth and nineteenth century entrepreneurs.[126] This dispute was between Sir John Edensor Heathcote and the younger, John Gilbert, although it is clear that the seeds of the dispute were sown during the lifetime of the elder John Gilbert. The elder John Gilbert had leased coal mines from Sir John Edenser Heathcote, at Brieryhurst, near Kidsgrove in 1792.[127] Subsequently, Heathcote accused the Gilberts of breaking several of the covenants contained in the lease, namely: failing to weigh the coal fairly; not distinguishing how much coal was sold at the pit and how much at the canal; and taking stone and bricks from the premises.[128]

The younger, John Gilbert was served with a writ of latitat, at Patricroft, near Barton-upon-Irwell, on 17th April 1797, and the matter was placed before the King's Bench.[129] The case was found in favour of Heathcote and John Gilbert had to pay compensation. The decision filled Gilbert with anger and a desire for revenge, that is reminiscent of the monumental rages that sometimes took hold of John Wilkinson.

He was clearly in the wrong, but he had a legitimate complaint against Heathcote, who broke his covenant and opened the Woodshuts Colliery in competition with the Gilberts.[130] One of John Gilbert's friends noted that he 'was in the habit repeatedly of expressing anger and dissatisfaction in reference to Sir John Edensor Heathcote and his Collieries.'

The animosity between the two flared up again in 1808. For in that year, John Gilbert gave notice of his intention to give up the colliery leases, but also of his requirement for Heathcote to keep an engine in operation to drain his other mines, as stipulated in the lease. Heathcote responded to this with a series of allegations of misconduct and notice to quit. Then, two years later, Heathcote's miners strayed under the Clough Hall estate and John Gilbert was presented with his opportunity for revenge. The build up to the actual act was described by Gilbert's friend:—

'the anger and resentment of Mr. Gilbert would often lead him to revengeful or malicious expressions, and frequently going to a situation in the room wherein they were seated at the time, where he had a better

The first edition of the Ordnance Survey map (1834) clearly shows the pivotal position of the Clough Hall estate astride the Trent and Mersey Canal. Nearby is Turnhurst where James Brindley settled after his marriage and lived until his death in 1772.

(The late Professor S.H. Beaver)

opportunity of observing the motions and operations of a fire engine (which) Sir John erected contiguous to Mr. G.'s works. . .'

This friend was also Gilbert's doctor and this explains the choice of words in the next section of the statement; for Gilbert bade him:—

'to view the movements of Sir John's engine, pressing him to observe, as he phraz'd it, that old Bitch and with apparent exultation desired him to see how slow she moved and on such occasions would metaphorically observe. . . that humans were afflicted with one incurable disease (which those of his friends' profession) could not cure, viz. the Dropsy. He (said that) he had more skill in this complaint than the Faculty. For although that dam'd old Bitch had already become dropsical and the disease was rapidly increasing, he would in the end radically cure her.'

The 'cure' involved John Gilbert's miners boring a hole from a lower level of his workings, into the level that Heathcote's miners had driven under the Clough Hall estate. This brought a vast quantity of water into Heathcote's Woodshut's colliery, which although his engine 'worked boath night and day, still it is not able to Lift out the said water.' This action on 5th October, 1811, effectively shut down Heathcote's Woodshuts colliery and Gilbert had acted within his rights.[131] Once again, Sir John Edensor Heathcote turned to the law, but John Gilbert's death in September 1812, robbed him of any chance of obtaining satisfaction in the courts.[132] The matter was finally settled by arbitration in 1813, when John Gilbert's executors were keen to complete the sale of the Clough Hall estate and the impending law suit was delaying matters.[133]

It could be argued that the sort of determination that is seen in its worst form in the dispute with Sir John Edensor Heathcote, was a necessary attribute of an entrepreneur. The business empire that was created by the Gilbert brothers, and continued in a more limited form by the younger, John Gilbert, could not have been created or sustained by anyone lacking a strong sense of purpose. At times, the tactics were underhanded and ruthless. The person capable of spreading the rumour that Hugh Henshall and Company were giving up the carrying business, when Worthington and Gilbert made their beginning, was a person who had advanced on his wits and not through advantage.[134] John Gilbert, John Gilbert, the younger and John Wilkinson, all came from the same mould and prospered through talent and application.

But among the other attributes needed by the successful business man and entrepreneur, was an eye for a good idea. Samuel Johnson said that 'the age is running mad after innovation; all the business of the world is to be done in a new way; men are to be hanged in a new way; Tyburn itself is not safe from the fury of innovation.'[135] John Gilbert's success, like that of John Wilkinson, and even now it appears James Watt, was more to do with business technique than inventive genius.[136] John Gilbert took the idea of the navigational level and used it successfully in a number of different enterprises. He took an interest in inclined planes, the theory of which was readily available in the works of the lecturer, James Ferguson.[137] He introduced the 'Ginny system' to North Staffordshire. This meant that the coal was conveyed underground in boxes on wheeled carriages, hauled up the shaft in the boxes, then placed on carriages for the journey by tram-road to a canalside wharf. It was noted that 'each waggon has one box (and) six waggons are brought from the pit by one horse.'[138]

A North Staffordshire tramroad employing the 'ginny system' as late as 1895, more than a hundred years after John Gilbert introduced the system to the area.   (British Rail)

But this search for a more efficient means of doing things was always tempered by the cost factor. The Gilbert brothers erected a water engine at Cheadle in 1759 as it was more economical to run than a steam engine and nearly as efficient. The same logic ensured that Lawton Saltworks made use of a water engine in 1800,[139] some twenty-two years after first employing a steam engine for brine pumping. At Kidsgrove, John Gilbert, the younger, erected a windmill in 1812, to grind the grain crops grown on the estate.[140] Yet a few miles away, a high-pressure Trevithick engine was being used for the same purpose.[141] The gap in terms of technology was immense, but in terms of efficiency, it was much smaller. This sort of practice highlights the most significant, single factor, that of 'frugality.' Another closely allied factor has been widely recognised, and Professor Crouzet noted it thus:—

'Enterprises increased their capital by ploughing back immediately, regularly and almost automatically the greater part, or even the whole of their profits. ... Thus most of the additional capital required for expansion was provided from (their) own resources, from the savings of the industrialists. The fact is so obvious as to be almost a cliché and the point is not worth labouring.'[142]

The motive of Thomas Gilbert (1688-1741/42) in participating in various mining and processing enterprises was to increase the size and value of his estate. He mortgaged his existing lands to provide the money required for the various enterprises, then used the profits to redeem the mortgage and to buy more land. Eventually, the estate would reach a point where it provided a very comfortable and secure income through rents and then the motivation for enterprise became limited. This can be demonstrated by reference to the Clough Hall estate, which in 1818, produced £735 in rents and £525 from the sale of coal.[143]

The younger, John Gilbert had realised his father's ambition, just as his uncle, Thomas, had realised that of his father. Thomas Gilbert became involved in various enterprises, in order to consolidate his property holding, whereas John was working to acquire property. Another motivation for Thomas Gilbert's enterprise, in the first half of the eighteenth century, was to pay for Thomas's legal training.

His legal knowledge and connections were to be a vital part in the organisation and financing of the numerous enterprises. The link and the need continued after Thomas's death in 1798, for in the will of the younger, John Gilbert, there are two significant bequests. One for £5,000 made to James Baron, 'Attorney of Wigan'; and another of £1,000, to James Siddel, his clerk.[144]

The two factors that enabled the Gilbert brothers to exceed the achievements of their father should be mentioned. One was the connection with the Gower-Bridgewater interest, which brought them numerous opportunities in a direct, or indirect way. The second was, that the brothers lived in the Canal Age and indeed did as much as any other individuals to promote it. As Phyllis Deane noted, the canals 'made a massive contribution to the first industrial revolution'[145] and the results are too well known to need reiteration here.

The purpose of the Gilberts was to secure wealth, land and social

Plan of the underground inclined plane initiated near Worsley by John Gilbert.

(*Author's Collection*)

position and their industrial endeavours did much to further this aim. The extent of their success can again be demonstrated by reference to the Clough Hall estate. By 1812, it was producing a yearly income of £1,260; and in the same year it was sold for £64,000.[146] This was a far cry from the £300 that was produced by the Cotton estate in 1742.

VII THE INHERITANCE

John Gilbert died on 3rd August 1795 at Worsley, 'a gentleman of the strictest honour and integrity, and universally respected by all ranks of people.'[1] At the time of his death, his interests were widespread and so intricately structured that no immediate realisation of his assets was possible. His were long-term investments and his will charged his two executors, John Gilbert (Junior) and Nathaniel Gould, with the task of maintaining, or disposing of his holdings, so that payments could be made in accordance with the clauses of his will. His wife, Lydia, received all his household goods; a cash payment of £100; a yearly income of £400; and a further payment of £1,000, payable on twelve months notice. As John's eldest son, Thomas had died before his father, no provision was made for him in the will, but his daughter, Alice was to be given £600 on marrying, or on reaching the age of twenty-four. Curiously, no provision was made for her sister Lydia, or brother, John,[2] who at the time was managing his uncle's pottery in Burslem.[3]

The eldest surviving son, the Reverend Robert Gilbert, received a quarter share of: his father's land at Stanton, in Derbyshire; the graphite, copper and lead mines, in Cumberland, Westmorland, Staffordshire and Derbyshire; and the smelting mills in Cumberland. He was also to receive a cash payment of £4,000, within three years of his father's death. The indications are that he sold most of these mining interests, some of them to his younger brother, John. A further £270 was paid out in small legacies to his associates and servants, including Robert Lonsdale ('my late servant') and Thomas Kent ('as a token of regard for him'). Both Lonsdale and Kent were in the employ of the Duke of Bridgewater. The residue and bulk of his estate was bequeathed to John Gilbert, Junior, including the Clough Hall property.[4]

Thomas Gilbert died three years after his brother. He bequeathed the Cotton estate to his eldest son, the Reverend Thomas Gilbert, and £2,500 to his other son's creditors. His widow was to receive household goods and £1,000 per annum, whilst her companion was given an annuity of £75. The only other beneficiaries were David Birds and Thomas Morris. They were to receive Thomas's shares in: 'all and every colliery, limeworks, lead mines and any other mines or minerals wherein he was concerned in conjunction with the Marquis of Stafford and the

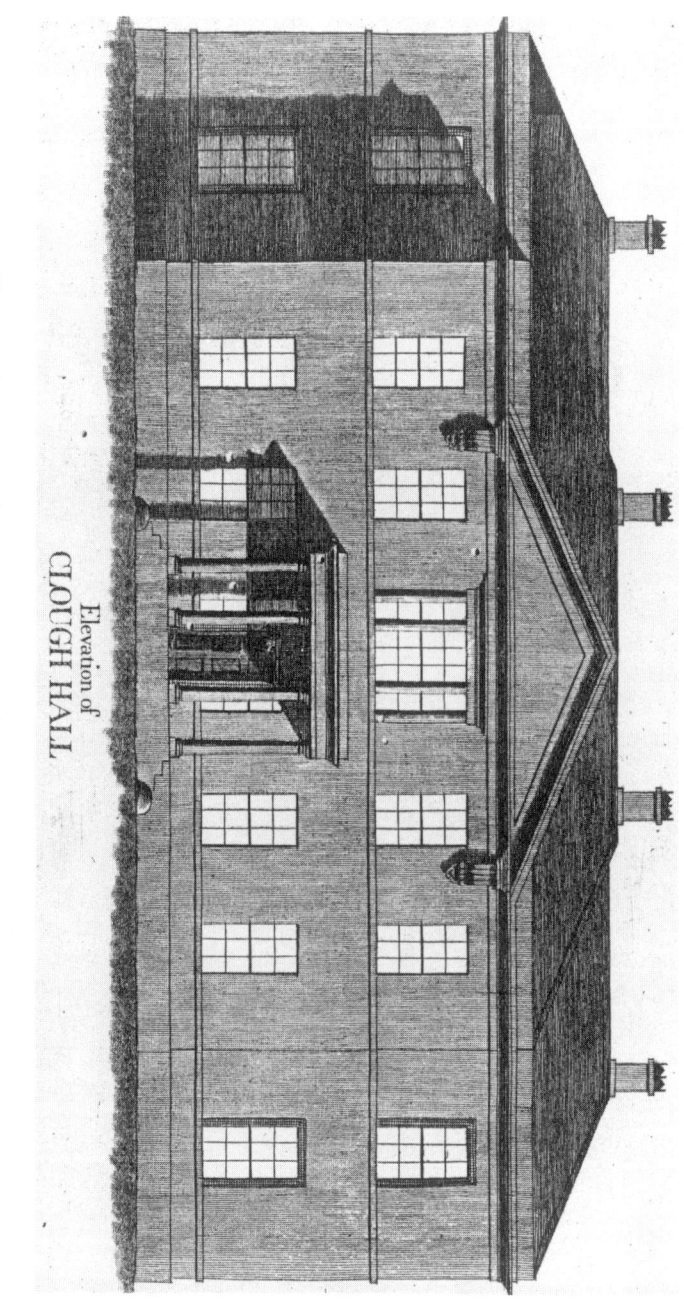

Elevation of
CLOUGH HALL

The 'magnificent mansion house called Clough Hall', built by the younger John Giolbert.
From the sale catalogue of 1812.
(*Staffordshire Record Office*)

140

representatives of his late brother, John Gilbert, or with any other person.' Exactly what relationship Thomas Gilbert had with Thomas Morris is unknown, but David Birds was his nephew, and it was he who also received Thomas's shares in the Trent and Mersey, Shropshire and Shrewsbury Canals.[5]

The deaths of both John and Thomas Gilbert marked an important change in the employment and life style of the Gilbert family. First, from this time onward they ceased to act as land agents or stewards and they started to employ such people, that is to say, they were firmly established as gentlemen. John Gilbert, Junior, fell out with the Duke of Bridgewater and left his employ before 1797.[6] The probable reason for this was that the Duke disliked his more independent ways and he 'had grown to expect unquestioning obedience to his every whim, at whatever cost to other people's feelings.'[7] The Duke's will, described in 1803 as an 'extraordinary' one, was designed to continue his influence beyond death and one of the clauses states that:—[8]

'nothing herein before contained shall extend or be constructed to extend at Law or in Equity to confirm any Lease or Leases granted by me to the late John Gilbert Esquire and continued to his son John Gilbert of a Farm called Worsley Hall Farm and a Mill and premises situated at Worsley Mills.'

Dr. Malet stated that John Gilbert, Junior was 'not up to carrying responsibilities similar to his father's, though he did manage to hold some of his father's firms and mining enterprises together.'[9] An examination of his subsequent career shows that this is an unjust evaluation for he launched and ran many enterprises in the more unfavourable economic climate of the early nineteenth century; and he realised his father's ambition of retiring to the Clough Hall estate. Perhaps the best judge of his capabilities was his father. John Gilbert, Senior wrote this of his son in 1784:

'My son John is lately became a miner and collier. He takes a great part of my own business of that sort from me which fits me well as I find I am not able or much inclined to slave so much as I have done. Jack went yesterday to my colliery at Harecastle and I expect him back tomorrow.'[10]

If John Gilbert, Junior lacked anything it was the ability to be self-effacing, the quality which had endeared his father to the Duke of Bridgewater and secured his generous patronage.

The younger John Gilbert owned mines at Whiston, Farnworth, Goldenhill and Kidsgrove, but of these the Kidsgrove mines were the most important. He drew a profit of £525 from the Kidsgrove mines,[11] compared with £144 from the Farnworth mines, in 1812.[12] A major business success was his securement of a contract with the limeburners at Froghall, to supply them with slack.[13] He also had coking ovens at Kidsgrove, which by 1808 were unable to keep pace with the 'demand for coakes.'[14] Considerable quantities of coal from his Kidsgrove mines went to the nearby pottery factories and Wedgwood and Byerley were among his customers.[15]

These interests in collieries were all inherited from his father, as was Marston saltworks and an interest in the canal carrying trade in salt. Later he purchased Newton Bank saltworks (in Middlewhich) with the adjacent iron foundry.[16] At the time of his death in 1812, he still held his father's interests in various Derbyshire lead mines, although by this time they were almost worthless. The one twelfth share in the Hill Carr Sough and Shining Sough lead mines produced a nominal profit of 13 shillings 10¾ pence in 1813, but for most years he had to bear an annual loss of £52. Three shares in the Cow Close lead mine, near Stanton also failed to produce a profit as the mine had become "wholly unproductive."[17]

By 1794, the younger John Gilbert had rented a 'potworks' in Burslem from a Mr. Fletcher.[18] This he worked until he stopped production and sold off various 'valuable utensils, raw materials and moulds' in 1803.[19] By the time of the sale he had purchased the pottery and subsequently he rented it out at £16 per annum.[20] How closely he was associated with the management of the works is difficult to establish, but his nephew (also called John Gilbert) was the resident manager from 1796 until sometime after 1801.[21] Presumably, he was installed there to learn the ways of business and the sale at the work in 1803, almost certainly marks the end of his association with the works.

One of the younger John Gilbert's most profitable involvements was with the trade in lime. Again, he inherited the basis of this interest from his father, namely 2 shares in the Caldon Lime Company and the limekilns at Cheddleton and Horsebridge. But he also extended his interests by erecting two limekilns and a coalyard, just outside Stone in 1796.[22] The limestone was brought by canal from Froghall Wharf and the coal sold from the yard came from the Kidsgrove collieries. By 1813, 'the greatest part of the town and neighbourhood of Stone (had) been for several years supplied with coals at this wharf.'[23] He also took over Newbold Astbury limeworks (to the north of Kidsgrove) in partnership with Robert Williamson.[24] Three years after this purchase, the limekilns were described as supplying 'a large district to the south-east of the county with this valuable article', but during the early part of 1808,

Gilbert and Williamson offered the limeworks on lease to anyone willing to work them.[25] The motivation for this development is revealed in an advertisement concerning the Horsebridge and Cheddleton kilns, which had previously been put up for lease. The would be lessee was made aware of the need to 'superintend' the concern himself, 'which is the only reason that induces the proprietors to let them.'[26] The younger John Gilbert retained his enterprises, but increasingly rented them out for a good profit, like the £40 per annum he received for the Stone limekilns.[27]

From 1800 onwards, the focus of the younger John Gilbert's enterprises was Kidsgrove where he built the impressive Clough Hall.[28] He consolidated his estate, but at the same time, he was looking for opportunities for investment further afield. Many of his investments were in land, including sizeable plots at Deansgate and Knott Mill in Manchester, bought in 1805. Other purchases of land were made in North Staffordshire at Biddulph and Stone. Two houses at Stone alone produced an annual rent of £65 and realised £1330 when sold by his trustees. In 1807, he bought a one tenth share in a hotel at Matlock Bath, then a rising spa town. Another purchase was a brewery at Prescot in Lancashire, secured through default on a loan made by John Gilbert and his business associate William Brett of Stone.[29] This association began in March 1802, when 'Mr William Brett of Stone, Grocer and John Gilbert, a gentleman of fortune and concerned in commercial pursuits, opened a bank at Stone as joint and equal partners under the firm of Brett and Gilbert.' Four years later they launched another bank at Cheadle, in partnership with John Higgs, a timber merchant, 'under the firm of Brett, Gilbert and Higgs'. This was quite a lucrative concern and in the early years the profit was said to have averaged £3,000 per year.[30] In 1800 there were about 370 country banks, which rose to 650 ten years later.[31] These two North Staffordshire banks had been established in the easy credit conditions, when the Bank of England was off gold between 1797 and 1815.[32] Such Banks were of particular importance as they helped to finance numerous industrial enterprises during this period.

John Gilbert had reached a point where he could not extend his profit from industrial enterprise without devoting more of his time to the supervision of such enterprises. The obvious solution was to lend some of his accumulated capital, with the actual business being transacted by Brett or Higgs. The two banks issued their own bank notes,[33] creating credit for those who wished to borrow from them thus encouraging local economic expansion. They were typical of the banks spawned by the wealth made in trade or manufacturing when 'it was difficult to tell to

CLOUGH HALL, MANSION, ESTATES
and COLLIERIES,

PARTICULARS

Of the MAGNIFICENT MANSION HOUSE, called

CLOUGH HALL;

And sundry Valuable Freehold and Leasehold Estates ; the HARECASTLE and other COLLIERIES, situated in the parishes of Audley, Woolstanton, and Norton-in-the-Moors, in the County of Stafford ; and in the parish of Astbury, in the County of Chester ;

CONSISTING OF

CLOUGH HALL,

Late the residence of JOHN GILBERT, Esqr. deceased,

Which is situated in the parish of Audley, with the Offices, Gardens, Pleasure Grounds, Woods and Plantations: Valuable Freehold and Leasehold Lands, Woods, a Mill, the Harecastle and other Collieries in hand, upwards of One Hundred and Twenty Freehold Houses, and sundry Freehold Farms and Lands let to Tenants, principally at Will ;

WHICH WILL BE

SOLD by AUCTION,

By Henshaw & Smith,

AT THE

ROE BUCK INN,

In NEWCASTLE-under-LYME, in the County of Stafford ;

On WEDNESDAY the 30th day of DECEMBER, 1812,

At THREE o'clock in the Afternoon,

In the SIX following LOTS ;

or in such other Lots as shall be then agreed upon.

The Estates may be viewed twenty-one days previous to the Sale upon application to Mr. EDMUND GOULD, at CLOUGH HALL, from whom particulars may be had; which may also be had at the Auctioneers', in Stafford ; at the place of Sale ; Lillyman's Hotel, Liverpool ; Royal Hotel, Birmingham ; King's Head Inn, Derby ; Castle Inn, Tamworth ; Bush Tavern, Bristol ; White Hart Inn, Bath ; George Inn, Newcastle-upon-Tyne ; Swan Inn, Hanley ; Red Bull, Lawton ; Legs-of-Man, Burslem ; or at the Offices of Messrs. Baron and Ditchfield, Wigan ; Messrs. Milne, Serjeant, and Milne, Manchester ; Robert Barbor, Esqr. Fetter Lane, London ; Messrs. Willis, Fairthorne, and Clarke, Warnford Court, London ; and of Mr. VERNON, Solicitor, Stone, at whose Office plans of the Estates may be seen, and further particulars obtained.

Newcastle-under-Lyme :---From the Office of C. Chester.

1812.

Title page from the Clough Hall sale catalogue, 1812.   *(Staffordshire Record Office)*

144

what extent a man was a specialized banker'.[34] Thomas Kinnersley, who bought the Clough Hall estate after the death of the younger John Gilbert, was a Newcastle ironmonger as well as the owner of the Old Bank, Newcastle. This fact was thrown in his face, when someone forged his One Pound banknotes and replaced his signature with that of 'T. Ironmonger.'[35]

The depression that followed the end of the Napoleonic Wars created real problems for the country banks, who had involved themselves mainly with long-term loans. The two banks had ceased to be profitable by 1814, when John Gilbert's executors discovered that the Stone branch had made a loss of £3,110 and Cheadle a modest profit of £50. In all the executors had to meet debts of £11,015 13s. 6d. owed to the bank, but in fact they were honouring the debts of their creditors who had been given credit in the form of banknotes. The two banks finally closed in August 1816, during the bank crisis of that year. Edward Trafford Nichols, who had taken John Gilbert's place as financial backer lost £22,000, 'brought on partly by bad debts owed to Brett and Gilbert.'[36]

The younger John Gilbert's progressive withdrawal from trade and industry was brought on by the realisation that he no longer had to lead the almost itinerant life required of an entrepreneur with widely dispersed interests. The new Clough Hall was the realisation of his father's dream and a statement about his own future. By devoting so much time and effort to his mines in the Kidsgrove area, he laid the foundations of the modern town itself. Kidsgrove was not his creation, in the sense that Etruria had been that of Josiah Wedgwood, but the degree of development in both cases was comparable. Etruria was described as 'a continuous street of about 120 workmen's dwellings adjacent, with an inn, and some houses of a better class, for farmers, clerks and others.'[37] At the time of the sale in 1812, the Clough Hall estate was comprised of over 300 acres with 'one hundred and twenty freehold Dwelling-houses for workmen.'[38] Like Wedgwood he was an employer of industrial labour, but at the same time a kind of squire figure.

Indeed, the younger John Gilbert played a very prominent part in the social life of this part of North Staffordshire. Some of his charitable works have already been mentioned,[39] but he also made contributions to a fund to purchase fire-engines for Burslem, Tunstall and Longport;[40] and he gave the highest individual annual subscription to the Dispensary and House of Recovery for the Staffordshire Potteries and Neighbourhood.[41] Apart from holding office as a Vice-President of the Newcastle-under-Lyme and Potteries Agricultural Society,[42] he was one of the stewards for

A row of houses built at Kidsgrove by the younger John Gilbert for his workmen. The photograph was taken in 1975. *(Peter Lead)*

the Newcastle and Pottery Grand Musical Festival, along with Lord Granville Leveson-Gower and other local dignitaries.[43] In addition he held a game licence, a further indication of an increasingly leisured existence.[44]

Such a life-style, involved him in the greater delegation of work and he employed two relatives, David Birds and Edmund Gould as his agents and assistants at Clough Hall.[45] The Reverend Thomas Gilbert (John's cousin) did exactly the same at Cotton, employing David Birds, William Birds and Thomas Birds. William Birds was the resident agent at Cotton, although he was known as the 'Bailiff' and he occupied the 'Bailiff's House' there.[46] He also employed a Mr. Walthall, possibly an attorney, who charged fees for doing his 'Business' at Cotton.[47] The younger John Gilbert even found time to engage in courtship, which resulted in his marriage to Elizabeth Horsefall, of the Parish of St. George, Hanover Square, London, in 1807.[48]

This John Gilbert has also been labelled as 'rather bigoted' and some accounts suggest that he carried out a campaign of religious persecution against the early Methodists in Kidsgrove.[49] The original account is somewhat more restrained in its accusations:—[50]

'as soon as God began to work, the enemy marshalled all his forces to raise opposition, and Mr. Gilbert was their Generalissimo, and roared

146

against them like a lion . . . He always walked with a staff, at the lower end of which there was a small paddle; and one night when they were very lively, he broke suddenly in amongst them, and shouted that he would have no meetings, or something to the like . . . (but) some of them were as courageous as he was, (and they) informed him that he had no right there, (as) they were not his premises, and that he came among a peaceable people in a hostile manner, with an unlawful weapon in his hand, (they knew he had his paddle with him). When he saw they were spirited men, and knowing the property did not belong to him, he left them, and never troubled them more.'

The writer continued to note that Gilbert's view of Methodism was in line with that of 'the great men of the land', who saw it as 'assuming a very serious character, and likely to produce mischievous effects in the nation, if not timely checked.'[51] The fact that the younger John Gilbert was a patriot could not be challenged. When the War with revolutionary France recommenced in 1803, numerous local landowners and manufacturers raised 'corps of infantry.'[52] One such company was the Clough Hall Volunteer Infantry, who before attending a church-parade to celebrate the victory at Trafalgar; 'requested their worthy Commander (John Gilbert) to remit one day's pay to the Patriotic Fund . . . for the relief of the sufferers in that ever memorable action.'[53] Two prints in Clough Hall showed Lord Nelson at the battles of the Nile and Trafalgar,[54] and John Gilbert also named the most powerful steam engine at Kidsgrove, the Nelson engine.[55] His regard for this national hero was such that he was the most enthusiastic supporter of the plan to erect an obelisk on Mow Cop in his honour. The obelisk was to be made of limestone from the Newbold Astbury limeworks, in which John Gilbert was a partner.[56]

When John Gilbert died in September 1812, he was the last of the Gilbert family to display any sort of entrepreneurial flair. Like his father, his interests were widespread and complicated and they could not be realised quickly. Three trustees were appointed to manage his interests; James Royds, Nathaniel Gould and David Birds.[57] As he left no children, his wife was the principal beneficiary under the terms of his will. She was to receive £2,000 at the time of his death and £6,000 for life; plus Clough Hall, provided she lived in it.[58] This she chose not to do and the bulk of the Clough Hall estate was sold to Thomas Kinnersley early in 1813, for £64,000.[59] He left a further £1,000 to his brother, the Reverend Robert Gilbert. His executors and trustees received cash gifts: James Royds (£500); Nathaniel Gould (£2,000) and David Birds (£2,000). Old business associates also benefited; the Wigan attorney, James Baron received £5,000; and his servant, James Siddel, the sum of £1,000. Alice Lander (née Gilbert) had £13,000 invested on her behalf; and her brother and sister-in-law, John and Sarah Gilbert, drew the interest from an investment of £25,000. Their children also had £1,000 held in trust for them.[60] Assuming an interest rate of five per cent, Alice Lander would have received an annual income of £650; and John and Sarah Gilbert, an annual income of £1,250.

Sarah Lander was the wife of George Lander, described firstly as a Birmingham haberdasher in 1807 and[61] then as a 'Gentleman, of Edgbaston' by 1821.[62] Presumably, this rise in station was occasioned by his wife's newly found income and later he became a Vice Consul for Spain and Portugal.[63] Interestingly, his surviving son, a George Moseley Lander qualified and practiced as a solicitor.[64] John and Sarah Gilbert inherited an estate at Great Broughton, near Chester from Sarah's family around 1803.[65] They appear to have settled there and led a comfortable life, drawing a handsome income from the estate and the investments made under the terms of John Gilbert's will.

The Reverend Thomas Gilbert, although he inherited the Cotton estate, chose not to live there. His stepmother lived there until her death and then the house and estate were let to a Mr. Errington. An advertisement published in 1818, offered a lease of the hall and estate 'for any term of years, not exceeding fourteen',[66] so clearly the Reverend Thomas Gilbert had no intention of living there. He held the living at Little Gaddesden from 1796 until 1813[67] and during his incumbency he was called upon to bury his patron—Francis, the third Duke of Bridgewater.[68] He was eventually evicted for non-residence, and subsequently depended on the rents from the Cotton estate and his income from his clerkship with the Privy Council. How much he drew from the Cotton estate is not known, but his income from the Caldon Low quarries alone averaged £282 for the years 1837 to 1842.[69] The Reverend Thomas Gilbert died unmarried in Paris in 1841[70] and the Cotton estate passed to his nephew (another Thomas Gilbert) who outlived him by a mere two years.[71] His widow offered the hall and estate for sale by auction in 1844[72] and it was bought by the Earl of Shrewsbury, a practising Catholic, who two years later offered the hall to Frederick William Faber and his fellow converts. Later the hall became a school and was incorporated in Cotton College, the oldest Catholic school in the country offering secondary education.[73] At the time of writing the former college buildings (including Thomas Gilbert's brick hall) are being

STAFFORDSHIRE.

VALUABLE FREEHOLD ESTATE FOR SALE.

PARTICULARS OF THE VALUABLE AND DESIRABLE

FREEHOLD ESTATE,

COMPRISING

THE SUBSTANTIAL BRICK-BUILT FAMILY RESIDENCE OF

COTTON HALL,

COMMODIOUSLY PLANNED,

WITH A SUITE OF HANDSOME WELL-PROPORTIONED APARTMENTS,

A CAPITAL RANGE OF ALL REQUISITE

DOMESTIC OFFICES, COACH HOUSE, AND STABLING FOR TWELVE HORSES,

LARGE WALLED GARDEN, WELL STOCKED WITH FRUIT TREES,

VINERIES,

GARDENER'S HOUSE, ICE HOUSE, BATH HOUSE AND BATH, AGRICULTURAL BUILDINGS,

AND BAILIFF's HOUSE.

THE ADVOWSON OF COTTON CHAPEL,

SITUATE WITHIN A MINUTE'S WALK OF THE HALL, SUBJECT TO THE LIFE OF THE PRESENT INCUMBENT,

TOGETHER WITH

338 ACRES OF MEADOW, PASTURE, ARABLE, AND WOODLANDS,

SUBDIVIDED INTO SUNDRY FARMS, WITH SUITABLE BUILDINGS.

AND PRESENTING IN THE WHOLE A PARK-LIKE APPEARANCE.

ABOUNDING WITH GAME, AND LYING CONTIGUOUS TO THE GAME PRESERVES OF THE EARL OF SHREWSBURY,

SITUATE IN THE PARISHES OF ALTON AND KINGSLEY.

A beautifully wooded, romantic, and healthful part of the Northern Division of the County of Stafford, one mile from Alton Towers, five miles from Cheadle, nine miles from Uttoxeter, Ashbourn, and Leek respectively, and possessing the great advantage of Canal Communication. The projected line of the Churnet Valley Railway will pass near the Estate.

ALSO SEVERAL OTHER

FARMS, LANDS, AND OTHER HEREDITAMENTS,

SITUATE IN THE SEVERAL PARISHES OF

ROCESTER, ELLASTONE, CHEADLE, CHECKLEY, IPSTONES, AND CAULDON, IN THE COUNTY OF STAFFORD.

TO BE SOLD BY AUCTION,

BY

MESSRS. CAPES AND SMITH,

AT THE ROYAL OAK INN, CHEADLE, IN THE COUNTY OF STAFFORD,

ON TUESDAY THE 20th DAY OF AUGUST, 1844,

AT THREE O'CLOCK IN THE AFTERNOON,

In Lots described in the annexed Particulars, or in such other Lots as will be mentioned at the Sale, and subject to Conditions.

A. J. CALDICOTT, PRINTER, DUDLEY-STREET, WOLVERHAMPTON.

Title page from the Cotton Hall sale catalogue, 1844.   *(Staffordshire Record Office)*

149

developed into a hotel, conference and leisure complex.

Adam Smith in *The Wealth of Nations* observed that 'the uniform constant and uninterrupted effort of every man to better his condition' was the greater motor of economic progress.[74] Of this the Gilbert family who had for two centuries striven to improve their economic and social status, were outstanding exemplars. Initially, it was by means of the piecemeal acquisition of land, which enabled loans for mining enterprises to be raised 'either on the strength of their own lands or from their farming friends and neighbours.'[75] It was a two-way flow as the purpose of their industrial ventures was to consolidate and add to their estates. Thomas Gilbert (1688-1741/2) would have resented being termed a 'yeoman', but he was typical of that group who did so much to develop industries and to bring about agricultural improvements. As C. Wilson noted:—[76]

'Where industrial opportunities offered the yeomanry were a nursery of enterprise. Yeoman leased mines in Northumberland, set up forges in Shropshire, turned clothiers in Yorkshire and Devon, and styled themselves potters in Staffordshire.'

The income from the Cotton estate and from extractive industries could also be invested in another way. The writer of Thomas Gilbert's obituary describes how he inherited a small estate at Cotton and 'endeavoured to improve it by the profession of law.'[77] This statement is rather misleading as it indicates that the choice was made by Thomas himself, whereas the original decision must have been made by his father, the elder Thomas. Thomas entered the Inner Temple in 1740[78] during his father's lifetime and it would have cost about £200 a year to keep him there.[79] As the Cotton estate was then worth about £300 per year, this represented a considerable investment of resources. But the rewards of a successful career in the law could be considerable. Sir Matthew Hale, Lord Chief Justice in the reign of Charles II owned Hales Hall (near Cheadle) and his grand-daughter was still living there in the early part of the eighteenth century.[80]

The path taken by Thomas Gilbert was a well-trodden route to social advancement, for 'even the bar, the highest rampart of social privilege in the professions, could be stormed by money and talent without birth.'[81] A prime example of advancement through the practice of law was that of Thomas Brereton, the son of an alehouse keeper, who married well and acquired an estate, and also sat for twenty-six years as a Member of Parliament for Liverpool.[82] The example of Joseph Banks, another attorney who also became a Member of Parliament, has already been

Clough Hall, c.1895. *(Derek Wheelhouse)*

described; but like Thomas Gilbert he founded 'a gentle family—too gentle indeed to succeed to the practice.'[83] Business was the means to an end, but not an end in itself.

Archdeacon Joseph Plymley recorded the gradual departure of the yeomanry and lesser gentry from eighteenth century Shropshire, when he wrote: 'The number of gentlemen of small fortune living on their estates, has decreased: their descendants have been clergymen or attornies, either in the country, or shopkeepers in the town of their own county; or more probably in this county, emigrated to Birmingham, to Liverpool, to Manchester, or to London.'[84] The Gilberts were part of this movement, but again it was a two-way flow. 'Manufactures and commerce, the profession of arms and of the law', wrote Plymley, 'raise men of small fortunes to affluence; and their riches enable them to concentrate the estates of others.'[85]

The same motive is to be found in the work of John and Thomas Gilbert as land-agents, or stewards. Not only did this work provide them with a secure source of income, it also allowed them numerous opportunities for launching various business enterprises promising a considerable financial return. This connection also led to Thomas Gilbert's parliamentary career, which required a secure and sizeable income, but brought about an accelerated social ascent. The Gilbert brothers were intent on making money. But when a writer said of Josiah Wedgwood that:

'He was the maker of his own fortune, and (that) his country has been benefited in proportion not to be calculated',[86] then he could also have been describing John and Thomas Gilbert.

Once fortunes had been secured, there was time for more relaxation and the adoption of a more comfortable way of life. John Gilbert's lifestyle had been frugal, but his son was able to enjoy a standard of living that was nothing short of luxurious.[87] When the Clough Hall estate sold for £64,000 in 1812, it provided a startling contrast with the few moorland farms that John Gilbert had inherited from his father in 1741/42. In addition to this estate, there were the other properties and enterprises that cannot be accurately valued. The younger John Gilbert's social standing was directly related to his wealth and by the time of his death he was the equal of any North Staffordshire gentleman. By 1812, the family were secure enough not to have to seek employment, as they could live very comfortably on rent receipts and the interest from investments.

NOTES TO CHAPTER I ORIGINS

1 Refer to family pedigree given as an appendix in *T&JG*.

2 Arthur Mee (Ed.), *The King's England: Staffordshire*, London (nd), p. 92.

3 F. J. Wrottesley (Ed.), *Ellastone Parish Register, Part 1, (1538-1700)*, SPRS, (1907), p. 44.

4 SHC (1935), p. 137.

5 F. J. Wrottesley, *Ellastone*, p. 96.

6 SHC (1900), p. 8.

7 D. M. Palliser, *The Staffordshire Landscape*, London (1976), pp. 102-103.

8 Type-script copy of this was loaned to me by the late Herbert Chester.

9 F. W. Wrottesley, *Ellastone*, pp. 55, 57, 60, 61, 67, 70, 73-75, 80 and 83.

10 Ibid., p. 67.

11 W. E. Tate, *The Parish Chest*, Cambridge (1960), p. 83-84.

12 F. W. Wrottesley, *Ellastone*, pp. 106 and 128.

13 Ibid., pp. 115-116, 118 and 127.

14 D. H. Pennington and I. A. Roots, *The Committee at Stafford, 1643-1645*, Manchester (1957).

15 PRO: S.P. 29/58/73..

16 F. J. Wrottesley, *Ellastone*, pp. 113 and 122.

17 Quoted in *The Cottonian*, Vol. 49, Part 1, No. 104 (Autumn 1960). Marriage Settlement (10th January 1661), between 'Thomas, son of George Gilbert, Yeoman of Ramsor and Elizabeth Morrice, of Lockwood, Staffs. I have been unable to trace the original.

18 F. J. Wrottesley, *Ellastone*, p. 140.

19 Ibid., pp. 148-149.

20 See reference 17 (above).

21 A stone lintel (from the original house) can be seen in the cellar of Cotton Hall (1989). It bears the inscription 'WM 1630 EM'.

22 SRO: D260/B/2/2/37.

23 Quoted in *The Cottonian*, Vol. 49, Part 1, No. 104 (Autumn 1960). I have also failed in my attempts to trace the original of this document.

24 O.S., *Derby and Burton-upon-Trent*, Southampton, 1974. Near Cotton is in grid square 0646.

25 SRO: D1343.

26 Ibid. See also *T&JG*, Chpt. 1, Note 35.

27 Thomas Whieldon (Josiah Wedgwood's partner) was a distant relative of John and Thomas Gilbert. See *T&JG*, Chpt. 1, Note 36.

28 Cloughead Colliery stood in Whieldon's Wood near Ipstones. See SRO: D554, Bundle 55.

29 SRO: D239/M/400.

30 SRO: D1343/6.

31 SRO: D554, Bundle 141.

32 Ibid.

33 P. W. L. Adams (Ed.), *Ellastone Parish Register, Vol. II*, SPRS, (1912), p. 213.

34 John Aikin (sometimes Aiken), *A Description of the Country From Thirty to Forty Miles Round Manchester,* Manchester (1795). Reprinted by David and Charles, Newton Abbot (1968), p. 183.

35 Thomas Pape, 'The Ancient Corporation of Cheadle', *TNSFC,* Volume LXIV (1929-30), pp. 16-17.

36 Ibid., pp. 20-23.

37 Ibid., p. 17.

38 Ibid., p. 13-15.

39 WSL: 68/5/49. Lease of Mines at Upper Elkstone.

40 Thomas Pape, op cit., p. 17-18. For the connection between the Cheadle, Leek and Hanley Corporations see *T&JG,* Chpt. 1, Note 49.

41 Herbert A. Chester, *The Iron Valley,* Cheadle (1979), p. 68.

42 Marie B. Rolands, *Masters and Men in the West Midland Metalware Trades before the Industrial Revolution,* Manchester (1975), pp. 73-74.

43 Herbert A. Chester, op. cit., p. 68.

44. Robert K. Dent and Joseph Hill, *Historic Staffordshire,* (1896). Reprinted by EP Publishing, Wakefield (1975), p. 265.

45 Ibid., pp. 264-265.

46 Peter Lead, 'The North Staffordshire Iron Industry, 1600-1800', *Jn. Historical Metallurgy Society,* Vol. II, No. 1. (1977), pp. 1-7.

47 Eric Richards, *The Leviathan of Wealth,* London (1973), p. 5.

48 John A. Robey and Lindsey Porter, *The Copper and Lead Mines of Ecton Hill, Staffordshire,* Cheddleton (1972), pp. 17-18.

49 D. H. Pennington and I. A. Roots, op. cit., p. 16.

50 R. A. Buchanan, *Industrial Archaeology in Britain,* Harmondsworth (1972), p. 87.

51 Robert Plot, *The Natural History of Staffordshire,* Oxford (1686). Reprinted by E. J. Morton, Didsbury (1973), p. 165. Plot also mentions that the ore was smelted at Ellastone.

52 H. Heckscher, 'The Place of Sweden in Modern Economic History', *EHR,* iv, p. 12.

53 SRO: D240/M/K/D and Plot, op. cit., p. 166.

54 SRO: D240/M/K/D.

55 SRO: D240/E/III/52.

56 Ibid.

57 Ibid.

58 SRO: D240/M/K/D.

59 Ibid.

60 Duke of Chandos—known as princely Chandos, he built a mansion at Canons, Edgeware, Middlesex at a cost of £250,000. This was the theme of Pope's epistle on bad taste.

61 SRO: D554/Bundle 55 and D239/M/400.

62 J. A. Robey and L. Porter, 'The Metaliferous Mines of the Weaver Hills, Staffordshire', *PDMHS,* Vol. 4, part 6, (December 1971), p. 240.

63 SRO: D554/Bundle 55.

64 SRO: D240/M/K/D.

65 J. A. Robey and L. Porter, 'The Copper and Led Mines of the Mixon Area, Staffordshire, *PDMHS,* Vol. 4, No. 4, (October 1970), p. 260.

66 J. A. Robey and L. Porter, '...Mines of the Weaver Hills', loc. cit., p. 418.

67 J. A. Robey, 'Two Lead Smelting Mills in North Staffordshire', *PDMHS,* Vol. 4, No. 3, (May 1970), p. 218.

68 SRO: D239/M/400.

69 SRO: D554/Bundle 55.

70 Abraham Rees (Editor), *The Cyclopaedia, or Universal Dictionary*, London (1819), Volume XVI, entry headed 'GILBERT, John'. I am grateful to Hugh Torrens for the loan of his copy.

71 H. J. Habakkuk, 'English Landownership, 1680-1740', *EHR*, X (1939-40).

72 SRO: D239/M/400.

73 Ibid.

74 Rees, op. cit. (GILBERT, John).

75 Aikin, op. cit., pp. 182-183.

76 Rees, op. cit. (See also W. K. V. Gale, *Boulton, Watt and the Soho Undertaking*, Birmingham (1968), p.3.

77 B&WP, John Gilbert to Matthew Boulton, 15th September 1755.

78 KEELE: Wedgwood Papers; 9281-11.

79 M. W. Greenslade and J. G. Jenkins (Editors), *A History of the County of Stafford*, Vol. II, Oxford (1967), p. 267.

80 Marie B. Rowlands, op. cit., pp. 141-142.

81 SRO: D1343/6.

82 For further information on Francis (supplied by Dr. Alma Kuiper-Ruempol). See *T&JG*, Chpt. 1, Note 90.

83 Christopher Rowell, *Tatton Park*, London (1978), p. 50.

84 Hugh Malet, *Bridgewater, The Canal Duke, 1736-1803*, Manchester (1977), pp. 51-58.

85 Rees, op. cit., (GILBERT, John).

86 N. W. Tinsley (Editor), *Kinglsey Parish Registers*, SPRS, (1968), p. 175: '3rd January, 1743. Mr. John Gilbert and Ms. Lyda Bill, both of the parish of Alton.

87 SRO: D554/Bundle 47.

88 According a pedigree at the College of Arms, London, Volume X, page 208; Thomas Gilbert married Anne Philips, daughter of Richard Philips of Hall Green, in the Parish of Checkley, on 27th January 1762. The marriage took place at Christ Church, (?), Co. Surrey. This is confirmed by an entry in the *Gentleman's Magazine*, 1762, p. 45. However, the *Gentleman's Mazazine*, 1761, p. 603, gives the date for the marriage as 24th December 1761.

89 SRO: D1343/6. Mrs. Elzabeth Gilbert (neé Philips) was buried at Alton in 1729.

90 *Gentleman's Magazine*, 1761, p. 603.

91 WSL: 109/33. (Copy presented in 1933 by F. H. Gilbert).

NOTES TO CHAPTER II LAND STEWARDS

1 Sir Maurice Powicke, *The Thirteenth Century*, Oxford (second edition, 1962), p. 323.

2 The steward, as the manager of the household, would move from one estate to another with his lord. Bailiffs were resident on the estates that they were responsible for.

3 Robert Plot, op. cit., p. 211.

4 Herbert Chester, *Iron Valley*, p. 44.

5 SRO: D554/Bundle 141.

6 The two standard studies on agents or stewards are: Edward Hughes, 'The Eighteenth-Century Estate Agent', in *Essays in British and Irish History*, (edited by H. A. Cronne, T. W. Moody and D. B. Quinn), London (1949); and G. E. Mingay, 'The Eighteenth-Century Land Steward', in *Land, Labour and Population in the Industrial Revolution*, (edited by E. L. Jones and G. E. Mingay), London (1967). The two authors opted for one of the alternative titles, but clearly there was no significant difference.

7 The Register of the Manchester School. 'Thomas and Robert , sons of John Gilbert, steward to His Grace the Duke of Bridgewater, Worsley, Lancashire.'

8 Rees, op. cit., (GILBERT, John).

9 SRO: D593/F/3/2/50.

10 SRO: D593/L/1/16.

11 See *T&JG*, Chpt. 2, Note II.

12 G. E. Mingay, op. cit., p. 7.

13 John Ward, *History of the Borough of Stoke-upon-Trent*, London (1843), p. 194.

14 SRO: D239/M/850.

15 SRO: D1343/6.

16 SRO: D554/Bundle 90.

17 SRO: D593/F/3/2/50.

18 SRO: D554/Bundle 148 and D1343/6.

19 SRO: D1343/6. ('Mr. Michael Barbor . . . of Stone).

20 WSL: William Salt Manuscript No. 522. (Barbors also belonged to the Cheadle Corporation).

21 Bedfordshire Record Office: R3/1954.

22 SRO: D593/L/1/16.

23 SRO: D554/Bundle 47.

24 See Gilbert family tree.

25 SRO: D593/C/23/4. (David Birds also worked for the younger John Gilbert at Clough Hall).

26 WSL: 93/1/22/41.

27 Rees, op. cit., LAND STEWARD.

28 Refer to Chapter 3.

29 Hugh Malet, op. cit., pp. 135-136.

30 Ibid, pp. 134-135. Robert Gilbert was not John Gilbert's eldest son as Dr. Malet states. Thomas Gilbert was the eldest son, and about thirty years of age at this time, which would have been the right sort of age for an agent to be appointed.

31 William Tunnicliff, *A Topographical Survey of the Counties of Somerset, Gloucester, Worcester, Stafford, Chester and Lancaster*, Bath (1789), p. 114.

32 Rees, op. cit., (GILBERT, John).

33 Tablet in Settrington Church.

34 Hugh Malet, op. cit., p. 145.

35 Howard Senar, *Little Gaddesden Parish Church*, Little Gaddesden (1980), p. 18. (He was incumbent from 1796 to 1813).

36 Robert Landsdale to James Loch (21st December 1843), quoted by Hugh Malet, op. cit., p. 161.

37 See Chapter 4 for suggestions why their relationship soured.

38 SRO: D593/C/23/4.

39 Based on Professor Mingay's figures, op. cit., p. 1.

40 Hugh Malet, op. cit., p. 138; but see SRO: D593/C/23/4.

41 Ann Kettle, 'The Struggle for the Lichfield Interest, 1747-68', *SHC*, Vol. 6, pp. 115-135.

42 SRO: D593/F/3/12/4/4.

43 Ann Kettle, op. cit., p. 135.

44 *Staffordshire Advertiser,* 12th January 1799.

45 S. M. Hardy and R. C. Baily, 'The Downfall of the Gower interest in the Staffordshire Boroughs, 1800-1830', *SHC,* (1950-1951), p. 300.

46 *Dictionary of National Biography,* p. 1025.

47 Rees, op. cit., 'Land Steward'. Once again, thanks to Hugh Torrens for the loan of his copy.

48 J. Lawrence, *The Modern Land Steward* (1801). Rees drew heavily from this source for his article on the 'Land Steward'.

49 Robert Robson, *The Attorney in Eighteenth Century England,* Cambridge (1959), pp. 84-103.

50 Hugh Malet, op. cit.

51 Rees, op. cit., 'Land Steward'.

52 According to Professor Chaloner, *People and Industries,* London (1963), p. 34, John Gilbert may have been in the Duke's service by 1753, which would have made him twenty-nine.

53 Rees, op. cit., 'Land Steward'.

54 Ibid.

55 W. A. Speck, *Stability and Strife,* London (1977), p. 41.

56 Rees, op. cit., 'Land Steward'.

57 *Staffordshire Advertiser,* 25th January 1806.

58 SRO: D593/L/1/15/5.

59 S. A. Broadbridge (Editor), *Journal of an Excursion to Wales, &c by Joseph Banks,* pp. 70-71, (unpublished manuscript for a book). I wish to record my thanks to the late Stan Broadbridge for allowing me to make a copy of this manuscript in 1976. It should be noted that the Duke only owned a portion of this 6,000 acres, something like 5-600 acres.

60 Ibid.

61 Ibid.

62 Ibid.

63 Ibid.

64 Ibid., p. 92.

65 Herbert A. Chester, *Cheadle: Coal Town,* Cheadle (1981), pp. 27-29.

66 John Aikin, op. cit., pp. 318-320.

67 Rees, op. cit., 'Lancashire'.

68 John Aikin, op. cit., pp. 320-321.

69 Ibid., p. 320.

70 Ibid., pp. 321-324.

71 Rees, op. cit.

72 A. W. Richeson, *English Land Measuring to 1800,* Cambridge, Massachusetts (1966), pp. 142-188.

73 Hugh Malet, op. cit., p. 45.

74 B&WP, John Gilbert to Matthew Boulton, 10th December 1765.

75 A. E. Musson and Eric Robinson, *Science and Technology in the Industrial Revolution,* Manchester (1969), p. 376.

76 *Dictionary of National Biography,* 'John Farey'.

77 J. F. Kirkaldy, *General Principles of Geology,* London (1971), pp. 15-16.

78 E. R. Hassal and J. P. Trickett, 'The Duke of Bridgewater's Underground Canals', *The Mining Engineer,* No. 37 (October 1963), p. 54.

79 B&WP, John Gilbert to Matthew Boulton, 17th January 1784.

80 Information supplied by the late W. Howard Williams.

81 *Monthly Magazine,* (1821), pp. 468-469.

82 *Gentleman's Magazine,* (1821), p. 381.

83 Rees, op. cit., 'Land Stewards'.

84 See Chapter 3.

85 B&WP; Box 5(XIII), Parcel F&G; Box 7, Parcel V; Box 4, Parcel G; and Box 2, Parcel G. (The drawings date from 1789).

86 Marston Saltworks, producing rock-salt, were near Northwich. For further details see Professor W. H. Chaloner, 'The Cheshire Activities of Matthew Boulton and James Watt, of Soho, near Birmingham, 1776-1817', in *Transactions of the Lancashire and Cheshire Antiquarian Society,* Vol. LXI (1949), pp. 126-131.

87 The Donnington Wood Engine.

88 B&WP.

89 Patent Number 730 (1758), Patent Office.

90 S. A. Broadbridge, op. cit., p. 79; and John Aikin, op. cit., p. 114.

91 Brindley's Notebooks, 30th June 1758.

92 Ibid., 'Cheadle 1759'.

93 Aikin, op. cit., p. 114.

94 Rees, op. cit., (GILBERT, John).

95 H. W. Dickinson and R. Jenkins, *James Watt and the Steam Engine,* (1927); reprinted by the Moorland Publishing Company, Ashbourne (1981), p. 138.

96 J. and W. H. Rankine, *A Biography of William Symington—Civil Engineer,* Falkirk (1862), pp. 55-56.

97 Charles Hadfield, *The Canals of the West Midlands,* Newton Abbot (second edition, 1969), p. 192 and 241-42.

98 G. Downs-Rose and W. S. Harvey, *William Symington,* London (1980), Chapter 4.

99 H. W. Dickinson and R. Jenkins, op. cit., p. 290.

100 G. Downs-Rose and W. S. Harvey, op. cit., p. 33.

101 H. W. Dickinson and R. Jenkins, op. cit., p. 290.

102 L. T. C. Rolt, *James Watt,* London (1962), p. 81.

103 G. Downs-Rose and W. S. Harvey, op. cit., p. 34.

104 Ibid., Chapters 6 and 7.

105 Hugh Malet, op. cit., pp. 151-152.

106 Frank Mullineux, *The Duke of Bridgewater's Canal,* Eccles (1959), pp. 26-28.

107 See Chapter 3.

108 (Lady) Katherine Euphemia Farrar, *The Letters of Josiah Wedgwood,* printed in three volumes (1903-06), Vol. II, p. 151.

109 John Ward, op. cit., pp. 351-352.

110 Frank Mullineux, 'The Duke of Bridgewater's Underground Canals at Worsley', *Transactions of the Lancashire and Cheshire Antiquarian Society,* Vol. 71 (1961), p. 158.

111 City Museum and Art Galley, Stoke-on-Trent; Enoch Wood's Scrapbook (1790-1836), p. 175. John Gilbert gave £15 to this fund, in 1795.

112 *Staffordshire Advertiser,* 13th February 1795.

113 A similar scheme was launched amongst the Shropshire ironmasters in 1796—see Arthur Raistrick, *Quakers in Science and Industry,* Newton Abbot (1968 reprint), p. 144.

114 *Cheltenham Chronicle and Gloucestershire General Advertiser,* 1st October 1812.

115 SRO: D593/F/4/3.

116 SRO: D593/F/3/5/53 and D593/F/3/7/1.

117 SRO: D593/F/3/7/1.

118 SRO: D593/F/3/2/69.

119 Hugh Malet, op. cit., p. 94.

120 Ibid., p. 38.

121 Ibid., pp. 38-39.

122 Ibid., pp. 95 and 138.

123 WSL: 93/13/41.

124 KEELE: Wedgwood Papers; 11-9515.

125 F. J. Wrottesley, (Editor), *Rocester Parish Register*, Vol. II, SPRS, (1909), p. 189. 'Buried...Mr. Francis Adams, who died at or near the seat of the Duke of Bridgewater.'

126 *Staffordshire Advertiser*, 12th January 1799.

127 Ibid.

128 Sir L. B. Namier, *The Structure of Politics at the Accession of George III*, London (1929), p. 53.

129 *Staffordshire Advertiser*, 12th January 1799.

130 Herbert A. Chester, *Cheadle: Coal Town*, pp. 23-24.

131 Robert Robson, op. cit., p. 71.

132 Herbert A. Chester, op. cit., pp. 23-24.

133 SRO: D239/M/400 and D239/M/402.

134 The grandfather of Sir Joseph Banks (1743-1820).

135 Edward Hughes, op. cit., p. 193.

136 Hugh Malet, op. cit., p. 27.

137 Northamptonshire Record Office: EB 1459.

138 Northamptonshire Record Office: EB 1461.

139 SRO: D593/C/23/4.

140 Information from Frank Mullineux, 3rd January 1978.

141 SRO: D239/M/850.

142 G. E. Mingay, op. cit., p. 10.

143 SRO: D593/F/4/3.

144 Robert Robson, op. cit. p. 85.

145 See Chapter Three.

146 SRO: D593/M/1/5.

147 Trevor D. Ford, 'The Speedwell Mine', *Derbyshire Countryside*, (April-May 1960), pp. 20-21, 47 and 55.

148 Rees, op. cit., (GILBERT, John).

149 Trevor D. Ford and J. H. Rieuwerts (Editors), *Lead Mining in the Peak District*, Bakewell (second edition, 1975), p. 84.

150 Somerset Record Office: DD/WG/BOX 15/5 and Hugh Malet, op. cit., p. 134.

151 Barrie Trinder, *The Industrial Revolution in Shropshire*, Chichester (1973), pp. 207-208.

152 Eric Richards, 'The Industrial Face of a Great Estate: Trentham and Lilleshall, 1780-1860', *EHR*, Vol. XXVII, No. 3, (August 1974), p. 415.

153 SRO: D593/B/2/7/22/1-2.

154 WSL: 93/7/41.

155 Eric Richards, '... Trentham and Lilleshall...', loc. cit., p. 415.

156 WSL: 93/20/41 a-c.

157 J. A. Robey, op. cit., p. 90.

158 SRO: D554/Bundles 91 and 154.

159 L. F. Helsby, A. J. Rushton and D. R. Legge, 'Water Mills of The Moddershall Valley,' *JSIAS*, Vol. 4. (1973), p. 25.

160 SRO: D593/C/23/4.

161 Hugh Malet, op. cit., p. 134.

162 See Chapter 4.

163 Rees, op. cit., 'James Brindley'.

164 Samuel Smiles, *Lives of the Engineers*, Vol. I., London (1862), p. 403. Smiles discounts the statements of two informed sources about this application as "untrue", basing his argument on an examination of Brindley's notebooks.

165 See Chapter 3.

NOTES TO CHAPTER III THE DUKE'S AND EARL'S CANALS

1 Charles Hadfield, *The Canal Age*, Newton Abbot (1968), pp. 1-4.

2 Ibid., p. 166.

3 Ibid., pp. 3-4.

4 An example is to be found in *Aris's Birmingham Gazette*, 14th September 1767.

5 Charles Hadfield, *The Canal Age*, p. 168.

6 Hugh Malet, op. cit., pp. 14-16.

7 J. Aikin, op. cit., p. 116.

8 *Manchester Mercury*, 21st July 1761.

9 Charles Hadfield, *British Canals: An Illustrated History;* fifth edition, Newton Abbot (1974), pp. 29-30.

10 Charles Hadfield, *The Canal Age*, p. 7.

11 Charles Hadfield, *British Canals: An Illustrated History*, p. 30.

12 J. Aikin, op. cit., pp. 106-109 and Joseph Priestley, *Historical Account of the Navigable Rivers, Canals and Railways of Great Britain*, London (1831), pp. 389 and 666.

13 Daniel Defoe, *A Tour through the Whole Island of Great Britain*, first published 1724-6. Edited version by Pat Rogers, Harmondsworth, (1971), p. 542.

14 J. Aikin, op. cit., p. 117.

15 Charles Hadfield, *British Canals: An illustrated History*, p. 30.

16 The first attempt to write a balanced account of the development of the Bridgewater Canal system was made by Frank Mullineux, in his booklet *The Duke of Bridgewater's Canal*, published in 1959. The first modern biography of the Duke of Bridgewater was Hugh Malet's, *The Canal Duke*, Dawlish (1961). This book was substantially revised and expanded, with the benefit of access to the Sutherland archives and appeared as: *Bridgewater: the Canal Duke, 1736-1803*, Manchester (1977). This last work added a forceful drip to help weather the persistent stone of Smile's legend; and succeeded in reducing the famous canal triumvirate of the Duke of Bridgewater, John Gilbert and James Brindley from three to two and a half.

17 Samuel Smiles, *Lives of the Engineers, Vol. I*, London (1862). Smiles devotes pages 305 to 476 to a detailed description of Brindley's life and works.

18 John Farey, (1766-1826), author of *Agriculture and Minerals of Derbyshire;* and a contributor to Rees' *Cyclopaedia*, including the article on canals.

19 Rees, op. cit., (GILBERT, John).

20 Samuel Smiles, op. cit., p. 403.

21 (Lady) K. E. Farrar, op. cit., Vol. II, pp. 319-320.

22 Note the gratuitous payment made in 1774.

23 SRO: Alton Parish Register (Bishop's Transcript, 1748-1755).

24 W. H. Chaloner, *People and Industries*, p. 34.

25 SRO: D1343/6.

26. For information on these early Welsh navigational levels see Stephen Hughes, 'The Development of British Navigational Levels', *Journal of the Railway and Canal Historical Society*. Vol. XXVII, No. 2 (July 1981), p. 2. For further information on John Rotten see: J. A. Robey, 'Copper Smelting in Derbyshire', *BPDMHS*, Vol. 4, part 5 (June 1971), pp. 348-49.

27 Rees, op. cit., (GILBERT, John).

28 The first useful stretch of the Sankey Navigation opened on 4th November 1757.

29 Rees, op. cit., (GILBERT, John).

30 Stephen Hughes, op. cit., p. 2.

31 M. J. T. Lewis, *Early Wooden Railways*, London (1970) p. 322. Patent Number 653 (9th February 1750): Machine for carrying coals from the coal walls to the bottom of the shaft, and from the mouth of the shaft to the heaps, and for other purposes. Michael Meinzies took out a further Patent (Number 762), dated 20th May 1761: for working mines of coal. Patent Office.

32 Hugh Malet, op. cit., p. 43.

33 Ibid., pp. 45-46.

34 Act 33 Geo II C.2. Hugh Malet, op. cit., pp. 45-48.

35 For further evidence regarding John Gilbert's arrival at Worsley see *T&JG*, Chapter 3, Note 35.

36 Act 32 Geo II C.2. A clause limited his sales of coal at Salford to a price of 4d a cwt. for forty years; but in fact the Duke fixed his price at 3½d a cwt. until mounting debts forced him to raise his prices. (Malet, pp. 49 and 81).

37 Act 33 Geo II C.2.

38 Brindley's notebooks. They are not in the main diaries but memoranda books. They range from 1754 to 1763 but cover only sections of that period. Those ranging from August 1754 to February 1758 are in the Birmingham Reference Library; and those covering the period March 1759 to October 1763 are at the Institution of Civil Engineers.

39 Brindley's notebooks. Under a heading 'Mr. Gilbert' (to whom the account would be submitted) 'July 1st (1759) at Worsley Hall 6 days'.

40 Hugh Malet, op. cit., p. 57.

41 This 'engine' is the subject of a short entry in one of Brindley's notebooks 'Cheadle 1759—Mobile Water Engine—May 17 1 day.'

42 J. Aikin, op. cit., p. 143.

43 Information from Hugh Malet, 5th June 1980.

44 S. A. Broadbridge, op. cit., p. 42.

45 Ibid., p. 84.

46 Ibid., pp. 80-81.

47 (Lady) K. E. Farrar, op. cit., Vol. II, p. 151.

48 Quoted in Charles Hadfield, *The Canals of the East Midlands*, Newton Abbot (1969), pp. 18-19.

49 Hugh Malet, op. cit., pp. 65-66 gives a full account of this episode.

50 *Manchester Mercury*, 21st July 1761.

51 Ibid.

52 *Annual Register, 1763.*

53 Hugh Malet, op. cit., pp. 72-76.

54 Brindley's notebook: 13th November 1763. Thomas Gilbert (John's eldest son) was fifteen years old at this time and apparently already helping his father. It was he who helped his father with the construction of the canal to Runcorn and not John (junior) as Hugh Malet states. (Malet, p. 126).

55 Hugh Malet, op. cit., p. 98.

56 Lady K. E. Farrar, op. cit., Vol. II, p. 199.

57 Hugh Malet devotes a full chapter to this dispute in his book.

58 WSL: SMS/478 (Folder G).

59 Charles Hadfield and Gordon Biddle, *The Canals of North West England*, Vol I, Newton Abbot (1970), p. 34.

60 Quoted in Hadfield and Biddle, op. cit., p. 34.

61 Hugh Malet, op. cit., pp. 133-137.

62 S. A. Broadbridge, op. cit., p. 92.

63 SRO: D593/I/1/33.

64 Barrie Trinder, op. cit., p. 126.

65 S. A. Broadbridge, op. cit., p. 63.

66 W. K. V. Gale and C. R. Nicholls, *The Lilleshall Company Ltd: A History 1764-1964*, Ashbourne (1979), p. 19. The tub boats on this branch were fitted with containers—see Charles Hadfield, *The Canals of the West Midlands*, p. 41.

67 Rees, op. cit., 'Canals'.

68 Barrie Trinder, op. cit., p. 126.

69 The remains of a wooden tub boat are featured in a photograph in *Waterways World*, June 1978, p. 46. A replica of a Shropshire tub boat was constructed (in wood) in 1977 and a photograph of its launching is to be found in *Waterways World*, May 1977, p. 31.

70 An iron tub boat which belonged to the Lilleshall Company (No. 749) is preserved at the Ironbridge Gorge Museum.

71 Charles Hadfield, *The Canals of the West Midlands*, pp. 155-157.

72 Hugh Malet, op. cit., p. 138.

73 J. Aikin, op. cit., p. 381 and S. A. Broadbridge, op. cit., p. 92.

74 Hugh Malet, op. cit., p. 138.

75 County Record Office, Northampton: EB 1461 (dated 1786).

76 SRO: D593/C/23/4.

77 County Record Office, Northampton: EB 1461 (dated 1803).

78 Hugh Malet, op. cit., p. 156.

79 Rees, op. cit., 'Land Steward'.

80 County Record Office, Northampton: EB1459, Day Book.

81 Charles Hadfield, *Canals of the West Midlands*, pp. 40 and 47.

NOTES TO CHAPTER IV THE GRAND TRUNK

1 Act: 10 Will. III c. 26 and M. W. Greenslade and J. G. Jenkins, op. cit., p. 285.

2 *Common's Journals*, XXX, pp. 720-1.

3 Sir Richard Whitworth, *Advantages of Inland Navigation*, (1766). Reprinted in J. Phillips, *A General History of Inland Navigation*, London (fifth edition 1805), p. 145.

4 Ibid., p. 133.

5 Jean Lindsay, *The Trent and Mersey Canal*, Newton Abbot (1979), p. 15.

6 Act: 6 Geo. III c. 96. (14th May 1766).

7 John Aikin, op. cit., p. 117.

8 Jean Lindsay, op. cit., p. 15.

9 *Collected Reports of John Smeaton*, Vol. I, p. 13. The reports are preserved in the Library of the Royal Society, London and the report on the Trent and Mersey (from Longbridge, near Burslem to Wilden) includes three schedules of landowners involved.

10 Charles Hadfield, *The Canal Age*, p. 4 and *British Canals*, p. 46.

11 Brindley's notebook contains the note (dated 15th February 1758):—'Surveying the Navigation from Long Brigg to Kinges Milles or inspection. Charges born work 12 days ½.' This appears to have been little more than a very general survey to determine the lie of the land. A further entry (dated 17th February) reads 'about the navigation 3 days.' Brindley was also working on a steam engine at Fenton at this time.

12 WSL: 93/23/41. This explodes the statement made by Samuel Smiles that James Brindley bought a share in his own right.

13 Brindley Notebooks, 10th May 1760. 'Bgnn to leavel from Hare Castle—4 days.' At this time the proposal was obviously to extend the canal from Longport into the southern flank of Harecastle Hill, so the coal could be exploited in the same manner as that employed at Worsley.

14 (Lady) K. E. Farrar, op. cit., Vol. I (1762-1770) and Vol. III, pp. 227-312.

15 I have been unable to trace a copy of this pamphlet and it does not appear amongst the list of Thomas Gilbert's pamphlets held by the British Library.

16 (Lady) K. E. Farrar, op. cit., Vol. I., pp. 19-23.

17 KEELE: Wedgwood Papers: Samuel Garbett to Josiah Wedgwood (18th April, 1765).

18 (Lady) K. E. Farrar, op. cit., Vol. I, pp. 37 and 41.

19 Ibid., Vol. III, p. 228.

20 Ibid., p. 229.

21 The 'Burslemites' were a small group of Burslem potters with Wedgwood as their leader, who were determined to have a canal to the River Trent.

22 For a portrait of Thomas Bentley, see Peter Lead, *The Trent and Mersey Canal*, Ashbourne (1980), p. 16.

23 This presumably refers to the Duke of Bridgewater's offer to meet all the costs of obtaining an Act of Parliament. (Lady K. E. Farrar, op. cit., Vol. III, pp. 230-231.

24 KEELE: Wedgwood Papers: 24153-32 and 24154-32.

25 T. S. Willan, *The Navigation of the River Weaver in the Eighteenth Century*, Manchester (1951), p. 90.

26 The surveys were carried out by Hugh Henshall and Robert Pownall. Levels were taken of the country between Winsford and Harecastle Hill by both Middlewich and Nantwich. The survey of an alternate route from Harecastle, through Middlewich to Northwich was paid for by the canal promoters. See T. S. Willan, op. cit., p. 90.

27 (Lady) K. E. Farrar, op. cit., Vol III, p. 238.

28 Ibid., p. 248.

29 T. S. Willan, op. cit., p. 91.

30 (Lady), K. E. Farrar, op. cit., Vol. I, pp. 69-70.

31 T. S. Willan, op. cit., p. 203.

32 (Lady) K. E. Farrar, op. cit., Vol. I, p.70.

33 Ibid., p. 73.

34 Ibid., pp. 72-73.

35 Eliza Meteyard, *The Life of Josiah Wedgwood from his private correspondence and family papers*, London (1865), Vol. I., p. 431.

36 For more on Whitworth and his scheme, part of which he constructed at his own expense see R. J. Dean, 'Sir Richard Whitworth and Inland Navigation,' *Journal of the Railway and Canal Historical Society*, Vol. XXVII, No. 4 (March 1982), pp. 42-46.

37 (Lady) K. E. Farrar, op. cit., Vol. III, p. 235. Whitworth was a true eccentric see *T&JG*, Chapter 4, Note 37.

38 SRO: D593/V/3/6 and Jean Lindsay, op. cit., p. 26.

39 *Journal House of Commons*, XXX, p. 453.

40 (Lady) K. E. Farrar, op. cit., Vol. I, p. 80.

41 *Journal of House of Lords*, XXXI, p. 350 and *Journal of House of Commons*, XXX, p. 649.

42 Geo. III c. 96, Royal Assent 14th May 1766. Copy in Hanley Reference Library.

43 *Aris's Birmingham Gazette*, 28th May 1766.

44 SRO: D593/T/1/35.

45 KEELE: Wedgwood Papers: 9281-11.

46 6. Geo. III c. 96.

47 (Lady) K. E. Farrar, op. cit., Vol I, pp. 85-7.

48 SRO: D554, Bundle 162 and WSL: 37/19.

49 (Lady) K. E. Farrar, op. cit., Vol. I, p. 134.

50 Ibid., p. 197.

51 Ibid., pp. 214-215.

52 John Thomas, *The Rise of the Staffordshire Potteries*, Bath (1971), pp. 87-88.

53 WSL: HM/19 (8th November 1774).

54 WSL: HM/37/19.

55 For further details on Hugh Henshall and Company see Peter Lead, *The Trent and Mersey Canal*, p. 12.

56 Pamphlet in the Wedgwood Papers at Keele, prepared by Order of the Canal Committee 24th-25th February 1785, entitled *A Statement of Facts respecting some Differences that have arisen betwixt His Grace the Duke of Bridgewater and The Proprietors from the Trent to the Mersey*.

57 Jean Lindsay, op. cit., p. 89.

58 Ibid.

59 WSL: HM 37/37. Letter from Richard Levitt to Edward Sneyd.

60 WSL: HM 37/38.

61 Information from Charles Hadfield.

62 WSL: HM 37/19. I am grateful to Arnold Gibson for drawing my attention to this important reference.

63 Josiah Wedgwood's Commonplace Book, Vol. 1, pp. 241-7 (E39/28408).

64 *The Gentleman's Magazine*, January 1795 carries an obituary and describes him as 'the proposer of the Grand Trunk Canal, and the chief agent in obtaining the Act of Parliament for making it.' Thomas Gilbert subsequently gave his support to the Company in its fight against the Commercial Canal scheme.

65 I have standardised my spelling on the first edition of the one-inch Ordnance Survey (1836) which uses 'Caldon' throughout.

66 See Peter Lead, *The Caldon Canal and Tramroads*, Tarrant Hinton (1979), p. 3.

67 PRO: Banks' Letters, Kew: B.C.1.30.

68 KEELE: Wedgwood Papers: 18438-25.

69 W. A. McCutcheon, *The Canals of the North of Ireland*, Dawlish (1965), pp. 69-74. *Reports of the late John Smeaton*, F.R.S., London (1812), Vol. ii, p. 279.

70 W. S. Chaloner, 'James Brindley and his Remuneration as a Canal Engineer', *Trans Lancashire and Cheshire Antiquarian Society*, Vols. 75 and 76 (1965-6), pp. 226-228.

71 KEELE: Wedgwood Papers. Josiah Wedgwood to John Wedgwood.

72 Caldon Canal Act: 16 Geo. III c. 32. Royal Assent 13th May 1776.

73 Herbert A. Chester, *Cheadle: Coal Town*, pp. 33-39.

74 SRO: D554, Bundle 162.

75 SRO: D239/M/1212 and D239/M/1217.

76 SRO: D554, Bundle 162.

77 For the opening date see Peter Lead, 'The Caldon Canal 1778-1978', *Cherry Eye*, Caldon Canal Society, No. 3, (Winter 1976-1977), pp. 3-5. A condensed version of this appears in Jean Lindsay, op. cit., p. 58.

78 SRO: D239/M/2139 and D239/M/2238.

79 SRO: D239/M/2139.

80 WSL: HM 37/19.

81 Act: 16 Geo. III c. 32.

82 M. J. T. Lewis, *Early Wooden Railways*, London (1970), p. 285.

83 WSL: HM/37/19 (9th January 1780).

84 Rees, op. cit., 'Canals'.

85 Act 23 Geo. III c. 33. Royal Assent 17th April 1783.

86 WSL: HM 37/19.

87 Rees, op. cit., 'Canals'.

88 WSL: HM 37/19.

89 Sir Lewis Namier and John Brooke, *The History of Parliament: The House of Commons, 1754-1790*, London (1964), p. 499.

90 Hugh Malet, op. cit., pp. 59-60.

91 Sir Lewis Namier, *The Structure of Politics at the Accession of George III*, London (1929), p. 54.

92 Charles Hadfield, *Canals of the West Midlands*, p. 26.

93 The townsfolk had to wait until 1797 for their branch canal to open.

94 *Staffordshire Advertiser*, 12th January 1799.

95 SRO: D868/10/26.

96 Sir Lewis Namier and John Brooke, op. cit., p. 500.

NOTES TO CHAPTER V FURTHER CANAL SCHEMES

1 Charles Hadfield, *The Canals of the West Midlands*, pp. 151-152.

2 H. M. Rathbone, *Letters of Richard Reynolds*, London (1852), p. 265.

3 W. H. Chaloner, 'James Brindley and his Remuneration as a Canal Engineer', loc. cit., pp. 226-228.

4 H. M. Rathbone, op. cit., pp. 93-94.

5 Barrie Trinder, *The Tar Tunnel*, Ironbridge (1973), p. 3.

6 Arthur Raistrick, *Dynasty of Ironfounders*, Newton Abbot (1970), p. 185.

7 R. M. and H. C. P. Larking, *The Canal Pioneers*, Goring-by-Sea (not dated), p. 27. (R. M. Larking is a descendant of John Gilbert, 1724-1795).

8 Ibid., p. 27.

9 Charles Hadfield, *The Canals of the West Midlands*, pp. 152-159.

10 J. Plymbley, *The Agriculture of Shropshire*, (1803), pp. 290-9.

11 33 Geo. III c. 113. Royal Assent 3rd June 1793.

12 The first cast iron aqueduct to come into service was the one of the Derby Canal, at Holmes, in Derby which was opened in February 1796. A month later Telford's aqueduct at Longdon was completed.

13 *Waterways News*, No. 100 (May 1980), p. 4.

14 Charles Hadfield, *The Canals of the West Midlands*, p. 160.

15 Desmond King-Hele, *Doctor of Revolution*, London (1977), p. 114.

16 Patent Office: Patent Number 1892 (19th June 1792).

17 Rees, op. cit., 'Canals'.

18 Michael Corfield, 'John Ward and the Kennet and Avon Canal: (Part 2)', in *Bristol Industrial Archaeology Society Journal*, Number 15 (1983), p. 23. Part I appeared in the same Journal, Number 14 (1981). I am grateful to Hugh Torrens for pointing this out to me and Michael Corfield for providing additional notes.

19 Rees, op. cit., 'Canals'

20 SRO: Alton Parish Register (Bishop's Transcript), 1748-1755. 'Marriage: Francis Ward of Cheadle and Miss Margaret Bill, 23rd December 1754, by John Bill, Rector of Draycott. In presence of Robert Bill and John Gilbert.'

21 Michael Corfield, 'John Ward . . ., pt. 2', p. 21.

22 Transcript from Michael Corfield. (Charles Dundas to John Rennie).

23 *Sherborne and Yeovil Mercury*, 13th October, 1794 (Transcript provided by Hugh Torrens).

24 Michael Corfield, 'John Ward . . ., pt. 2, p. 23.

25 Charles Hadfield, *Canals of the West Midlands*, pp. 151-154.

26 Michael Corfield, 'John Ward . . ., pt. 2', p. 21.

27 Ibid., p. 23.

28 Hugh Torrens, 'The Somersetshire Coal Canal Caisson Lock', *Journal of the Bristol Industrial Archaeology Society*, No. 8, (1975), pp. 4-10.

29 Michael Corfield, 'John Ward . . ., pt. 2', p. 29.

30 *Bath Herald*, 9th June 1798.

31 Rees, op. cit., 'Canals'.

32 Hugh Torrens, op. cit., p. 2.

33 Ibid., pp. 2-3.

34 National Library of Scotland, John Rennie's Reports, Volume 2, Number 76.

35 Charles Hadfield, *The Canals of the West Midlands*, pp. 159-160.

36 SRO: D554, Bundle 162.

37 John Farey, *General View of the Agriculture and Minerals of Derbyshire*, Vol. III, London (1817), pp. 304, 329-330, and 392-3.

38 SRO: D554, Bundle 162.

39 Hanley Reference Library: SP 138.6.

40 *Staffordshire Advertiser*, 25th June 1796.

41 *Staffordshire Advertiser*, 8th October 1796

42 For a more complete account of the Commercial, Leek and Uttoxeter Canals, see Peter Lead, *The Caldon Canal and Tramroads*, pp. 19-21 and 22-40.

43 Charles Hadfield, *The Canal Age*, pp. 42-44.

44 *Manchester Mercury*, 4th May 1762.

45 Charles Hadfield and Gordon Biddle, *The Canals of North-West England*, Vol. II, p. 263.

46 SRO: D1343/6.

47 Pedigree registered at the College of Heralds (1886): John Royds (1729-1799) and his eldest son, John Royds (1755-1823).

48 Rochdale Canal Minute Book, Rochdale Canal Company, Manchester.

49 B&WP: Box 4, Parcel G. (4th June 1791).

50 Rochdale Canal Minute Book.

51 Ibid.

52 Ibid.

53 34 Geo. III c. 98. Royal Assent 4th April 1794.

54 SRO: D593/C/23/4.

55 SRO: D260/M/E/428.

56 Letter from G. Bowyer, himself an old boatman to William Jack (17th July 1960). I am grateful to Bill Jack for allowing me to transcribe this letter.

57 This photograph is included in Peter Lead, *Trent and Mersey Canal*, photograph and caption number 20.

58 SRO: D260/M/E/428.

59 Photographic copy of the sale notice (dated 1826) in Hanley Reference Library: SP 867.

60 W. K. V. Gale and C. R. Nicholls, op. cit., p. 26.

61 WSL: 93/23/41.

62 SRO: D239/M/1703.

63 KEELE: Wedgwood Papers: 29912-49.

64 WSL: 93/23/41.

65 William Marshall, *The Review and Abstract of the County reports to the Board of Agriculture from the several Agricutural Departments of England; Western Division*. York, (1818), p. 141. This is contained in Holland's report compiled in 1808. This is a very early reference to iron boats on canals and the earliest known instance of their use on the Trent and Mersey Canal. For further information on such boats see: Philip Weaver, 'Iron Boats on the Canals', *Journal of the Railway and Canal Historical Society*, Volume XXIV, No. 3, (November 1978), pp. 97-99; and Peter Lead, 'Early Iron Boats—the North Staffordshire Connection', *Journal of the Railway and Canal Historical Society*, Vol. XXVIII, No. 2, (July 1984), p. 94.

66 *Staffordshire Advertiser*, 7th March 1812.

67 KEELE: Wedgwood papers: 9679-52.

68 John Farey, op. cit., p. 436.

69 SRO: QR/UBI.

70 SRO: D239/M/2146.

71 SRO: D239/M/2140.

72 Harry Hanson, *The Canal Boatmen, 1760-1914*, Manchester (1975), p. 17; also William Tunnicliff, op. cit., pp. 113 and 116.

73 T. S. Willan, op. cit., p. 131.

74 For a picture of such chutes, see Peter Lead, *Trent and Mersey Canal*, picture 13.

75 T. S. Willan, op. cit, p. 131.

76 Ibid.

77 KEELE: Wedgwood Papers: 9671-52

78 SRO: QR/UBI.

79 KEELE: Wedgwood Papers: 9672-52.

80 Ibid., 9679-52.

81 Charles Hadfield and Gordon Biddle, op. cit., p. 26(n).

82 Laurent's Map of Manchester (1793), Central Reference Library, Manchester.

83 Thomas Kent's General Account with His Grace the Duke of Bridgewater for the Year 1791 (MS Chetham Library). Thomas Kent was the Duke's Chief accountant for the Worsley estate and the Bridgewater Canal.

84 WSL: 93/23/41.

85 Ibid.

86 Harry Hanson, op. cit., p. 29.

87 Robert Nicholls, *Ten Generations of A Potting Family,* London (1931), pp. 104-105.

88. Letter from Helen F. Ladd, Reference and Information Librarian, City Library, Worcester (dated 27th February 1979).

89 Freight (including coal) was being delivered to the Bartington area of Cheshire by 1793. (Information for Hugh Malet.)

90 SRO: D593/M/16/1/1.

91 The Trent and Mersey Canal passed through and under (by means of the Harecastle Tunnel) the Clough Hall estate.

92 John Phillips, op. cit., p. vi.

93 Aikin, op. cit., p. 536.

94 V. I. Tomlinson's, 'Salford activities connected with the Bridgewater Canal', *Transaction of the Lancashire and Cheshire Antiquarian Scoiety,* Vol. 66 (1956), p. 86. Tomlinson is in fact quoting F. H. Egerton, who was often in the Duke's company prior to his death in 1803.

95 *Staffordshire Advertiser,* 12th January 1799.

96 WSL: 93/13/41.

NOTES ON CHAPTER VI ENTERPRISE AND INNOVATION

1 See Chapter 1.

2 SRO: D554, Bundle 55.

3 SRO: D260/B/2/2/37.

4 W. K. V. Gale, op. cit., pp. 3-4.

5 H. W. Dickinson and R. Jenkins, op. cit., p.25.

6 W. H. Chaloner, 'Isaac Wilkinson, Potfounder'; in *Studies in the Industrial Revolution presented to T. S. Ashton,* Edited by L. S. Pressnell, London (1960), pp. 23-51.

7 Hugh Torrens, *The Evolution of a Family Firm: Stothert and Pitt of Bath,* Bath (1978), pp. 1-22.

8 Herbert Heaton, 'Financing the Industrial Revolution', originally published in the *Bulletin of the Business Historical Society,* Vol. XI, No. 1, (February 1937). Reprinted in Francois Crouzet, *Capital Formation in the Industrial Revolution,* London (1972), p. 89.

9 Robert Sherlock, *Industrial Archaeology of Staffordshire,* Newton Abbot (1976), pp. 59-60.

10 Peter Mathias, *The First Industrial Nation,* London (1969), p. 151.

11 SRO: D260/B/2/2/37.

12 J. Aikin, op. cit., pp. 79-80.

13 Ibid., p. 79.

14 Ibid., p. 80.

15 SRO: D240/M/K/D/63.

16 John A. Robey and Lindsey Porter, *The Copper and Lead Mines of Ecton Hill, Staffordshire*, p. 19.

17 SRO: D240/M/K/D/63.

18 SRO: D260/B/2/2/37.

19 SRO: D240/M/K/D/63.

20 Robey and Porter, *The Copper and Lead Mines of Ecton Hill, Staffordshire*, pp. 38-39.

21 SRO: D260/B/2/2/37.

22 SRO: D240/M/E/III/45.

23 At the time of Thomas Gilbert's death in 1741/42, there were even proposals to make a rabbit 'burrough . . . on Alton Common', and a partnership was envisaged to facilitate this.

24 SRO: D240/E/III/52.

25 SRO: D240/M/E/III/45.

26 SRO: D554/Bundle 57.

27 SRO: D239/M/850.

28 Robey and Porter, *The Copper and Lead Mines of Ecton Hill, Staffordshire*, pp. 24-25.

29 Ibid.

30 Ibid., p. 78.

31 Ibid., p. 68.

32 S. A. Broadbridge, op. cit., pp. 61-62.

33 See Chapter 2.

34 Brindley's Notebook, 'On Wednesday Night—7 Mar. Mr. Brindley to be at J. Gilbert to go to Ecton the next morning', (NOT IN BRINDLEY'S HANDWRITING).

35 William Efford, *Gentleman's Magazine*, February 1769, p. 61.

36 Robey and Porter, *The Copper and Lead Mines of Ecton Hill, Staffordshire*, p. 28.

37 J. A. Robey and L. Porter, 'The Metalliferous Mines of the Weaver Hills, Staffordshire', p. 420.

38 Ibid., p. 421.

39 Ibid., p. 420-421.

40 Ibid., p. 421.

41 SRO: D554/Bundle 142.

42 SRO: D1229/D/1/1.

43 Brindley's Notebook.

44 SRO: D1229/D/1/1.

45 SRO: D1229/D/1/1-2.

46 Herbert A. Chester, *Cheadle: Coal Town*, pp. 35-36.

47 Robert Hurst was Mrs. Lydia Gilbert's (John's wife) uncle. The Goldenhill estate was conveyed to him in 1760, after it had been purchased by the partnership which included the two Gilbert brothers.

48 SRO: D1229/D/1/1.

49 SRO: D1229/D/1/1-2.

50 SRO: D1229/D/1/1.

51 This dispute is described later in this Chapter.

52 SRO: D240/K/Bundle D.

53 SRO: D240/K/Bundles C and D.

54 16 Geo. III c. 32. Royal Assent 13th May 1776.

55 SRO: D554/Bundle 84.

56 SRO: D554/Bundles 84 and 85.

57 16 Geo. III c. 32. Royal Assent 13th May 1776.

58 WSL: 93/23/41 and John Farey, op. cit., pp. 435-436.

59 WSL: 93/23/41.

60 SRO: D239/M/2139.

61 See also—*Staffordshire Advertiser,* 24th March 1804. This mentions 'four very valuable LIME KILNS . . . in the possession of messrs. Gilbert & Co.'

62 The first limekilns at Froghall basin were not erected until 1786, at a cost of £312-12s-4d. (WSL: HM/37/19.)

63 SRO: D239/M/2146.

64 SRO: D239/M/2143.

65 WSL: 93/7/41.

66 KEELE: Wedgwood Papers: 9281-11.

67 WSL: 93/23/41.

68 WSL: 93/23/41.

69 Graphite is used in the so called 'lead pencils' and was formerly mistaken for lead, hence its alternative names of 'plumbago' or 'black lead'.

70 William Tunnicliff, op. cit., p. 107.

71 B&WP; John Gilbert to Matthew Boulton, 28th June 1765.

72 B&WP: John Gilbert to Matthew Boulton, 31st August 1765.

73 B&WP; John Gilbert to Matthew Boulton, 7th September 1765.

74 B&WP; John Gilbert to Matthew Boulton, 15th October 1765.

75 (Lady) K. E. Farrar, op. cit., Vol. I, p. 191.

76 Samuel Parkes, *Chemical Essays,* London (1815), p. 134.

77 John Farey, 'A First Report to Henry Bankes Esq. (as owner), & to him and Sir Joseph Banks Bart and the several other gentlemen, associated with them (as occupiers) of the Ward of or Black Lead Mine in the Manor of Borrowdale in Cumberland', 7th September 1818, p. 11. (Dorset Record Office: D/BKL.)

78 Samuel Parkes, op. cit., p. 133.

79 John Farey, . . . 'Black Lead Mine' . . . , pp. 11-15.

80 Hugh Malet, op. cit., p. 134-135.

81 Samuel Parkes, op. cit., p. 137.

82 John Farey . . . 'Black Lead Mine . . . ', p. 15.

83 Ibid., p. 16.

84 Rees, op. cit., 'Black Lead'.

85 *Manchester Mercury,* 16th July 1782.

86 *Staffordshire Advertiser,* 18th February 1815.

87 W. Wallace, *Alston Moor, Its Pastoral People: Its Mines and Miners,* Newcastle (1890), p. 124.

88 Paul N. Wilson, 'The Nent Force Level', *Trans. Cumberland and Westmorland A. &A. Soc.,* Vol. LXIII, n.s. (1963).

89 W. Wallace, op. cit., p. 124.

90 Paul N. Wilson, op. cit.

91 W. Wallace, op. cit., p. 125.

92 There are numerous similarities between the career of John Taylor (1779-1863) and John Gilbert. For a full account of his life see: *John Taylor, mining entrepreneur and engineer, 1779-1863*, by Roger Burt, Hartington (1977).

93 Roger Burt, op. cit., p. 35.

94 W. Wallace, op. cit., p. 23.

95 Ibid.

96 See Chapter Four.

97 Phyllis Deane, *The First Industrial Revolution*, Cambridge (1965), p. 121.

98 B. L. Anderson, 'The Attorney and the Early Capital Market in Lancashire', in Francois Crouzet, *Capital Formation in the Industrial Revolution*, London (1972), p. 228.

99 Information from Mr. A. R. Muir.

100 B. L. Anderson, op. cit., p. 228.

101 R. W. Chapman (Editor), *Boswell, Life of Johnson*, London, (1970), p. 1078.

102 WSL: 93/23/41.

103 WSL: 93/23/41-42.

104 Samuel Smiles, op. cit., pp. 350-351.

105 Brindley's Notebook.

106 Samuel Smiles, op. cit., p. 351.

107 (Lady) K. E. Farrar, Vol. III, p. 294.

108 W. H. Chaloner, 'Salt in Cheshire, 1600-1870', *Transactions of the Lancashire and Cheshire Antiquarian Society*, Vol. 71 (1961), p. 71.

109 Ibid.

110 Ibid.

111 S. A. Broadbridge, op. cit., p. 85.

112 Rees, op. cit., 'John Gilbert'.

113 W. H. Chaloner, 'The Cheshire Activities of Matthew Boulton and James Watt, of Soho, near Birmingham, 1776-1817', in *Transactions of the Lancashire and Cheshire Antiquarian Society*, Vol. LXI (1949), pp. 122-124.

114 *Staffordshire Advertiser*, 28th March 1818.

115 Boulton and Watt Engine Book, Birmingham Central Reference Library.

116 W. H. Chaloner, 'The Cheshire Activities of Matthew Boulton and James Watt . . .', p. 122.

117 WSL: HM/37/19.

118 Boat Register (1795), Cheshire County Record Office.

119 J. Aikin, op. cit., p. 141.

120 WSL: 93/23/41.

121 Phyllis Deane, op. cit., p. 49.

122 SRO: D260/M/T/4.

123 John Ward, op. cit., p. 129.

124 ·Hugh Malet, op. cit., p. 141.

125 SRO: D593/C/23/4.

126 A. N. Palmer, 'John Wilkinson and the old Bersham iron works', *Transactions of the Cymmrodorion Society* (1897-8), pp. 27-28. John Wilkinson and his brother William are described as two 'clever, determined, and most intractable men'; who during the course of dispute, hired rival gangs of men to remove, or smash the machinery contained in the Bersham iron works, which they worked as partners.

127 Newcastle-under-Lyme Museum: Document Number 8454.

128 Heathcote Papers (in possession of the family in Yorkshire). I am grateful to Mr. David Dyble for allowing me to see these documents which relate to the dispute between Sir John Edensor Heathcote and the Gilberts.

129 Ibid.

130 Ibid., The mine was opened c. 1800.

131 Ibid.

132 *Staffordshire Advertiser*, 19th September 1812. 'On Thursday morning the 10th inst. at Cheltenham, John Gilbert, Esq., of Clough Hall in this county.'

133 WSL: 44/66/41.

134 See Chapter 4.

135 R. W. Chapman, op. cit., p. 1211.

136 A recently discovered document shows that James Watt went to some trouble to suppress evidence of earlier experimental work that could have been used to challenge his patent. (Information from Dr. Hugh Torrens who is to cite the document and other evidence in a forthcoming article.)

137 *Gentleman's Magazine*, Volume 47 (1777), pp. 14-15.

138 Heathcote Papers. The system had been introduced by 1797 and remained in use in the area until the early twentieth century. See caption and picture 23, Peter Lead, *The Trent and Mersey Canal*, Ashbourne (1980).

139 *Staffordshire Advertiser*, 7th June 1800. 'The brine...is raised from two pits contiguous to the pans by a water engine at a very trifling expence.'

140 Ibid., 7th November 1812.

141 Peter Lead and Hugh Torrens, 'The Introduction of the Trevithick Steam Engine to North Staffordshire', in *Journal of Trevithick Society*, No. 8 (1981), p. 27.

142 Francois Crouzet, 'Capital Formation in Great Britain during the Industrial Revolution'; in his book *Capital Formation in the Industrial Revolution*, p. 188.

143 WSL: 93/22/41.

144 WSL: 93/23/40-41.

145 Phyllis Deane, op. cit., pp. 75-80.

146 WSL: 93/23/41.

NOTES ON CHAPTER VII THE INHERITANCE

1 *Manchester Mercury*, 4th August 1795.

2 PRO: S. PROB. 11/1266; IP/149.

3 P. W. L. Adams (Editor), *Burslem Parish Register, Part II (1761-1809)*, Wolstanton (1913), pp. 495, 515 and 526.

4 PRO: S. PROB. 11/1266; IP/149.

5 WSL: 93/13/41.

6 Cheshire Record Office: DFI/167.

7 Hugh Malet, op. cit., p. 144.

8 SRO: D593/C/23/4.

9 Hugh Malet, op. cit., p. 146.

10 B&WP: John Gilbert to Matthew Boulton, 17th January 1784.

11 WSL: 93/23/41.

12 Ibid.

13 KEELE: Wedgwood Papers; 9679-52.

14 Ibid., 9672-52.

15 Ibid. (In 1790, Josiah Wedgwood took into partnership his three sons, John, Josiah and Thomas, and his nephew Thomas Byerley. Later the firm was known as Josiah Wedgwood, Sons and Byerley.)

16 WSL: 93/23/41.

17 WSL: 93/23/40-41.

18 City of Stoke-on-Trent Museum and Art Gallery, Enoch Wood's Scrapbook (1794-1836), p. 12.

19 Ibid., p. 73.

20 WSL: 93/23/41.

21 P. W. L. Adams, op. cit., pp. 495, 515 and 526.

22 Information from the 1796 Inclosure Act for Stone, provided by Norman A. Cope.

23 WSL: 93/29/41/C.

24 This Robert Williamson was the son of the Robert Williamson, who had participated in the purchase of the Goldenhill estate in 1760 with John and Thomas Gilbert. His mother was the widow of James Brindley, who remarried following the engineer's death.

25 William Marshall, op. cit, p. 140.

26 *Staffordshire Advertiser*, 24th March 1804.

27 WSL: 93/23/41.

28 John Ward, op. cit., p. 129 and SRO: D239/M/1703-1705.

29 William Salt Library: 93/24/41. In the *Stafforshire Advertiser*, 30th March 1822, William Brett is described as a 'Grocer, Dealer and Chapman of Stone.'

30 WSL: 93/24/41.

31 Peter Mathias, op. cit., p. 169.

32 Ibid., pp. 168-169.

33 WSL: 93/24/41.

34 Peter Mathias, op. cit., p. 170.

35 *Staffordshire Advertiser*, 24th October 1810.

36 WSL: 93/24/41.

37 John Ward, op. cit., p. 443.

38 *Staffordshire Advertiser*, 24th October 1810.

39 See Chapter 2.

40 Enoch Wood's Scrapbook, loc. cit., p. 53 (1799).

41 Ibid., p. 92 (1806).

42 *Staffordshire Advertiser*, 25th January 1806.

43 *Staffordshire Advertiser*, 29th September 1810.

44 Ibid.

45 KEELE: Wedgwood Papers; 9674/9675-52.

46 WSL: 93/21/41 and 93/29/41; also *Staffordshire Advertiser*, 22nd August 1818.

47 WSL: 93/29/41.

48 The following extract for the register of the Parish of St. George, Hanover Square was provided by the Rector W. M. Atkins (20th February 1981): 'John Gilbert, Esq., of the Parish of Woolstanton in the County of Stafford, Bl., and Elizabeth Horsefall of this Parish, Widow. 2nd May 1807.'

49 Hugh Malet, op. cit., p. 145.

50 Richard Timmis, *Some Account of the Rise and Progress of Wesleyan Methodism in Kidsgrove*, (1842), p. 21. Copy in local pamphlets, Vol. 32, Hanley Reference Library.

51 Ibid., pp. 21-22.

52 John Ward, op. cit., p. 59.

53 *Staffordshire Advertiser*, 7th December 1805.

54 SRO: D239/M/1705.

55 Heathcote Papers (with family in Yorkshire). This engine was erected by John Rose at Clough Hall, between 1804-05, the parts being supplied by the Coalbrookdale Company. (Shrewsbury Public Library: MSS 336 and 337.)

56 *Staffordshire Advertiser*, 7th December 1805.

57 WSL: 93/20/41.

58 Ibid.

59 Ibid. The Foxholes estate (at Audley) was not included in the estate bought by Kinnersley.

60 Ibid.

61 Ibid.

62 From registers of the School of King Edward the Sixth, Birmingham; cited in H. C. P. and R. M. Larking, op. cit., p. 2.

63 Ibid., p. 1.

64 Ibid., pp. 1-2.

65 *Staffordshire Advertiser*, 30th May 1795. 'Monday was married Mr. Gilbert of Burslem to Miss Bennet of Great Broughton, near Chester.

66 *Staffordshire Advertiser*, 22nd August 1818.

67 Howard Senar, op. cit., p. 18.

68 Letter from Howard Senar (4th January 1982). 'I have checked the registers to establish who officiated at the (burial) service. I think that it was almost certainly the Rev. Thomas Gilbert. He did not at that time sign individually that he had officiated, but the entry is in his writing as far as one can judge.'

69 SRO: D554/27a.

70 Foster's *Alumi. Oxon.*, Vol. II, p. 523.

71 SRO: D1343/6.

72 SRO: D554/27a.

73 *Cotton College* (Prospectus 1980), pp. 2-3.

74 Quoted in W. A. Speck, *Stability and Strife*, London (1977), pp. 139-140.

75 Phyllis Deane, op. cit., p. 49.

76 C. Wilson, *England's Apprenticeship*, London (1965), p. 125.

77 *Staffordshire Advertiser*, 12th January 1799.

78 Sir Louise Namier and John Brooke, op. cit., Vol. II, p. 86.

79 Edward Hughes, 'The Professions in the Eighteenth Century', in *Durham University Journal*, Vol. xliv (1952), p. 48.

80 Thomas Pope, op. cit., p. 12.

81 Geoffrey Holmes, 'The Professions and Social Change in England, 1680-1730', *Proceedings of the British Academy*, Vol. LXV (1979), p. 352.

82 Ibid., p. 347.

83 Robert Robson, *The Attorney in Eighteenth-Century England*, Cambridge (1959), p. 71.

84 William Marshall (Editor), op. cit., p. 227.

85 Ibid., pp. 227-228.

86 John Aikin, op. cit., p. 536.
87 SRO: D239/M/1705.

BIBLIOGRAPHY

Manuscript Sources
There is no single accumulation of documents relating to the Gilbert family, so the search for information has been widespread, prolonged and often unfruitful.

(a) In Public Repositories
County Record Office, Stafford.
D239/D240/D260/D554 (Bill Papers)/D593 (Trentham Papers)/D868/D1229 and D1343. Boat Register (1795).

William Salt Library, Stafford.
William Salt Manuscripts/Hand Morgan collection and the Bird Papers.

Northamptonshire Record Office.
Ashbridge (Bridgewater) Papers.

Birmingham Reference Library.
Boulton and Watt Papers. Boulton and Watt Engine Book. Brindley's notebooks.

University of Keele—Library.
Wedgwood Papers. Sneyd Papers.

Institution of Civil Engineers, London.
Brindley's notebooks.

Cheshire Record Office.
DFI 167 (Will of Mrs. Lydia Gilbert). Boat Register (1795).

Bedfordshire Record Office.
R3/1416 to R3/1954 (Farey's correspondence as steward at Woburn).

City Museum and Art Gallery, Stoke-on-Trent.
Enoch Wood's scrapbook.

Public Record Office, London
Will of John Gilbert (1724-1795): S. PROB. 11/1266 IP/469.

Somerset Record Office.
Waldegrave Manuscripts DD/WG.

(b) In Private Hands
Heathcote Papers (with the family in Yorkshire).

Rochdale Canal Company.
Minute books, etc. Rochdale Canal Company, 75 Dale Street, Manchester.

Cotton College.
Maps of Cotton estate and correspondence with members of the Gilbert family (1920-1930).

Journals and Newspapers:
Staffordshire Advertiser
Gentleman's Magazine
Aris's Birmingham Gazette
Manchester Mercury
Monthly Magazine
Derby Mercury
Waterways World

Books:
Aikin, John. *A Description of the Country From Thirty to Forty Miles Round Manchester,* Manchester (1795 - reprinted 1968).
Adams, P. W. L. (Editor), *Ellastone Parish Register, Vol. II,* Staffordshire Parish Register Society (1912).
Broadbridge, S. A. (Editor), *Journal of an Excursion to Wales & c by Joseph Banks,* (unpublished manuscript).
Buchanan, R. A. *Industrial Archaeology in Britain,* Harmondsworth (1972).

Burt, Roger. *John Taylor, mining entrepeneur and engineer, 1779-1863,* Hartington (1977).
Chaloner, W. H. *People and Industries,* London (1963).
Chapman, R. W. (Editor), *Boswell, Life of Johnson,* London (1970).
Chester, Herbert A. *The Iron Valley,* Cheadle (1979).
Chester, Herbert A. *Cheadle: Coal Town,* Cheadle (1981).
Crouzet, Francois. *Capital Formation in the Industrial Revolution,* London (1972).
Deane, Phyllis, *The First Industrial Revolution,* Cambridge (1965).
Defoe, Daniel. *A Tour through the Whole Island of Great Britain,* (1724-6).
Dent, Robert K. and Hill, Joseph. *Historic Staffordshire,* (1896).
Dickinson, H. W. and Jenkins, R. *James Watt and the Steam Engine,* London (1927), p. 25.
Dictionary of National Biography.
Farey, John. *The Agriculture and Minerals of Derbyshire,* (1817).
Farrar, Lady Katherine Euphemia. *The Letters of Josiah Wedgwood,* printed in three volumes (1903-06).
Ford, Trevor D. and Rieuwerts, J. H. (Editors). *Lead Mining in the Peak District,* Bakewell (second edition, 1975).
Gale, W. K. V. *Boulton, Watt and the Soho Undertakings,* Birmingham (1968).
Gale, W. K. V. and Nicholls, C. R. *The Lilleshall Company: a history, 1764-1964,* Ashbourne (1979).
Greenslade, M. W. and Jenkins, J. G. (Editors). *A History of the County of Stafford,* Vol. II, Oxford (1967).
Hadfield, Charles. *The Canal Age,* Newton Abbot (1968).
Hadfield, Charles. *The Canals of the West Midlands,* Newton Abbot, (second edition, 1969).
Hadfield, Charles. *British Canals: An Illustrated History,* Newton Abbot (fifth edition, 1974).
Hadfield, Charles and Biddle, Gordon. *The Canals of North West England,* Newton Abbot (1970).
Hanson, Harry. *The Canal Boatmen, 1760-1914,* Manchester (1975).
King-Hele, Desmond. *Doctor of Revolution,* London (1977).
Larking, R. M. and H. C. P. *The Canal Pioneers,* Goring-by-Sea (c. 1965).
Lawrence, J. *The Modern Land Steward* (1801).
Lead, Peter. *The Caldon Canal and Tramroads,* Tarrant Hinton (1979).
Lead, Peter. *The Trent and Mersey Canal,* Ashbourne (1980).
Lewis, M. J. T. *Early Wooden Railways,* London (1970).
Lindsay, Jean. *The Trent and Mersey Canal,* Newton Abbot (1979).
McCutcheon, W. A. *The Canals of the North of Ireland,* Dawlish (1965).
Malet, Hugh. *Bridgewater: The Canal Duke, 1736-1803,* Manchester (1977).
Marshall, William. *The Review and Abstract of the County Reports to the Board of Agriculture From the Several Agricultural Departments of England: Western Division,* York (1818).
Mathias, Peter. *The First Industrial Nation,* London (1969).
Mee, Arthur. *The King's England: Staffordshire,* London (n.d.).
Meteyard, Eliza. *The Life of Josiah Wedgwood from his private correspondence and family papers,* London (1865).
Mullineux, Frank. *The Duke of Bridgewater's Canal,* Eccles (1959).
Musson, A. E. and Robinson, Eric. *Science and Technology in the Industrial Revolution.* Manchester (1969).
Namier, Sir Lewis. *The Structure of Politics at the Assession of George III,* London (1929).
Namier, Sir Lewis and Brooke, John. *The History of the House of Commons, 1754-1790,* London (1964).
Nicholls, Robert. *Ten Generations of A Potting Family,* London (1931).
Palliser, D. M. *The Staffordshire Landscape,* London (1976).
Parkes, Samuel. *Chemical Essays, Vol. 5,* London (1815).
Pennington, D. H. and Roots, I. A. *The Committee at Stafford, 1643-45,* Manchester (1957).
Plot, Robert. *The Natural History of Staffordshire,* Oxford (1686).
Plymley, J. *The Agriculture of Shropshire* (1803).
Priestley, Joseph. *Historical Account of the Navigable Rivers, Canals and Railways, of Great Britain,* London (1831).
Raistrick, Arthur. *Dynasty of Ironfounders,* Newton Abbot, (1970 reprint).
Rathbone, Hannah May. *Letters of Richard Reynolds, with a Memoir of his Life,* London (1852).

Rees, A. (Editor). *The Cyclopaedia, or Universal Dictionary*, London (1819).
Rees, William, *Industry before the Industrial Revolution*, Cardiff (1968).
Richards, Eric. *The Leviathan of Wealth*, London (1973).
Richeson, A. W. *English Land Measuring to 1800*, Cambridge, Massachusetts (1966).
Robey, John A. and Porter, Lindsey, *The Copper and Lead Mines of Ecton Hill, Staffordshire*, Cheddleton (1973).
Robson, Robert. *The Attorney in Eighteenth Century England*, Cambridge (1959).
Rolt, L. T. C. *James Watt*, London (1962).
Rowell, Christopher. *Tatton Park*, London (1968).
Rowlands, Marie B. *Masters and Men in the West Midland metalware trades before the Industrial Revolution*, Manchester (1975).
Senar, Howard. *Little Gaddesden Parish Church*, Little Gaddesden (1980).
Sherlock, Robert. *Industrial Archaeology of Staffordshire*, Newton Abbot (1976).
Smiles, Samuel. *Lives of the Engineers*, Vol. I, London (1862).
Speck, W. A. *Stability and Strife*, London (1977).
Tate, W. E. *The Parish Chest*, Cambridge (1960).
Thomas, John. *The Rise of The Staffordshire Potteries*, Bath (1971).
Tindsley, Norman W. (Editor), *Kingsley Parish Registers*, Willenhall (1968).
Torrens, Hugh. *The Evolution of a family firm: Stothert and Pitt of Bath*, Bath (1978).
Trinder, Barrie. *The Industrial Revolution in Shropshire*, Chichester (1973).
William Tunnicliff. *A Topographical Survey of the Counties of Somerset, Gloucester, Worcester, Stafford, Chester and Lancaster*, Bath (1789).
Wallace, W. *Alston Moor, Its Pastoral people: Its Mines and Miners*, Newcastle (1890).
Ward, John. *History of the Borough of Stoke-upon-Trent*, London (1843).
Willan, T. S. *The Navigation of the River Weaver in the Eighteenth Century*, Manchester (1951).
Wilson, C. *England's Apprenticeship*, London (1965).
Wrottesley, Reverend F. J. (Editor). *Ellastone Parish Registers, Part I (1538-1700)*, Stafford (1907).
Wrottesley, Reverend F. J. (Editor). *Rocester Parish Register, Vol II*, Denstone (1909).

Articles:
Anderson, B. L. 'The Attorney and the Early Capital Market in Lancashire'; first published as Chapter 3 of J. R. Harris (ed.), *Liverpool and Merseyside: Essays in the Economic and Social History of the Port and its Hinterland*, London (1969).
Bolton, J. 'Stone—Canal Town', *Waterways World*, (March 1982).
Chaloner, W. H. 'The Cheshire Activities of Matthew Boulton and James Watt, of Soho, near Birmingham, 1776-1817', in *Transactions of the Lancashire and Cheshire Antiquarian Society*, Vol. LXI (1949), pp. 126-131.
Chaloner, W. H. 'Isaac Wilkinson, Potfounder', in L. S. Pressnell (Editor), *Studies in the Industrial Revolution presented to T. S. Ashton*, London (1960).
Chaloner, W. H. 'Salt in Cheshire, 1600-1800', *Transactions of the Lancashire and Cheshire Antiquarian Society*, Vol. 71 (1961).
Corfield, Michael, 'John Ward and Kennet and Avon Canal: Part 1', in *Bristol Industrial Archaeology Society Journal*, No. 14 (1981), pp. 28-35.
Corfield, Michael, 'John Ward and the Kennet and Avon Canal: Part 2', in *Bristol Industrial Archaeology Society Journal*, No. 15 (1983), pp. 20-28.
Dean, R. J. 'Sir Richard Whitworth and Inland Navigation', *Journal of the Railway and Canal Historical Society*, Volume XXVII, No. 4 (March 1982).
Ford, Trevor D. 'The Speedwell Mine', *Derbyshire Countryside* (April-May 1960).
Habakkuk, H. J. 'English Landownership, 1680-1740', *Economic History Review*, Vol. X.
Hardy, S. M. and Baily, R. C. 'The Downfall of the Gower interest in the Staffordshire Boroughs, 1800-1830', in *Collections for a History of Staffordshire*, (1950-1951).
Hassal, E. R. and Trickett, J. P. 'The Duke of Bridgewater's Underground Canals', *The Mining Engineer*, No. 37 (October 1963), pp. 45-57.
Heaton, Herbert. 'Financing the Industrial Revolution', *Bulletin of the Business Historical Society*, Vol. XI, No. 1 (February 1937).
Heckscher, H. 'The Place of Sweden in Modern Economic History', *Economic History Review*, Vol. iv.
Hughes, Edward. 'The Eighteenth Century Estate Agent', in *Essays in British and Irish History*, (Edited by H. A. Cronne, T. W. Moody and D. B. Quinn), London (1949).

Hughes, E. 'The Professions in the Eighteenth Century', in *Durham University Journal*, Vol. X/iv (1952), pp. 46-55.

Hughes, Stephen. 'The Development of British Navigational Levels', *Journal of the Railway and Canal Historical Society*, Vol. XXVII, No. 2 (July 1981).

Kettle, Ann. 'The Struggle for the Lichfield Interest, 1747-68', in *Collections for a History of Staffordshire*, Vol. 6 (1970).

Lead, Peter. 'The Caldon Canal, 1778-1978', *Cherry Eye* (Caldon Canal Society), No. 3, (Winter 1976-1977).

Lead, Peter. 'The North Staffordshire Iron Industry, 1600-1800', *Journal of the Historical Metallurgy Society*, Vol. 11, No. 1 (1977).

Lead, Peter. 'Early Iron-Boats—the North Staffordshire Connection', *Journal of the Railway and Canal Historical Society*, Vol. XXVIII, No. 2, (July 1984), p. 94.

Lead, Peter and Torrens, Hugh. 'The Introduction of the Trevithick Steam Engine to North Staffordshire', in *Journal of the Trevithick Society*, No. 8 (1981).

Mingay, G. E. 'The Eighteenth-Century Land Steward', in *Land, Labour and Population in the Industrial Revolution*, (Edited by E. L. Jones and G. E. Mingay), London (1967).

Mullineux, Frank. 'The Duke of Bridgewater's Underground Canals at Worsley', *Transactions of the Lancashire and Cheshire Antiquarian Society*, Vol. 71 (1961).

Palmer, A. N. 'John Wilkinson and the old Bersham iron works', *Transactions of the Cymmrodorion Society* (1897-8).

Pape, Thomas. 'The Ancient Corporation of Cheadle', *Transactions of the North Staffordshire Field Club*, Vol. LXIV, (1929-1930), pp. 4-30.

Richards, Eric. 'The Industrial Face of a Great Estate: Trentham and Lilleshall, 1780-1860', *Economic History Review*, Vol. XXVII, No. 3 (August 1974).

Robey, J. A. 'Two Lead Smelting Mills in North Staffordshire', *Bulletin Peak District Mines Historical Society*, Vol. 4, Part 3 (May 1970).

Robey, J. A. 'Copper Smelting in Derbyshire', *Bulletin Peak District Mines Historical Society*, Vol. 4, Part 5 (June 1971).

Robey, J. A. and Porter, L. 'The copper and Lead Mines of the Mixon Area, Staffordshire', *Bulletin Peak District Mines Historical Society*, Vol. 4, Part 4 (October 1970).

Robey, J. A. and Porter, L. 'The Metalliferous Mines of the Weaver Hills, Staffordshire', *Bulletin Peak District Mines Historical Society*, Vol. 4, Part 6 (December 1971).

Tomlinson, V. I. 'Salford activities connected with the Bridgewater Canal', *Transactions of the Lancashire and Cheshire Antiquarian Society*, Vol. 66 (1956).

Torrens, Hugh. 'The Somersetshire Canal Caisson Lock', *Journal of the Bristol Industrial Archaeology Society*, No. 8 (1985), pp. 4-10.

Weaver, Philip. 'Iron Boats on the Canals', *Journal of the Railway and Canal Historical Society*, Vol. XXIV, No. 3 (November 1978).

Wilson, Paul N. 'The Nent Force Level', *Transactions of the Cumberland and Westmorland A & A Society*, Vol. LXIII, n.s. (1963).

LIST OF SUBSCRIBERS
[Subscribers for more than one copy have the numbers indicated by figures within brackets.]

Mr. P. H. Abell, Peel, Isle of Man.
Mr. W. R. Akerman, St. Leonards-on-Sea.
Mr. Austen Albu, Hassocks, Sussex.
Mr. John S. Allen, Stourton.
Mr. Paul Anderton, Newcastle-under-Lyme.
Mr. A. Armstrong, Somerford, Congleton.
Mr. George Atkinson, St. Albans.

Mr. Allan Baker, Newcastle-under-Lyme.
Mr. R. K. Bartlett, East Molesey.
The Barracks Trust, Newcastle-under-Lyme.
Mrs. E. Beaver, Eccleshall, Staffs.
Mr. Graham Bebbington, Trentham, Staffs.
Mr. R. J. Bebbington, Newcastle-under-Lyme.
Mr. Maurice Berrill, Edinburgh.
Mr. N. W. Bertenshaw, Kings Heath, Birmingham.
Mr. Herbert D. Bickley, Welwyn, Herts.
Mr. G. Biddle, Levens, Kendal.
Birmingham University—Main Library [2].
Mr. S. Blackford, Sutton, Surrey.
Basil Blackwell Ltd., Oxford.
Miss Gaye Blake-Roberts, Stone, Staffs.
The Boat Museum—Archive Centre, Ellesmere Port.
The Boat Museum Shop, Ellesmere Port [6].
Mr. A. Bonson, Congleton.
Dr. and Mrs. Peter Borrell, Garmisch-Partenkirchea, W. Germany.
Mr. Joseph Boughey, Wallasey.
Mr. Grahame Boyes, Richmond, Surrey.
Mr. A. W. Brackenbury, Cheadle Hulme.
Miss Margaret Breeze, Meir Heath, Staffs.
Mr. David Brown, Tamworth [2].
Mr. C. A. Buchanan, Bridgewater, Somerset.
Mr. J. S. P. Buckland, London.
Business Archives Council, London.

Mrs. E. J. Carr, Greenford, Middlesex.
Mr. Eddie Cass, Manchester.
Chapter and Verse Bookshop, Cardiff.
Cheshire Libraries and Museums Department, Chester.
Cheshire Libraries and Museum (Salt Museum), Northwich.
Mrs. Christine Chester, Foxt, Staffs.
Mr. R. Chester-Browne, Culcheth, Cheshire.
Mr. M. A. Clarke, Accrington.
Mr. E. G. Cobb, Salford.
Colonel M. H. Cobb, Cullompton.
Mrs. H. Cope, Oakamoor, Staffs.
Mr. B. O. Corbett, Burgess Hill, W. Sussex.
Mr. Roger Cragg, Coventry.
Mr. J. B. Crawford, Witney.
Professor D. W. J. Cruickshank, Alderly Edge.

Mr. Michael S. Darby, Harborne, Birmingham.
Mr. I. Davidson, Warrington.
Mrs. Mary Davidson, Worcester.
Mr. J. Dixon, York.

Mrs. Mary Dowler, Hook Gate, Staffs.
Mr. J. E. Dunn, Hereford.
Miss W. M. A. Dwyer, Cotton, Staffs.

The Economists' Bookshop, London.
Mrs. K. M. Evans, Sutton Coldfield.
Mr. Roger Evans, Childwall, Liverpool.

Mr. M. R. Fairbrother, Stamford.
Mr. John Fisher, Leek.
John and Margaret Fletcher, Bolton.
Mr. Martin Lister Franks, Newcastle-upon-Tyne.

Mr. E. H. Garland, Erith, Kent.
Mr. Arnold Gibson, Biddulph, Staffs.
Mr. Michael J. Gilkes, Brighton.
The Archives, University of Glasgow.
Mr. K. C. Godden, Newcastle-under-Lyme.
Mr. D. C. Goodacre, Ipstones, Staffs.
Mr. E. W. Gordon, Brewood, Stafford.
Mr. D. T. Goselthine, Whipsnade.

Mr. Charles Hadfield, South Cerney.
Mr. Rodney Hampson, Newcastle-under-Lyme.
Mr. John Hancock, Biddulph, Staffs.
Mr. and Mrs. Stuart Hargreaves, Tittenley Farm, Market Drayton.
Reverend J. B. Harrop, Foxt, Staffs.
Mr. R. P. Haskings, Tilehurst, Reading.
Mrs. D. R. Haszard, Milford, Stafford.
Mr. Ian K. Heath, Stone, Staffs.
Mr. Nigel James Heathcote, Newcastle-under-Lyme.
The Reverend Dr. R. L. Hills, Hyde, Cheshire.
Mr. D. J. Hodgkins, Amersham.
Mr. Stanley A. Holland, Selly Oak, Birmingham.
Dr. J. R. Hollick, Hartington, Derbyshire.
Mr. Brian Edward Hopkinson, Kenilworth.
Mr. H. Horton, Oldham.
Mr. R. S. Howard, Leeds.
Dr. J. M. T. Howat, Rawtenstall.
Howplan Ltd., Bath Cottage, Cotton [6].
Mr. Peter M. Hughes, Huddersfield.
Mr. Robert Humm, Stamford.
Mr. Humphrey G. W. Household, Folkstone.
Mr. Alexander Hunter, Greasby.
The Huntingdon Library, San Marino, California, U.S.A.
Mr. R. A. Hutchings, Warminister.

Mr. A. G. Jackson, Stourbridge.
Mr. A. E. Jarvis, Liverpool.
David and Pauline Jenkins, Stone, Staffs.
Mr. Basil Jeuda, Macclesfield.
Mr. Peter Johnson, Leicester.
Mr. R. C. Jones, Northampton.
Mr. A. E. Jordan, Corby.
Mr. P. A. E. Jump, Bedford.

The Library, University of Keele.
Mr. M. F. Keef, Ross-on-Wye.
Mr. R. N. Kirk, St. Albans.
Miss Helen R. Kneebone, Congleton.

Lancashire County Library [4].
Mr. Christopher L. Law, Dudley.
Claude and Margaret Law, Halesowen.
Mr. G. R. Peter Larwrence, Harpenden.

Mrs. Ann C. Lead, Stone, Staffs.
Mrs. B. M. Lead, Newcastle-under-Lyme.
Peter Lead, Stone, Staffs. [21].
Mr. John Leaper, Harrow.
Mr. James Leese, Rode Heath, Cheshire.
Mrs. S. A. Leeson, Ipstones, Staffs.
Leicester University Book Shop.
Mr. Paul Leppard, Newcastle-under-Lyme.
Mr. C. R. Lester, Stafford.
Mr. F. M. Light, Uxbridge.
The Lilleshall Company.
Mr. Robert K. Loraine, Upper Hartfield.
Mrs. Lucy C. Lovatt, Dudley.

The Hon. W. H. McAlpine, Henley on Thames.
Mr. Angus McInnes, University of Keele.
Dr. I. McKim Thompson, Pershore.
Dr. B. H. G. Malet, Minehead.
Manchester Ship Canal Company.
Mr. Robert W. Miller, Bolton.
Mr. Brian Mills, Tadworth.
Mr. P. R. Mitchell, Coulsdon.
Michigan State University Library, East Lansing, Michigan, U.S.A.
Dr. Philip Morgan, University of Keele [2].
Moorland Publishing Company, Ashbourne [2].
Mr. P. Morris, Newcastle-upon-Tyne.
Mrs. C. E. Mullineux, Worsley.

Newcastle-under-Lyme Borough Council.
Newcastle-under-Lyme Borough Museum.
Newcastle-under-Lyme School Library—Wendy Butler [2].
Mr. Leslie Norman, Newbury.

Mr. R. Oakley, Bridgewater, Somerset.
Mr. Michael Oxley, Worksop.

Mr. W. J. D. Parkhouse, Coleford.
Mr. and Mrs. G. Parkyn, Grampound, Cornwall.
Mr. I. R. Patterson, Melksham.
Mr. B. Pearson, Manchester.
Mr. Alan Perks, Bewdley.
Mr. E. C. Perry, Teanford, Staffs.
Mrs. P. M. Pitts, University of Keele.
Mr. Basil E. Poole, Brierley Hill.
Mrs. J. M. Potter, Madeley, Staffs.
The Public Record Office, Kew.

Dr. Arthur Raistrick, Skipton.
Mr. P. J. G. Ransom, Lochearnhead, Scotland.
Dr. G. A. Rawlins, Garn Dolbenman.
Mr. G. G. Reed, Condover, Shropshire.
Mrs. Isabella M. Reid, Wanlockhead, Scotland [4].
Mr. Michael R. Reynolds, Chippenham.
Mr. M. J. Rigby, Norley, Cheshire.
Mr. D. G. M. Roberts, Hassocks, Sussex.
Mr. P. Robinson, Museum of Science and Industry, Birmingham.

William Salt Library (Mr. Dudley Fowkes), Stafford.
Science Museum, South Kensington, London.
Fred Scott, Bradford.
Mr. James Reginald Shaw, Cheadle, Staffs.
Dr. Edwin A. Shearing, Malvern.
Mr. J. B. Sheldon, Nuthall, Nottingham.
Mr. W. G. Short, Cheadle, Staffs.

Mr. William L. Short, Leighton Buzzard.
Shropshire County Library, Shrewsbury [16].
Mr. G. Slattery, Canterbury.
Dr. Denis Smith, Woodford Green, Essex.
Mrs. F. Smith, Farley, Staffs.
Mr. M. Smith, Stapleford, Nottingham.
Mr. J. A. Smithies, Lancaster.
Sneyd High School Library, Newcastle-under-Lyme.
Mr. Robert Speake, Audley, Staffs.
Mr. G. J. Spencer, Brentford.
Dr. Roger W. Squires, Rotherhithe, London.
Staffordshire County Library, Stafford [25].
North Staffordshire Field Club Library, Hanley, Staffs.
Mr. D. M. Stakes, B.W.B., Leeds.
Mr. Francis A. Stanier, Penkhull, Staffs.
Dr. F. B. Stitt, Little Hayward, Staffs.
Mr. D. G. Stuart, Burton-on-Trent.
Mr. A. E. Swinscoe, Peterchurch, Hereford.

Mr. D. H. Tew, Oakham.
Vera and Sidney Till, Dudley.
Reverend D. A. Tipper, Belmont, Hereford.
Dr. Hugh S. Torrens, University of Keele.
Mr. D. B. Tracey, Siddington, Cheshire.
Reverend Peter Travis, Newcastle-under-Lyme.
Mr. Stanley Tyson, York.

Mr. Michael Veissid, Shrewsbury.
Mr. M. Vickers, Lowestoft.
Mr. Alan P. Voce, Tiverton.

National Waterways Museum, Gloucester.
Mr. Maurice A. Wade, Longport, Staffs.
Mr. Anthony E. Wood, Foxt, Staffs.
Mr. Robert M. Westmorland, Roundhay, Leeds.
Mr. Derek J. Wheelhouse, Biddulph, Staffs.
Mr. Mark Whitby, Whitby and Bird, London.
Mr. R. H. Whittle, Goring-on-Thames.
Mr. Gerald S. Wootton, Endon, Staffs. [2].
Mr. A. A. Wright, Congleton.
Total Subscription Edition = 286 copies.